# GKN

# GKN

*The Making of
a Business*

## 1759–2009

A John Wiley & Sons, Ltd., Publication

Published in 2009 by John Wiley & Sons Ltd
© 2009 GKN

*Registered office*
John Wiley & Sons Ltd, The Atrium, Southern Gate, Chichester, West Sussex, PO19
8SQ, United Kingdom

For details of our global editorial offices, for customer services and for information about
how to apply for permission to reuse the copyright material in this book please see our
website at www.wiley.com.

*Library of Congress Cataloging-in-Publication Data*
A catalogue record for this book is available from the Library of Congress.

A catalogue record for this book is available from the British Library.

ISBN 978-0-470-74953-1

Set in 12.5 on 15.25 pt Adobe Garamond by SNP Best-set Typesetter Ltd., Hong Kong
Printed in Great Britain by TJ International Ltd, Padstow, Cornwall.

*For Helen, James and Harry*

# Contents

*FOREWORD BY THE CHAIRMAN* XI

*ACKNOWLEDGMENTS* XV

*CHAPTER 1*
Iron Men and an Iron Lady 1

*CHAPTER 2*
World Leader 15

*CHAPTER 3*
The Steel Age 25

*CHAPTER 4*
Keen, Guest and Nettlefolds 45

*CHAPTER 5*
The Empire-Builder from Merthyr 63

# CONTENTS

*CHAPTER 6*

Depression and Rearmament   73

*CHAPTER 7*

The Fight for Steel   85

*CHAPTER 8*

Metal Bashing   97

*CHAPTER 9*

Constant Velocity   107

*CHAPTER 10*

White Heat and Cold Comfort   121

*CHAPTER 11*

Crossroads   133

*CHAPTER 12*

In Face of Strife   141

*CHAPTER 13*

Farewell to a Hot Forger   149

*CHAPTER 14*

A Pallet Pool Is Born   157

*CHAPTER 15*

Shot Down   167

*CHAPTER 16*

On the Front Line   179

*CHAPTER 17*

Baptism of Fire   193

*CHAPTER 18*

Transformation   207

*CHAPTER 19*

The Japanese Connection   225

*CHAPTER 20*

An Era Ends   241

*CHAPTER 21*

A Stake in Westland   251

*CHAPTER 22*

Reformation   263

*CHAPTER 23*

Lift-off   275

*CHAPTER 24*

Courtroom Battle   289

*CHAPTER 25*

Acquisition Drive   301

*CHAPTER 26*

Parting of the Ways   311

*CHAPTER 27*

Rump or Fillet   323

*CHAPTER 28*

Moving South, Driving East   335

*CHAPTER 29*

The Ultimate Challenge   345

*CONCLUSION*   353

*SELECT BIBLIOGRAPHY*   357

*INDEX*   359

# *Foreword by the Chairman*

The year 1759 is known in British history as "The Year of Victories" because of the extraordinary spate of land and sea battles fought and won by the British in those 12 months. Horace Walpole, the English scholar, was moved to declare that the year was "the most glorious in the annals of our history".

Considering the momentous events of that year – it was said that "the church bells never stopped ringing" – it is little wonder that the foundation of an ironworks in the Welsh Valleys passed without much notice. Today, 250 years later, we can deploy the wisdom of hindsight to recognise the significance of that enterprise.

From it sprang a company – our company, if I may for a moment address the many employees and former employees who might read this book – which has survived and grown to the global business it is today. As recounted vibrantly here by Andrew Lorenz, the chronicle of GKN's progress is rich in character and action, but it also reflects the patterns of history that led Sir Winston Churchill to note that no-one could understand the future without knowing the past.

What does GKN's past tell us about its future? Above all, that this is a company which time and again has successfully responded to change in order to stay ahead of the game. From iron to steel, from steel to fasteners, from fasteners to general engineering and industrial services and on to automotive, defence and, ultimately, aerospace – GKN has moved through the decades and up the value chain.

We have evolved geographically too. As the balance of economic growth has shifted – from Britain and its Commonwealth in the 18th and early 19th centuries to America, the rest of Western Europe and Japan in the 20th and on to the emerging powers of Asia, Latin America and Eastern Europe in the 21st century – GKN has moved with it and frequently ahead of it. Today, our people span the globe, from the West Coast of the USA to the eastern shores of Japan, from northern China through Europe to South Africa, Argentina and Australia. GKN is a truly global corporate citizen.

Every book is, to an extent, a child of its times. Therefore, at this most testing of times and with due recognition to the vast majority of GKN people who live and work beyond British shores, I would like to bring one message from the book back home.

From the earliest days of the industrial revolution, this company has done much to advance manufacturing industry. It has developed countless engineers in many lands and valued them in periods, particularly recent years, when their contribution has been overlooked in favour of ostensibly more glamorous occupations.

Over the past quarter of a century, no country was more seduced by the vision of the financial service-led "post-industrial society" than Britain. Today, as this country reawakens to the importance of a balanced commercial and industrial base, GKN's experience is more relevant than ever.

Roy Brown

# *Acknowledgments*

I would like to thank all those GKN directors and senior company officers, past and present, who helped with their time, experience and knowledge to bring to life the events since 1945.

For GKN's history pre-1945, I am indebted to Edgar Jones' two monumental and comprehensive studies of the company from its origins.

A further invaluable source were the interviews with Lord Brookes by John Cockcroft in 1972 and 1974, which are rich in describing his involvement with the group.

For all their assistance, I am grateful to Simon Hardaker, Judith Felton, Kristina Monaghan, Carole Mount and David Smith.

Finally, may I thank Peter Baillie, without whom I could not have written this book.

Andrew Lorenz

# CHAPTER 1

# Iron Men and an Iron Lady

The company that became GKN was forged in the first fires of the Industrial Revolution.

On 19 September 1759, nine Welsh and West Country merchants and businessmen established a partnership to build a pig iron works at a site high in the Welsh Valleys, near Merthyr Tydfil. They called the venture the Dowlais Iron Company, after its location. It was capitalised at £4000 (equivalent to about £240,000 in 2009). Its avowed purpose, according to its deeds of partnership, was to deal in "the Art, Mystery, Occupation and Business of an Iron Master and Iron Manufacturer".

Early visitors were astonished by their achievement and those of peers who set up other ironworks nearby. Merthyr, said one observer, was "a mountain valley ... peopled in the teeth of every obstacle ... the triumph of fact over probability".

Dowlais's founders built a blast furnace into the hillside next to a stream. The blast was provided by bellows driven by a waterwheel, fed from a pond which was created by damming the stream. The water supply was irregular – in times of water shortage, workers had to tread the inside of the waterwheel to maintain the blast furnace supply.

By the end of 1760, its first full year of operation, the furnace's average weekly output was 18 tons of iron. Its modest size and primitiveness were typical of the numerous similar iron works springing up round the country. Three other works were founded around the same time in the Merthyr area alone.

The Dowlais partners inherited leases, previously acquired by one of their number from the Dowager Viscountess Windsor, granting the holder mineral rights over her property for 99 years from 1 May 1749. The annual rental was fixed at £31 – a tiny sum even in those days, because it was based on the value of land in a pre-industrial economy. There was no conception of what the venture could become, and what the land it occupied might therefore be worth.

Dowlais's potential was not lost on John Guest when he arrived in Merthyr six years after the forming of the partnership. Guest was tall, well-built and keen to get on in business. He was also steeped in the young iron industry. He hailed from the village of Broseley in Shropshire – in the heart of Coalbrookdale, where in 1709 Abraham Darby had demonstrated that coke could be used to fuel a blast furnace rather than the traditional charcoal. One historian described Coalbrookdale as "the chief centre of dispersion for the new race of ironmasters".

Darby's discovery dramatically reduced the industry's costs and therefore its barriers to entry. It liberated aspirant iron makers from the need to site furnaces near woods and forests, sources of charcoal but far from the other raw materials required for their trade. The Merthyr area, rich in easily accessible reserves of coal, iron ore and limestone, was one of many localities which came into its own as a result.

The area attracted the young Guest, who had learned the skills of smelting and refining and used a small income from farming to diversify into brewing, coal-dealing and working a small forge. In the process, he earned a reputation for being able to command the loyalty and trust of his employees.

Not that he was an instant success. His first major ironworks venture in Merthyr soon began to struggle and he sold out of it in 1766, barely a year after it was started. However, Isaac Wilkinson, his partner in the venture, was one of the original Dowlais investors. Wilkinson introduced Guest to Dowlais's three executive partners and on 30 April 1767, they offered the 45-year-old Guest the post of works manager. He took the job.

Guest brought several members of his family from Shropshire to help him run the works. He took a direct interest for the first time in 1781 when he used savings from his wages to buy out one of the partners. That year, he built a second blast furnace. Guest retired in 1786, a year before his death, and his son Thomas and son-in-law William Taitt took over the management and became the principal partners, owning half the company.

Guest and Taitt divided the main jobs between them. Guest took over his father's post of works manager while Taitt became the company salesman and Dowlais's first accountant. Each man was paid £150 a year. Guest added a refinery and foundry to the plant, which could now, for the first time, genuinely be described as a works.

By 1787, Dowlais's capital had increased to £38,000 and output reached 1800 tons. Like its peers, Dowlais benefited from the successive wars – the Seven Years' War which ended in 1763 and the American War of Independence from 1775 to 1783 – which created ready demand from the British Army and Navy for cannon and musket balls. The armaments business was highly lucrative – it enabled Dowlais's profits to reach almost £2500 in 1763 – not a bad return on the £4000 invested less than five years earlier. Not for the last time in the company's iron and steel history, war drove profitability.

Peace, on the other hand, repeatedly proved a depressant. A slump ensued in July 1763, within six months of the Peace of Paris that ended the Seven Years' War. Likewise, the iron industry suffered a severe downturn in the two years following the end of the War of Independence. The period was, however, noteworthy for one development: Dowlais began to export small amounts of iron to the new United States of America. The shipments were carried down the valleys to the port of Cardiff by mule train. Future exports to the USA followed a speedier route.

While it expanded in absolute terms, Dowlais was not a relative success. Its owners failed initially to invest to capitalise on technological advances, such as the puddling and rolling process invented by Henry Cort in 1784 which significantly speeded the manufacturing process by improving iron quality and removing intermediate stages such as preliminary refining. Puddling, which involved the heating, refining and stirring of a brick-lined bath of pig iron into a molten ball of wrought iron, was highly labour-intensive but also highly skilled. The "gentleman puddler" was the aristocrat of the iron industry. As Dowlais lagged behind other works which were early adopters of the process, its owners lost confidence in the business. In 1792, the Guest family and Taitt even offered to sell their majority holding back to one of the original partners for £25,000, and when those negotiations fell through the partners offered the whole business to a larger rival for £60,000. The offer was declined.

In 1793, the French Revolutionary War triggered a surge in demand for iron armaments which both benefited Dowlais and stimulated further expansion in the local industry, including the construction of a blast furnace at Brymbo in Denbighshire.

Transportation was improved by the opening of the Glamorganshire Canal in 1794, the first major canal in Wales, which ran from Merthyr to Cardiff. All the Merthyr ironmasters contributed to its cost but the financing, and subsequent usage, was dominated by Richard Crawshay, owner of Cyfarthfa, the largest ironworks. Now there were no more mule trains.

But despite the local industry's overall growth, there was no hiding the fact that Dowlais had fallen behind its local rivals.

That all changed during one week in November 1798, when Taitt and Guest installed a new steam engine made by (Matthew) Boulton and its inventor, (James) Watt. The steam engine revolutionised the industry by opening the way to large, integrated ironworks where the machinery was so heavy that it could no longer be driven by waterwheels. The steam engine was not only much more powerful, but it was infinitely more reliable: it was not at the mercy of the elements.

Taitt, the driving force of the business, followed this critical investment by switching to Cort's puddling and rolling process, enabling Dowlais to enter the growing market for bar iron. As a result, Taitt was able to extend his product and, therefore, his customer base.

Dowlais now began its rise to pre-eminence. To weaken Crawshay's hold on the transport system, Taitt and two fellow ironmasters agreed to build a private tram-road from Merthyr to Abercynon, near Cardiff, a distance of nine-and-a-half miles. When it was completed in 1802, one horse would pull five loaded trams with a total payload of 10 tons of iron. On 21 February 1804, the Merthyr Tram-road earned a place in industrial history when it was used by the first steam locomotive designed and built by Richard Trevithick. It took 4 hours 5 minutes to make the journey.

By then, more than 25 blast furnaces studded the Valleys and their annual iron output of at least 35,000 tons accounted for more than a quarter of the iron made in Great Britain. If Britain was fast becoming the workshop of the world, then GKN's home town was one of the largest workshops in Britain. "At night," wrote a contemporary still struggling to acclimatise to the new industrial landscape, "the view of the town is strikingly singular. Numbers of furnaces and truly volcanic accumulations of blazing cinders illuminate the vale, which combining with the incessant roar of the blasts, the clangour of ponderous hammers, the whirl of wheels, and the scarcely human aspect of the tall gaunt workmen seem to realise, without too much aid from fancy, many of our early fears."

By the time Wellington defeated Napoleon at Waterloo in 1815, Dowlais had four blast furnaces and could produce 15,600 tons of pig iron a year. Thanks to the steam engine and the technique of coke smelting, the later furnaces were larger and more efficient.

Taitt died in November that year, eight years after Thomas Guest. Josiah John Guest, Thomas's 30-year-old son, became the company's leader and controlling shareholder.

Josiah Guest had had a difficult childhood. His mother died when he was a small boy, and he was brought up in Dowlais by an elderly nanny. He went to Bridgnorth Grammar School in Shropshire and then joined the company, where he was trained by its general manager, John Evans. His father's death pitched him into a leading management role at the age of 22. He remained in Taitt's shadow for eight years, but with Taitt's death there was no question on whose skills and judgment the future of Dowlais depended.

Fortunately for the business, Josiah Guest proved more than equal to the challenge. When he died in 1852, one obituary writer paid fulsome tribute to his talents – his "extraordinary capacity for business, his mechanical ingenuity and his judgement in mercantile transactions". Hyperbole aside, Guest proved to be an exceptional industrialist.

Like his father and grandfather – and, indeed, many of the South Wales ironmasters – he was a Methodist, although he did not take his Wesleyan faith to quite the extent of Thomas Guest senior and his brother, also named Thomas, who both became local preachers. And he could be hard. In 1810, when iron industry prices dropped by more than 10% while a bad harvest pushed up wheat prices, Guest decided that he had to maintain operating margins as far as possible. So he cut the wages of the Dowlais workers. They promptly walked out in what was the first ever strike at the plant.

Dowlais was shut down for two weeks. Then some of the men, effectively starved into submission, accepted the lower wage rate and the drift back to work began. To encourage the others, Guest allowed the first men back to choose their place of work. After five weeks, the strike was over.

Guest suffered a personal tragedy in 1817 when his wife Maria died at the age of 23, only nine months after the couple had married. For the following 16 years, he put his personal life aside to focus on building the business.

Dowlais needed all Guest's single-minded determination and his business acumen, because the ending of the Napoleonic Wars also marked a sea-change in Britain's iron industry. Post-1815, output from the vastly-expanded capacity which was a legacy of the good times generally increased faster than demand and prices gradually declined. The ironmasters could no longer rely on being carried along by a favourable tide. They had to out-perform their rivals in order to survive, never mind prosper.

Dowlais's profitability fluctuated widely and wildly. In 1815, the company made £15,021. Over the ensuing 25 years to 1840, profits fell as low as £4711 in 1829 and rose as high as £129,160 in 1837. But at least the business remained profitable – unlike many of its competitors. And while the 1837 peak was exceptional, it also reflected the generally higher level of profit achieved by Dowlais in the mid-to-late 1830s as Josiah Guest led the company to the forefront of the industry.

This was the first age of the train – at the root of Dowlais's success lay the explosion in railway construction. By 1821, Dowlais had made a name for itself as a maker of rails. In May that year, the chairman of Britain's first railway, the Stockton & Darlington – famous for the runs of George Stephenson's Rocket – wrote to Guest seeking his views on "Tram-roads and Rail-roads".

In 1830, the year in which Britain's railway boom really began, Guest laid down the so-called Big Mill, a specialised piece of machinery designed to roll bar iron into rails. The railway boom continued for two decades. Activity peaked with the "Railway Mania" of 1836–37, when Parliament authorised the construction of almost 1500 miles of track. Dowlais made 20,000 tons of rails a year in this period, and demand continued at a high level until 1850.

Almost from the outset, Guest also looked overseas for rail business. In 1832, the company won its first orders from the US – the Baltimore & Susquihanna Railway and the Harlaam Railroad in New York were early customers. In 1836, Guest broke into the Russian market with a contract to supply the St Petersburg-Pauloffsky Railway. Russia was an important source of business for some years. Guest also supplied the East India Company.

Guest drove Dowlais through this boom with a top management team strengthened by the addition of one crucial new member: his second wife, Charlotte – Lady Charlotte Elizabeth Bertie, only daughter of the ninth Earl of Lindsey. Charlotte Guest proved to be not only a most loving and supportive wife to Guest and a mother of 10 children but, as Edgar Jones wrote in the first volume of his encyclopaedic history of GKN, "a remarkable business-woman of courage, application and insight".

Like Guest, she had endured a lonely childhood – in her case, at Uffington, near Stamford on the Lincolnshire/Rutland border. Her father was aged 68 when she was born and died when she was six years old. Her mother's second husband was a vicar who had no love for young Charlotte. In the remarkable Journal that she kept from the age of 10 until she was 79, she wrote: "I have been brought up alone and never have associated with children or young persons of my own age, nor had I ever anyone with whom to share my early joys and griefs ... Though I know many whom I love and esteem, I have never found a kindred soul to whom the whole of my heart may be opened."

She might have found that soul in the shape of Benjamin Disraeli, the future Tory prime minister, with whom she had a brief romance in early 1833. He described her as "very clever, [worth] £25,000 and domestic". She thought him "wild, enthusiastic and very poetical".

Within days of parting from Disraeli, Charlotte met Josiah Guest at the London home of one of the Dowlais shareholders. Guest did not share Disraeli's politics – he had been Liberal Member of Parliament (MP) for Honiton for five years from 1826. But politics was immaterial to Charlotte.

The couple embarked on a whirlwind romance. They married on 29 July 1833, honeymooned on the South coast and at Brighton, and then travelled to Dowlais House in Merthyr. It was a far cry from rural Lincolnshire. "By the time we reached the house, it was quite dark, and the prevailing gloom gave full effect to the light of the blazing furnaces which was quite unlike all I had ever before seen or even imagined", Charlotte wrote. Her husband was worried that the sight might frighten his new bride. But she was made of sterner stuff. "I am iron now," she wrote. "And my life is altered into one of action, not sentiment."

Charlotte learned Welsh, immersed herself in the business – including going down the company's coal mines – and took on the roles of company secretary and accountant. She did not turn her back on metropolitan high society, but she kept a strict sense of priorities. Jones recounts one scene when Charlotte was attending a social event in London and a messenger from Dowlais delivered a long tin case containing the year's accounts. Amid the crinoline dresses and the small talk of the chattering class, Charlotte sat down to check the Dowlais figures and calculate its profits.

Thanks to Dowlais, her own conversational partners came from a more interesting background than the average London aristocratic crowd. Charles Babbage, the scientist and inventor of the punching machine, the first calculator, was one who gave her sound advice: "He placed strongly before me the necessity of looking at great leading points and not allowing myself to be discouraged and perplexed by comparatively insignificant details ...". She retained a firm grasp of the big picture.

Charlotte called her husband "Merthyr" – a nickname which affectionately and accurately embodied the fact that man and place were synonymous. Guest provided the township of Dowlais with houses, churches, schools, a library and educational facilities for the employees. He was chairman of the local railway company and of the first Merthyr Board of Health.

When the Great Reform Bill of 1832 was enacted to widen the electoral franchise and reflect the rise of new towns and cities, it created a parliamentary constituency of Merthyr Tydfil. Guest became the town's first MP. He defended the seat in 1837 and was subsequently re-elected, unopposed, at four general elections. In 1838, he became a Baronet and was known thereafter as Sir John Guest. Charlotte was upset – she thought that he deserved a peerage.

If Guest's lesser ennoblement reflected an establishment prejudice against industry which existed even in early Victorian days, his combination of business and politics made a useful connection which was lost in Britain during the 20th century, to the country's cost.

Politically, Guest was for cheap and efficient government, free trade, the abolition of the Corn Laws which artificially inflated corn and food prices, and further Parliamentary reform. He was, however, opposed to the radicals who advocated the establishment of trade unions and who endorsed the Chartist movement's calls for universal male suffrage and other, more radical, reforms.

South Wales in general, and Merthyr in particular, was a hotbed of Chartism in the 1830s, and the movement there reached its peak in 1839 with a spate of peaceful protests followed by riots in Ebbw Vale and Newport. Fear ran high – even among the Guests. One night in October, fearing an imminent attack on Dowlais House itself, they sent their children away for safety and brought in up to 100 special constables to guard against possible assault. But the threatened mob never materialised.

The disturbances did not affect development of the business. Guest consistently invested in new capacity and the new technology that underpinned cost-effective expansion. Some of the innovations were his own, such as the "running-out" furnace which allowed molten iron to be run directly into the refinery instead of letting it cool and have to be reheated twice during the process – a significant saving of both coal and labour costs. By 1839, Dowlais had 17 blast furnaces and Guest built a second iron plant next to the first, naming it the Ifor Works after his and Charlotte's eldest son, Ivor Bertie Guest.

In the process, Dowlais finally superseded Cyfarthfa as the largest ironworks in Merthyr. Under Richard Crawshay's heirs, Cyfarthfa had rested on its laurels as by far the largest and, initially, the most modern ironworks in the area. While Guest was building up Dowlais, Cyfarthfa slipped back through under-investment and lack of commitment by its owners.

Dowlais overtook Cyfarthfa in output during the mid-1830s and by the end of the decade was firmly established for the first time as the foremost Merthyr ironworks. But the Guests had little cause to celebrate. They were all too aware that the original 99-year lease granted to Dowlais's founding fathers was only eight years from expiry. And they were not hopeful of securing a new agreement. For Sir John and Lady Charlotte, the Guest hold on Dowlais seemed to be terminally weakening.

CHAPTER 2

# World Leader

Sir John Guest had premonitions about the lease renegotiation long before its expiry date of 1 May 1848 began
to loom seriously large. Indeed, he viewed the prospect
of renegotiation with foreboding and began at a very
early stage to prepare himself and his wife for the worst
outcome. "At luncheon, Merthyr again talked of renting
some country place and weaning himself from Dowlais,"
Charlotte recorded in September 1837.

"He is the first in the Trade ... for the works are a
wonder to all who see them. He feels that the lease is expir-
ing, that other works are springing up with prospects of
rivalling Dowlais, and that at 52 he has not the energy and
activity to sustain a higher position than we have already
gained."

For all Guest's natural concerns about the competition,
the lease was the real canker gnawing at his confidence in
the future. His fears were well-founded. Dowlais's relations
with its landlord, John, second Marquis of Bute, were not
good. In fact, they were dire.

Lord Bute had inherited the Dowlais freehold from his father, the first Marquis, who had married Lady Windsor's daughter. The father had died in 1814, and his heir was ill-disposed to Guest and the Dowlais Company from the outset. Bute could immediately see that the terms of the lease – notably the level of annual rent – were remarkably favourable to the thriving commercial enterprise that Dowlais had become.

This resentment was exacerbated by his dislike of aspects of Dowlais's operation, in particular its management of the company's coal reserves. In this, he was at least partly justified. The ironworks had access to substantial coal deposits. These, combined with Guest's awareness that Bute was most unlikely to offer lease renewal on acceptable terms, encouraged the Dowlais chairman to remove the best coal as quickly and cheaply as possible, regardless of wastage. As a result, substantial quantities of coal were lost in the process of extraction, much to Bute's annoyance. The two men were on a collision course. Guest knew that, if the apparently inevitable clash happened, there could only be one outcome.

But he did not yet allow his increasing concern about the lease to obstruct his vision of what Dowlais needed to perpetuate its success. By the mid-1830s, it was clear to Guest and some of the other local ironmasters that they needed a better transport link to Cardiff than either the Glamorgan Canal or the Tramroad could provide. They needed a railway.

In October 1834, Guest met Isambard Kingdom Brunel, creator of the Great Western Railway, to discuss the feasibility of a rail link from Cardiff to Merthyr. A year later almost to the day, the Taff Vale Railway Company was inaugurated with both Guest and his brother Thomas on the governing committee.

The following year, the company obtained an Act of Incorporation authorising construction of the line, which was to be built by Brunel. John Guest became chairman. The railway reached Merthyr on 12 April 1841 and immediately brought the ironworks a prime artery to the great markets of England. Dowlais gained most of all. It was the Taff Valley's largest freight customer and by the mid-1840s was using the railway to carry 70,000 tons of goods a year. Of the iron carried on the Railway by then, 80% was from Dowlais.

The combination of lower costs, helped by the Taff Valley line, and buoyant demand as railway building surged through the decade, propelled Dowlais through the 1840s. It became a very major supplier of rails to the Great Western and a number of other companies, initially in southern England but gradually throughout the country.

The rails varied considerably in length and weight, according to the demands of each customer, although there was a gathering trend for longer, heavier product for the simple reason that it lasted longer. Although Dowlais did not regain the exceptional profit level of the "railway mania" period in 1836–37, it continued to produce very healthy results.

By the late 1840s, Dowlais had more than 7300 employees manning 18 blast furnaces, which disgorged almost 90,000 tons of iron a year. One local observer remarked that it was "by far the largest establishment of the kind either in this district, or in any country on the face of the globe". This was not mere hyperbole. From its modest origins, through the smoke and flame and cacophony of industrial revolution, the Guests' company had emerged at the pinnacle of its profession, a British world leader.

Yet John Guest now teetered on the brink of losing it all. As 1848 approached, he cut back investment in order to maximise immediate returns. No new blast furnaces were built; adoption of new techniques was minimal. Guest's efforts remained focused on trying to negotiate acceptable terms for renewing the lease, but he became increasingly convinced that Bute would make this impossible.

Bute's motivation went beyond the understandable desire to ensure that, this time, the terms of a new lease would adequately reflect the value that Dowlais would derive from it, while incorporating an element of compensation for historic underpayment. Bute harboured a grand design of his own: he wanted to develop Cardiff as a major port which would yield substantial duties to his estate and he reckoned that Dowlais could help to finance this expansion – either through the lease costs that Guest (or a new leaseholder) would pay, or through the profits that would accrue directly to him should Guest walk away without a replacement.

Jones writes that Bute nursed a "deep, brooding dislike of the Guests, which manifested itself in unrealistic demands and fickle changes of mind, and his conviction that he was being defrauded of his rightful inheritance. The obsessional distrust and suspicion of this myopic and solitary aristocrat overwhelmed any sound business principles in dealings with the Guests and produced a series of half-truths, broken promises and fruitless deals."

Formal negotiations between the two parties began around 1841, but no progress was made for almost two years. In 1843, the Guests thought they were on the brink of reaching a settlement, only to be told that Bute had changed his mind. Two more years of frustration passed before Bute tabled a new set of conditions which Charlotte Guest reported were "as we expected, quite preposterous".

This was no overstatement. Bute demanded a royalty of 4s 6d per ton of pig iron and 7s a ton on bar iron (now Dowlais's main product because of the rail boom), £9000 a year in rent, very limited mining rights and a one-off payment of £80,000. And the lease was to run for no more than 42 years.

By now, it was clear to the Guests that Bute intended to present them with a choice which was, in reality, no choice. Either John Guest must agree to commercially prohibitive terms or give up the company that had been his life's work. In late 1846, the Guests paid the huge sum of £354,000 [almost £30 m at 2009 prices] for their retirement home, Canford Manor and associated lands near Wimborne in Dorset. Another £30,000 went on fees for extending and modifying the high-Gothic property – a large bill, but then the architect Charlotte engaged was Sir Charles Barry, designer of the Houses of Parliament.

Guest continued the negotiations with Bute for another year. But as Christmas 1847 approached, he, Charlotte and the minority shareholders decided enough was enough. Bute would give no ground. Therefore the lease would expire and with it would go their Dowlais Iron Company.

The company that became GKN has faced a number of crises in its long history. But this was the closest that it has ever come to oblivion. On the shortest day of the year, 21 December 1847, Charlotte spent what she described as "the longest day" of her life. With her husband, she toured the Dowlais site for one last time.

"I wanted once more, while they were in operation, to go through the dear old works, leaning as old on my dear husband's arm," she wrote. "I knew it to be my last day at Dowlais in its glory." Together, they were saying goodbye.

Now the harsh mechanics of winding down the works began. Three blast furnaces were blown out. Rail stocks were piled alongside process equipment brought up from the mines for sale. Coal trams were shunted round the pit heads.

Then something quite unexpected happened. On 20 March, Charlotte visited friends at Bournemouth. One of the group was Lady Shrewsbury, who remarked that she had read in that day's paper that Lord Bute had died suddenly at Cardiff Castle. The calm of the genteel gathering was shattered by Charlotte's reaction. "I shrieked rather than exclaimed, 'Lord Bute!' My agitation was so great that I could hardly breathe. Tears stood in my eyes and for many minutes I trembled violently."

Some of the gathering may have thought – mistakenly – that she was crying in sorrow for the deceased aristocrat. Those who suspected otherwise may have viewed Charlotte's reaction as inappropriate. But then they had not been facing the imminent end of their working life. And they had not just received an eleventh-hour, fifty-ninth minute reprieve.

Bute's death immediately cleared the way for a settlement. Outline agreement on the terms of a new lease was reached on 21 April 1848 – 10 days before the old lease expired. The Guests returned to Dowlais on 11 July to a heroes' welcome: "Here were several arches and flags put across the road for us to pass under," recorded Charlotte. "At the Lodge was a triumphal arch, made of flowers and evergreens and flags."

Nevertheless, it took almost five years for the details of the lease to be agreed. It was finally signed by Charlotte on 18 January 1853. By then, John Guest was dead. Beset by poor health and further weakened by the struggle over the lease, he died on 26 November 1852, 45 years after taking over management of the ironworks.

Like other Victorian ironmasters, Guest was no saint – he made little contribution to improving health in the area, for example. But he played an important part in educational development, founding a school for the workers' children which expanded into a fully-fledged institution combining a nursery, primary and secondary school and a night school for employees.

During the recurrent bouts of serious disease, notably cholera, which afflicted the area, he organised and funded schemes for improved sanitation. He also wanted to "improve" his workforce morally, inculcating into his employees the values of "respectability". With this objective in view, he made loans available to privileged workers to enable them to buy their homes from the company. One of his last acts was to open a savings bank for his workers. The other was to buy out the last independent shareholder in the company and secure absolute control.

Guest was buried in St John's Church, Dowlais. The inscription, written by Charlotte, read: "Beneath rests the mortal part of Sir Josiah John Guest ... who through honest paths placed himself at the head of the Iron Manufacture of Great Britain, raised into importance this populous and flourishing district, and was himself an example of what, in this free country, may be attained by the exercise of skill, energy and perseverance."

An even more eloquent epitaph was the Iron Works itself. Dowlais at the time of Guest's death epitomised the power and the dark glory of the Industrial Revolution. One visitor to the plant observed: "The scene is strange and impressive in broad daylight, but when viewed at night is wild beyond conception. Darkness is palpable ... The vivid glow and roaring of the blast furnaces near at hand – the lurid light of distant works – the clanking of hammers and rolling mills, the confused din of massive machinery ... the wild figures of the workmen, the actors in this apparently infernal scene – all combined to impress the mind of the spectator wonderfully."

Charlotte Guest had effectively taken over leadership of the company during her husband's long illness. She was now chairwoman – the first and, so far, the only female leader of the business. She was aged 40. Her devoted self-education in the business now served her well: she knew the company inside out.

With John Evans, Guest's right-hand man and Dowlais's works manager, she rebuilt the rundown plant at a cost of more than £100,000 and ran the company until 1855, when she remarried. One of her first challenges was to face a strike over pay by Dowlais miners. "I am not afraid of the men," she said. "I will be their master." The miners abandoned their claim and returned to work.

But even the redoubtable Charlotte suffered doubts about Dowlais's future. Early in 1854, those concerns became particularly acute. "Other districts, with apparently better resources, are opening up," she noted. "Unless we keep quite ahead as to improvements and the most advantageous and enlightened system of working, we shall be quite unable to keep any position at all – much less than we now occupy at the head of the trade – and this will involve continuous labour and immense skill and energy."

The perceived pressures led her to decide to sell the company. It was valued at £400,000 – but financial markets were depressed, ruling out the prospect of an offer anywhere near that level. As a result, Charlotte and her advisers turned to the idea of leasing the works at an annual rental.

They had barely begun to explore this option when fate again lent a hand. In March 1854, the Crimean War broke out between Britain and Russia. Charlotte and her advisers met at her London house in Suffolk Street, just off Trafalgar Square and concluded that because of "the present state of the money market and following the declaration of war, it was hopeless to attempt to carry out any [leasing] scheme".

So Charlotte Guest remained in full control of Dowlais. She brought her late husband's two trustees – George Clark and Edward Divett – into more active management of the business. Divett's involvement was short-lived. A banker and MP for Exeter, he had withdrawn from the company by the time – 10 April 1855 – that Charlotte married

Charles Schreiber, who she met after he had been appointed tutor to her eldest son.

After the marriage, Charlotte moved from Dowlais House to London and handed the chairmanship to her son, Lord Wimborne, who had little interest in the business. Her legacy was a company which, after the vast rebuilding effort of recent years, was the largest ironworks in the world. With Evans having resigned from the company and retired, leadership of Dowlais was taken over by Clark. He proved a worthy successor.

CHAPTER 3

# The Steel Age

George Clark effectively became chief executive of Dowlais on Charlotte Guest's retirement, and held that position for 38 years. He had substantial powers – Guest's will gave his trustees the authority to choose managers for the company or to run the business themselves. The son of a chaplain at the Royal Military Hospital in Chelsea, he was educated at Charterhouse School, embarked on a medical career but abandoned it in favour of civil engineering. He worked under Brunel on the construction of the Great Western Railway and then, in the mid-1840s, spent several years in India where he made studies for sewerage systems in Bombay while also pushing for the country's first railway.

In 1848, Clark returned to England to join the Board of Health, rising to become one of its three Commissioners. He became close friends with Sir John Guest, whom he probably met through his wife, Ann Price Lewis, a descendant of one of the original Dowlais Iron

Company partners. That friendship led to Guest appointing Clark as one of his trustees.

Despite his civil engineering expertise, Clark knew nothing about iron-making when, at the age of 45, he answered Charlotte Guest's call for support. Undaunted, he then took control of the manufacturing operations while Henry Bruce, who replaced Divett as Clark's co-director, focused on the commercial side. Bruce was based in London, while Clark took up residence with his wife Ann in Dowlais House, living over the shop. "A master who is not regularly resident cannot expect to know very much of what his agents do – although he may flatter himself to the contrary," Clark wrote to Bruce.

Clark quickly made a significant contribution to the wider community, as well as to the company itself. He was elected to the Merthyr Board of Health in 1857, and brought to bear his knowledge of the most modern water and drainage systems. Within months, he helped to promote a Bill for the construction of the Merthyr Tydfil Waterworks. Filter beds were built and standpipes provided throughout the town. In 1862, a reservoir was opened.

The new infrastructure produced clear health benefits. The death rate in Merthyr fell from 36 per 1000 people in 1851–52 to 25 per 1000 in 1866. Child (under five) mortality dropped from 527 per 1000 to 434 per 1000 over the same period. The average age at death rose from 17.5 years to 24.5 years.

The final element in the works that Clark inspired was an extensive sewerage system. The urgent need for one became apparent in 1866, when cholera returned to ravage the town, killing 115 people in eight weeks. At Clark's instigation, the Board of Health built 55 miles of sewers by autumn 1868, enabling householders to install lavatories for safe waste disposal. Cholera was finally banished from Merthyr.

In his role as *de facto* chief executive of Dowlais, Clark conceived the corporate strategy, set the agenda and oversaw the operation of the business. He established a system for heads of departments to file monthly reports on their section. He was clear about his role – it was to head the company, not to manage its operations on a day-to-day basis. However, where he identified a major issue affecting the business, he could be totally hands-on. In the mid-1860s, when Dowlais was paying about £50,000 a year in rail charges, he negotiated the freight rates down. Above all, his perceptive judgment of men and their abilities proved vital. He selected highly-competent specialists to manage the detailed, daily running of the works.

First and foremost among these was William Menelaus, a Scottish engineer, whom Clark appointed General Manager in 1856 and who remained in that vital post until 1882. Menelaus had joined the company five years earlier, aged 33. His first major assignment under Clark was to provide a complete and highly-detailed analysis of Dowlais's competitive position.

The "Dowlais Works Report", which Menelaus completed in November 1857, concluded that the company was in danger of becoming a fallen giant. "Within the last four years, at nearly every works in Wales, the makes and yields of furnaces have been improved and rapid strides [were being made] in the way of producing cheaper pig iron," Menelaus wrote. "Dowlais is standing still instead of taking the lead, as from her site and position she ought; she is quietly falling into the rear. To remedy this state of things, a great effort is necessary and also a considerable outlay of capital."

The £100,000-plus invested by the Guests after agreement on the lease renewal had restored Dowlais's scale, but that was all. The works had 17 blast furnaces, making an average 107 tons of pig iron a week. But these levels had been unchanged for several years. About 57 hundredweight of coal was needed to produce a ton of iron – more than at many other South Welsh furnaces. Moreover, Menelaus found, the iron quality was "very irregular and often inferior".

To increase output and efficiency, Clark and Menelaus had first to overcome the irregular supply of raw materials. To replace declining local supplies of iron ore, they concluded large contracts with more distant providers, many of them in Westmorland. They bought 60 new wagons to transport the ore from Cardiff, and freed up capacity by buying 30 cheaper wagons to handle all cinder and other works traffic. As a result, the furnaces were regularly supplied and a 10,000-ton stockpile could be accumulated.

The company's own mines could not cope with demands for higher output without being expanded, but this would take years. So Dowlais immediately contracted with a firm in nearby Aberdare to supply 200 tons of coking coal a day for five years. Clark and Menelaus then sank two new pits, which opened in 1863 and 1866. In the meantime, they acquired the nearby Penydarren Ironworks. They had no use for the actual business, which was struggling to survive against the likes of Dowlais; its attraction was that it owned two coal fields and an iron ore field, with reserves totalling about 1.5 m tons. The acquisition was completed in June 1859 for almost £60,000.

The addition of Penydarren's abundant reserves – 135,700 tons of coal and 6900 tons of ore were raised in the first year of Dowlais's ownership – transformed Clark and Menelaus's attitude to the coal trade. Menelaus recommended to Clark that the company become a fully-fledged participant in the "sale coal trade". Clark, having confirmed with his deputy that Dowlais had sufficient quality and quantity of deposits to satisfy its demands and to leave a substantial surplus for sale, approved the new venture.

Menelaus contended that the ironmaster who owned collieries would always enjoy a cost advantage over the coal-miner who had no ironworks, on the grounds that the iron company could provide more regular employment. He also believed firmly that coal-trading would increase Dowlais's power over its mineworkers: "When an ironworks only raises sufficient coal for daily use in iron-making, the men [miners] have always the power to inflict grievous loss upon the master by simply idling, keeping the furnaces and forges short of coal ... Dowlais has on several occasions suffered severely from the conduct of the colliers in this way. If, however, the works raises a considerable quantity of coal beyond its requirements for iron-making, the power of the men to inflict loss is lessened."

In the ironworks itself, five blast furnaces were repaired and one was completely rebuilt, with new boilers being added in some places to improve efficiency further. The renovations boosted output by 48% and cut fuel consumption by 22%. Menelaus calculated that the annual fuel bill saving could reach £28,000.

Most challenging of all, Menelaus had to tackle the gulf between Dowlais's pig iron output and its capacity to convert pig iron into bar iron. The improved blast furnaces could now turn out almost 3000 tons of pig iron a week, but the puddling furnaces and mills could not exceed 1200 tons. Menelaus reckoned that the company's profitability depended on raising their output, because refining and finishing was where the vast majority of value could be added. Finished iron capacity had to be increased to 2000 tons a week, he concluded.

Part of the capacity expansion came from increasing the rolling mills' efficiency and flexibility, but the puddling furnace was a much harder nut to crack. Effectively, output increases could only be realised there through duplication. So Menelaus increased the number of furnaces and forges to meet the immediate need.

However, Menelaus was looking further ahead. He anticipated another quantum leap in production capability and was determined that Dowlais should be equipped to provide it and reap the commercial rewards. He therefore recommended to Clark that they build a new mill, a very large one – powerful enough to roll between 1000 and 1500 tons of iron a week.

"In the production of wrought iron, the means of producing large sizes and great lengths has not kept pace with the requirements of engineers," Menelaus wrote. "It may be fairly anticipated that when machinery of sufficient power has been erected, a demand for large sizes will follow which will command a high price from the difficulty of obtaining iron of this description. With this in view, the New Mill is designed of thrice the power of any mill in the kingdom."

The new super-mill was called the Goat Mill, apparently because many of its workers belonged to the Dowlais Company of the Glamorgan Engineers, whose coat buttons showed a goat's head in relief. It took two years to build. Its engine beam and driving wheel were carried entirely by cast iron framing, the first time that cast iron had been used in this way. The engine had twice the power of any existing engine in Britain. It drove three mills, one of them capable of turning out 1000 tons of rails a week. Menelaus accurately anticipated that the mill could roll rails up to 70 feet long.

The Goat Mill may have cost £50,000 but it paid back the investment handsomely, because it enabled Dowlais to make rails more cheaply than its competitors while maintaining their quality. The mill's size and efficiency meant it could mass-produce heavier, longer rails to a consistently good standard. "Unless a rolling mill turns out a regular and uniform quantity of finished iron, there is an end to all economy," Menelaus said after the Goat Mill was up and running.

In some product areas – notably girders and deck beams – the Goat Mill's scale made Dowlais virtually the sole UK supplier. Before the end of the Crimean War, for instance, the works won a government order for deck beams for floating batteries which were 50 feet long.

The Goat Mill was the largest single element in a huge capital spending programme masterminded by Clark and Menelaus between 1854 and 1859. In total, Dowlais invested almost £162,000 during this period [about £13.2 m in 2009 terms]. As a result, the business was loss-making in some of those years but the foundations were laid for future prosperity. From the mid-1860s, Dowlais's profits increased steadily to almost £198,000 in 1870, while its output rose to almost 166,000 tons in that year, mainly focused on rails and related products.

The one area that consistently defied Menelaus's productivity-enhancing efforts was puddling, the intermediate phase between the blast furnaces and the rolling mills. Menelaus was not alone in experiencing this intractability: iron-makers throughout the world suffered from the same problem. Menelaus told the South Wales Institute of Engineers in October 1857: "Puddling has remained ... since its invention, almost without improvement ...

"Science and practice have alike failed ... Here is a process which absolutely costs nearly one half of the value of the material operated upon, to change very slightly its chemical condition, a large proportion of the cost being for manual labour of the most severe kind, of which the supply barely keeps pace with the demand."

Increasing skilled labour shortages and the cost-inflexibility of puddling meant that a report in *The Times* on 14 August 1856 was read with intense interest throughout the iron industry. The story covered a paper delivered three days earlier to the British Association at Cheltenham by one Henry Bessemer, an engineer who had devised a method of making steel. In his paper, Bessemer detailed a process whereby compressed air was blown into the bottom of a brick-lined furnace – a converter – containing molten pig iron. Through the consequent chemical reaction, the pig iron was purified into steel while the impurities formed a slag.

The Bessemer process promised to render puddling obsolete. As a result, Menelaus recorded: "Iron makers went mad with excitement." A steel rush ensued as iron-makers tried to secure licences from Bessemer. Menelaus was in the forefront: accompanied by Edward Riley, Dowlais's chemist, he raced to London for discussions with the inventor.

On 27 August 1856, Menelaus and Riley secured for Dowlais the first licence to use Bessemer's patent. The company paid Bessemer £10,000 in return for the right to make 20,000 tons of steel a year for 10 years with a royalty of one farthing [a fraction of one pence] per additional ton providing total output was less than 70,000 tons.

The licensing agreement proved somewhat academic, in the sense that it took years for Dowlais's steel output remotely to approach 20,000 tons. In fact, before late 1865, Dowlais was unable to produce any steel at all. The first steel rail was rolled at Dowlais in 1858 from an ingot supplied by Bessemer's works at St Pancras, London. Much to the delight of the puddlers who were watching, it broke while still hot. Subsequent attempts suffered the same fate. Other iron-makers who had rushed to secure licences encountered the same problem.

The brittleness was due to the chemical composition of the pig iron fed into the converters. The "acid" process of steel-making required iron ore with very low phosphorus and sulphur content, and the ingots produced at Dowlais during this period vastly exceeded these very low levels. As a result, the steel was liable to crack and could not be rolled.

It took Menelaus and his team almost 10 years to isolate the problem and resolve it. In July 1865, after Dowlais had at last obtained suitable ore to prevent the brittleness, steel-making began in earnest. The works began to produce bars which were rolled into rails and supplied to London & North Western Railway (LNWR) for testing. LNWR – and other railway operators – were cautious adopters. In 1866, Dowlais made only 2257 tons of steel.

At this juncture, confident that Dowlais had at last overcome the technical problems of commercial steel-making, Menelaus carried out a survey of the company's workforce. In 1866, the company had 7719 male employees, 1482 of them under the age of 18, and 781 female, of whom 297 were under 18. By contemporary standards, this was quite progressive. Menelaus wrote: "Practically no children are employed under 10 years of age. There are no girls under 10 and the few boys, nine in all, are the sons of very poor parents to whom the earnings are of importance.

"The labour at which these children are employed is healthy; they either work in the open air or under large and airy sheds, and the employment is by no means hard; as they are for the most part taken on as a help to their parents, and very little work is expected of them. Of children between the ages of 10 and 13 years, there are employed 505 boys and 64 girls. Most of the boys work in the collieries and mine works."

Menelaus concluded that there had been a great improvement in working conditions over the previous 20 years. Women were generally being replaced by men or machinery. Because wages were slowly rising, it was no longer necessary to send children to work at such young ages. Women were increasingly concentrating on bringing up children rather than supplementing their husband's income at the ironworks. He believed that his report reflected not just the workforce profile at Dowlais, but "may be taken as a fair sample of the South Wales ironworks generally".

By 1869, Dowlais had installed six 5-ton converters, making the works one of the biggest Bessemer plants in Britain. The previous year, an increasingly confident Menelaus told the Institution of Civil Engineers in London that "even the best wrought iron ever made was far inferior to Bessemer metal, at least for rails. In adopting steel for Bessemer rails there was one great security: bad steel, in the sense of impure steel, could not be made into rails."

However, the price of steel rails held back their market penetration. Steel rails in 1869 were known to cost up to £70 a ton, against £7 a ton for wrought iron rails. But when the Bessemer patent with its royalty payments expired in 1870, the price differential began to narrow dramatically. That was the breakthrough year for Dowlais: it made more than 20,000 tons of steel for the first time and never looked back. Within a decade, its steel output had almost quadrupled to more than 83,000 tons.

At first, steel was made solely by the Bessemer method. But shortly after the Bessemer process had been perfected, the Siemens Steel Company began operating Britain's first commercial open-hearth steelworks at Landore, a process invented by Sir William Siemens. Unlike Bessmer's method, the Siemens system involved slowly converting a mixture of steel scrap and molten pig iron in a large bath heated by a regenerative gas furnace.

Siemens and his brother Frederick then developed a gas producer which used the gases emitted during the coke-making process to be used to fire the furnace, and the hot waste gases given off during steel-making to be used to pre-heat the incoming fuel and air. This generated huge fuel cost savings, making the steel-making process commercially viable.

In 1871, to ensure that Dowlais benefited from any commercial opportunities provided by the Siemens break-through, Menelaus built only the second open-hearth furnace in Britain, after the pioneering Landore plant itself. Although Dowlais continued to be dominated by steel made under the Bessemer process, by the early 1880s it was producing a significant amount from the open-hearth method.

However, the company was also facing increased competition, both from Britain – where younger firms with newer technology were expanding – and overseas. German, American and Belgian steel-makers, with the latest equipment and sites hand-picked for optimum efficiency, began to constitute a serious competitive threat.

Dowlais entered a joint venture with two of the new competitors – the Consett Iron Co. in the UK and Germany's Krupp – to buy the Orconera Iron Co. in Bilbao in order to secure supplies of iron ore that was almost free from sulphur and phosphorus, which could wreck an open-hearth furnace. But this deal itself highlighted how Dowlais's first mover advantage had now become a competitive disadvantage.

Dowlais used the original steel-making process, known as the "acid" process, in which the furnace brick linings were made of acid materials. As a result, phosphorus present in the pig iron oxidised to form phosphoric acid and was not removed. So manufacturers had to use low-phosphorus ore.

But in the late 1870s, two British engineers devised a new method, the "basic" process, which cut steel-making costs because it allowed producers to use iron ore that was high in phosphorus. Such iron ore was still plentiful in the UK, but could not be used by first-generation technology works such as Dowlais.

In the basic process, the open-hearth furnace was lined with dolomite, a form of limestone. This reacted with the phosphoric acid in the pig iron to produce a compound which could be removed as "slag", cooled, ground up and sold as fertiliser. As a result, modern steelworks could now be built close to the large reserves of iron ore in Britain which were high in phosphorus, vastly reducing the plants' transport costs compared with Dowlais, which was now shipping in ore from Spain.

Menelaus's health began to fail in the late 1870s, and he died on 30 March 1882 while on holiday at Tenby in Wales. He was 64 and had run Dowlais under Clark for more than a quarter of a century. He was the first great engineer in the history of what became GKN.

Menelaus left the very substantial sum of £250,000 [almost £22 m at 2009 prices], but his personal life was scarred by the tragedy of losing his wife to a fatal fever only nine weeks after their wedding. He later adopted his two nephews, the eldest of whom became an MP and judge. He combined supreme engineering prowess with a considerable interest in the arts, and assembled a collection of pictures which was bequeathed to Cardiff

Town Council. Today, they form part of the National Gallery of Wales.

His engineering achievements were legion. Apart from what he achieved at and for Dowlais itself – the innovative process developments epitomised by the first application of the Bessemer process – he made a massive contribution to the engineering profession. In 1881, he was awarded the prestigious Bessemer Gold Medal for services to the steel industry. Co-founder and first president of the South Wales Institute of Engineers, he also played a formative role in establishing the Iron and Steel Institute. Its Journal paid due tribute to him in its obituary: "It is perhaps no exaggeration to say that there was no more indefatigable worker in the manufacture of iron and steel, no-one who had more thoroughly mastered it in the best practical way, and few if any who enjoyed at Dowlais and elsewhere a stronger and better reputation."

Menelaus's final achievement, rare for many business leaders before and since, was consummately to manage his own succession. Edward Martin had been apprenticed to Menelaus in 1860 at the age of 16, and worked for the Dowlais Company for 10 years before leaving, as deputy general manager, to gain experience and career advancement at other iron and steel companies. Menelaus, knowing his health was waning, re-recruited Martin in 1881 as his deputy and heir-apparent. When he died, Martin duly succeeded him.

Martin was already a leading figure in the steel industry, having played a significant part in bringing the "basic" manufacturing process into commercial operation. In 1884, he won the Bessemer Gold Medal for this work. He soon identified new opportunities for Dowlais in related sectors.

Under Menelaus, Dowlais had already diversified into markets such as tin plate, laying down three tin plate mills in 1879. Martin went much further. In 1885, he designed and built a plant for making steel sleepers to replace the traditional timber variety. They were a particular export success in India, where insects ate timber sleepers, and other colonial markets. Dowlais and other steel-makers were also able to substitute steel for iron in railway accessories, initially for the likes of signal post masts and point control rods, later for much larger structures such as bridges, viaducts and stations.

The largest source of demand remained the replacement of iron by steel rails. By 1879, most rail companies had gone over completely to steel rails. The last iron rail made in Dowlais was finished in 1883. The following year, Dowlais turned out more than 138,000 tons of steel. Demand was boosted further by the gradual realisation that engineers had overestimated the likely life of steel rails. Under the increasing pressure of rising rail traffic and heavier rolling stock, rail replacement became a thriving market.

But Dowlais's increasing competitive disadvantage meant that it could not reap full benefit from the rising demand. The company could not recover the high profitability it had enjoyed in the early 1870s. Dowlais experienced extreme cyclicality in its profitability from the mid-1870s. Profits peaked at around £250,000 in 1874, troughed at £60,000 the following year, recovered to almost £200,000 in 1882, plunged back to mid-1870s levels around 1887, rose again to just over £246,000 in 1890, then slipped once more in the early 1890s.

The overall numbers masked a change in the balance of group profits. Steel's contribution waned as Dowlais's competitive disadvantages told. Coal accounted for an increasing proportion of the surplus. Its contribution increased from 6% of profits in steel's halcyon days of the early 1870s to 60% in 1894.

Dowlais was not the only British steel-maker to struggle. J. Stephen Jeans, an astute observer of the industry in the late 19th and early 20th centuries, attributed the domestic industry's relative decline to the rise of overseas competition: "Our hold on foreign markets is loosening year by year, while we retain a firmer grip on our colonial markets," he wrote with foresight. "But it will not be overlooked that the time is certainly to ultimately arrive when our principal colonial possessions, and India, will largely supply their own needs."

Overall industrial production told a similar story. Average annual real growth rates in British output fell from 3.5% in the 1850s to 2.1% in the 1870s, 1.8% in the 1890s and 1.5% in the early 1900s. In 1887, America overtook Britain in steel production volumes and its output of steel rails was double that of the UK. In mainland Europe, huge German steel-makers such as Krupp satisfied domestic demand and, increasingly, won export orders – some of them from British and Australian customers which had previously bought from UK steel-makers.

However, Dowlais faced a double impact: it was disadvantaged not only against overseas rivals, but against newer, more modern competitors at home. Sited remotely, having to transport both its ore and its finished product more than 20 miles by rail and with blast furnaces and rolling mills that dated from mid-century, the company could no longer compete with integrated works located close to raw material sources which were benefiting from lower transport costs and greater economies of scale.

Clark and Martin realised that the company was facing terminal decline and that dramatic action was needed to save it. In 1887, they conceived a plan for a large new, integrated steelworks that could at least match their rivals. It was nicknamed "Dowlais by the sea".

Clark and Martin decided to site the new plant near Cardiff docks, so that raw material imports could be transported directly from freighters to the furnaces and finished products moved efficiently by sea or rail. They identified a greenfield location on open moorland called East Moors, which had easy access to the Great Western Railway's main Paddington–Cardiff line. A 99-year lease was taken at £1200 a year, and another on a wharf at Roath Dock for £1500 a year.

Martin designed the new works, and in March 1888 construction of the foundations for three blast furnaces began. The first two furnaces went into operation just under three years later on 4 February 1891. Lord and Lady Wimborne performed the opening ceremony. Each furnace had a capacity of more than 1000 tons a week. The third blast furnace was completed in 1892 and a fourth added five years later.

The steelworks themselves, comprising six Siemens open-hearth furnaces, opened in September 1895. Clark and Martin did not want to compete with the Dowlais works in the rail market, so they targeted shipbuilding. Slabbing and plate mills were installed at the same time as the Siemens furnaces were laid down, and the works pushed into the plate steel business, also targeting boiler-makers and construction girders. The shipbuilding market was high-growth, and became even more buoyant in the early 20th century because of naval rearmament. And as architects and engineers turned increasingly to structural steelwork in place of timber, demand for East Moors' plate grew further.

The new works was among the most advanced in Britain. Seven hydraulic cranes were installed at Roath Dock to unload the ore from Spain. By using a greenfield site, Martin could maximise the efficient layout of the manufacturing processes.

Dowlais-Cardiff had two drawbacks. Partly because of the success of the Orconera supply venture, it used the acid steel process which had been adopted by Dowlais and not the basic method used by its more modern rivals, at home and particularly overseas. As a result, wrote Edgar Jones, it missed "the sustained inventive attention which others focussed on the basic method.

"Since both American and German steelworks were predominantly organised around the basic system and were responsible for generating a host of innovations, it is likely that British concerns which remained wedded to acid technology fell progressively behind in the race for efficiency."

The efficiency gains that the East Moors plant could have achieved were further compromised by the company's continued operation of the antiquated Dowlais works. While Clark and Martin did not suggest closing the 140-year-old plant at a stroke – an action which would have caused huge unemployment in the Merthyr area – they did plan a phased shutdown which would have allowed them to switch steel-making to the new plant.

But in 1892, while East Moors was still under construction, Clark retired. He was 83 and had presided over the company for almost four decades. In that time, Dowlais had made a massive contribution to Britain's industrial development. In many respects, it had become to the steel industry what Coalbrookdale had been to the first iron masters: an educational centre and training ground for people who became some of the country's leading engineers and metallurgists. "The company assumed a significance beyond its mere commercial standing," Jones concluded. Such was George Clark's legacy.

Clark's retirement left a vacuum which Lord Wimborne, throughout Clark's tenure the absentee owner-chairman of the company, now partially filled. His influence was significant – but not beneficial to the business. Crucially, he refused to countenance the closure of Dowlais, apparently insisting that it was the company's duty to its original community to keep the works going regardless of cost and sensible economics. The effect was to blunt Dowlais-Cardiff's competitive edge while merely postponing the inevitable at Dowlais itself and therefore making its eventual closure all the more painful.

"A policy which recognised the inevitability of Dowlais's decline as a steel-producing works and gradually transferred plant to Cardiff and offered incentives to the workforce to migrate to Cardiff would have prevented much of the harrowing unemployment that ultimately occurred when the steelworks finally closed," wrote Jones.

More critically still, Wimborne's supremacy spelled the end for the Dowlais Iron Company's independence. Its great custodians were departing the scene.

East Moors opened the same year as Lady Charlotte Guest died, at the age of 83. She had gone blind in her last years, but still produced a red woollen scarf every day, which was then given to a London cabman. When she was not knitting, she would recite Chaucer at length. No eminent Victorian, she nevertheless occupies a singular and overlooked place in British industrial history.

Charlotte Guest's death was followed three years later, on 2 February 1898, by that of George Clark. The way was now clear for Wimborne to pursue his own objectives. These soon boiled down to one aim: to sell the business.

Wimborne's intention was partly prompted by fears that John D. Rockefeller and Andrew Carnegie, the American oil and steel titans, were planning an assault on the British market. "It is obvious that American competition, by reducing prices, would affect most seriously the prospects of English steel companies," Wimborne wrote to Martin in April 1899. "It therefore seems to me that advantage should be taken of the present exceptionally favourable time. If Dowlais is to be bought out as a company, no time should be lost."

He need not have worried. Dowlais had a buyer, ready and waiting. Step forward, Arthur Keen.

# CHAPTER 4

# Keen, Guest and Nettlefolds

The man who created Guest, Keen & Nettlefolds was born on 23 January 1835 in Cheshire. Arthur Keen was a classic first-generation Victorian entrepreneur. The son of a yeoman-farmer and innkeeper, Keen had barely any education and joined the London & North Western Railway as a clerk in the great rail hub of Crewe. He was promoted at the age of 22 to the post of goods agent, which was based in Smethwick, near Birmingham. Keen thus began a working lifetime's association with the town, which was fast becoming a city.

Keen was not an engineer. He had no formal qualifications at all. What he did possess was a razor-sharp eye for a business opportunity. Around 1856, Keen was introduced to Francis Watkins, an American who had journeyed to Britain to try to sell the rights to a nut-making machine of his own invention. The commercial matchmaker was Thomas Astbury, a wealthy iron-founder and cannon-maker. Appropriately enough, Keen married Astbury's daughter two years later in Smethwick Chapel.

Astbury backed the two men to form Watkins & Keen, a maker of nuts and bolts. Demonstrating from the very outset an awareness of the competitive advantages to be gained from process technology, they imported American machinery which was so superior to that of their home-grown rivals that, within two years of its formation, their company employed 500 people. It outgrew its original base and, about 1860, moved into the London Works in Smethwick, which had been vacated by the failure of a firm of structural and railway engineers. The small, two-storey offices at London Works were to become the home and headquarters of GKN.

In April 1864, Watkins & Keen floated on the stock market and changed its name to The Patent Nut and Bolt Company (PNB). A former mayor of Birmingham became chairman and a later Mayor of Salford became deputy chairman: Arthur Keen understood intuitively the value of connections. He rapidly embarked on a spate of acquisitions to expand the company. The first was a West Bromwich nut and bolt maker which also owned an ironworks and foundry in South Wales – the Cwmbran Iron company.

Keen made no bones about his objective: he planned to corner the Birmingham nut, bolt and rivet market through a combination of acquisitions and price-cutting designed to drive rivals into his arms or out of the business. Amid the red-blooded and distinctly unregulated capitalism of the late 19th century, this plan delivered substantial shareholder value. Or, as one local newspaper put it at the time, Keen's strategy "has consistently been to absorb or exclude, and it was so managed that in exclusion his competitors were absolutely disarmed".

Nevertheless, Keen did not attain total dominance. Major competitors survived and thrived, including F.W. Cotterill and John Garrington & Sons, founded in Darlaston in the Black Country in 1810 and 1830 respectively, and Bayliss, Jones & Bayliss of Wolverhampton. Watkins & Keen set horizons well beyond the West Midlands, however.

The partners scoured the world for export markets, selling into the colonial territories of Australia, New Zealand and Canada, albeit without great success. Like Dowlais, they won business in Russia. But their most sustained success came in mainland Europe – not with their nuts and bolts, but through licensing continental manufacturers to use the American machines that they patented for use in Europe.

Watkins retired from the board in 1867, although he continued to work as an overseas salesman. The pair remained close – Keen gave one of his sons the Christian names Francis Watkins. The former rail clerk now dominated the company, even though he did not actually become chairman for another 28 years. During that period, he extended his influence into many aspects of West Midlands commerce and politics. "Mr Keen generally got his way, both in business and public affairs," observed one contemporary. He was "cautious to a degree, and yet always enterprising, gifted also with an intuitive knowledge of men and a born organiser".

A supreme networker, he became chairman of the Birmingham and Midland Bank (which later became the Midland, one of Britain's big four clearing banks); he was a vice-president both of the Institution of Mechanical

Engineers and the Iron and Steel Institute, and director of a number of engineering companies in addition to his own.

A combination of his networking skills and the very real needs of his company led Keen to Dowlais. Through the 1880s and into the 1890s, Keen became increasingly concerned about the PNB's dependence for its raw material on the wrought iron that was still being produced by its Cwmbran works. He eventually decided that, in order to continue to compete successfully, Cwmbran must be converted to steel-making.

To do that, Keen needed steel technology. There were only two ways to acquire it – employ experts to advise him on how to design the best new plant, or buy an existing steel-maker. Having failed to find a suitable target, Keen chose the former route. And one of the experts he consulted was Edward Martin.

Once he had talked for a while with Martin, Keen changed his plan of action. From Martin, he learned that Wimborne was ready to sell the Dowlais Company. Keen knew Dowlais – it had been a bar iron supplier to PNB. Dowlais was a steel-maker with two works, one of them new, and a clutch of profitable coal mines – it was the perfect fit. Keen moved fast. Preliminary negotiations began in autumn 1899. In September, Wimborne's industrial interests were consolidated into a new, private limited liability company with registered capital of £1.1 m. This reconstruction cleared the way for a sale.

On 27 March 1900, Keen made public his intention to acquire the Dowlais Company. It would be a reverse takeover, because Dowlais was larger than PNB. Dowlais produced statements showing that its average annual profit over the 10 years to 1898 was £84,000, and Keen initially offered £1.6 m for the business. He subsequently reduced the price slightly to £1.53 m – £138 m in 2009 money.

The deal completed a few months later. In the first July of the 20th century, a new public limited liability company, with the registered number 66549, was formed to acquire the businesses of the Patent Nut & Bolt Co. Ltd and the Dowlais Iron, Steel and Coal Co. It was called Guest, Keen & Co.

On its creation, Guest, Keen raised £3 m through three £1 m issues – of ordinary shares, preference shares and debenture stock. Wimborne's £1.53 m was paid in instalments of between £100,000 and £350,000, the last tranche coming a year after the establishment of the new group.

Keen also did rather well: PNB shareholders received £1 m for their interests, of which £200,000 was in ordinary shares and £400,000 each in prefs and debentures. Since Keen owned 590 PNB pref shares and 4380 ordinary shares, he emerged with holdings of 2.95% and 21.9% in the respective equity classes.

He did not pause to count his gains. Instead, concerned about the threat of high-tech US competitors, he embarked on a search for an American steel company which Guest, Keen could buy. Keen rapidly reached outline agreement for a merger with United States Steel Corporation (the forerunner of US Steel) but the deal then fell through.

Instead, Keen turned to a target much, much closer to home. He determined that Guest, Keen's first acquisition should be none other than Nettlefolds, the highly-successful maker of screws and other nuts and bolts based opposite the London Works at Heath Street, on the other side of the Birmingham Canal.

Nettlefolds had stuck closely to its knitting in the three-quarters of a century since John Sutton Nettlefold, an ironmonger, founded a wood screw-making business in 1826 at Sunbury-on-Thames. That year, Nettlefold published the first of what was to become a series of industry-leading price lists for his range of screws. The list contained 184 varieties of screw in different gauges, made of iron, brass or copper. The smallest sold for eight old pence per dozen, the largest for a not-inconsiderable 16 shillings (about 80p).

In the early 1830s, in order to be closer to his raw material suppliers, Nettlefold decided to move his factory to Birmingham, the centre of the screw trade. His crucial breakthrough came in 1854, when he bought the exclusive UK rights to the Sloane patent from America for using automatic lathes to make woodscrews with gimlet points. Until then, screws had had a blunt end.

The patent and the machines to capitalise on it did not come cheap. Together, they cost £30,000. On top of that, Nettlefold had to build a new type of factory, large enough to provide the economies of scale to repay his hefty upfront investment.

He had to borrow some of the money he needed from his brother-in-law, Joseph Chamberlain Senior, who owned a London-based shoe-making business. Nettlefold & Chamberlain (N&C) was born.

Chamberlain Senior sent his son, also called Joseph, to look after his interests in the Birmingham firm. Similarly, Nettlefold installed his brother, Edward, to oversee the firm and appointed his son, Joseph Henry, as works manager. The company therefore became an archetypal family partnership in the forefront of 19th century industrialisation.

The new factory was built on the border of Birmingham and Smethwick, in Heath Street. Nettlefold and Chamberlain then embarked on an expansion drive, taking out a series of competitors while integrating vertically upstream, into both iron-making and wire-drawing and rolling. It built an ironworks at Hadley Castle in Shropshire, from which it derived its "castle" trademark.

The heavy investment in automation paid off because it made possible huge increases in output. In 1865, the company produced 70% of Birmingham's total weekly output of 18,720,000 woodscrews, which exceeded the entire national output of screws in 1850. By 1873, N&C's wood screw output was up to 21,600,000 weekly – 1,036,800,000 of screws a year – with more than 730 varieties of iron screw alone. It also made a gamut of other fasteners: nuts, bolts, rivets, hooks, eyes, split linch and cotter pins, washers and hinges – a product range which continued well into the second half of the 20th century.

Nettlefolds' list prices remained unaltered from the early 1850s until 1954. The company changed prices by varying the discounts it gave to wholesalers, according to the state of the market and the extent of the competition. This technique was made possible by the high degree of control the company wielded over its home market.

In June 1870, after diversifying into nuts and bolts, N&C was on the receiving end of an informal bid approach – from Arthur Keen. The partners turned him down, and

Joseph Chamberlain drew up a strategy for exporting to continental Europe.

Chamberlain's marketing approach would have impressed an early 21st-century MBA. Before launching into France, he enhanced his basic knowledge of the language by reading French literature in the original and hiring a Frenchman for conversation over breakfast. When he began selling, he quoted in decimalised weights and measures and packaged screws in French blue wrapping paper rather than in English green.

The French preferred screws nicked and wormed, not turned as the English did, so he had them made accordingly. "No work is worth doing badly, and he that puts his best into every task that comes to him will surely outstrip the man who waits for a great opportunity before he condescends to exert himself," Chamberlain said, referring to what we might today recognise as the continuous improvement ethic.

Chamberlain did benefit in his French foray from one exceptional if temporary event: the siege of Paris in the Franco-Prussian War of 1870–71 cut off one Paris-based rival of Nettlefolds from its customers. Nevertheless, his record of establishing N&C in export markets was formidable – by the mid-1870s, it was exporting throughout mainland Europe and to Russia, the US, Canada, Japan, India, Australia and New Zealand.

At home, Chamberlain demonstrated the political skills that he employed to great effect in his second career. He became Mayor of Birmingham and, when some Birmingham businessmen attempted to start up a rival screw-maker, Chamberlain used the local media in a bid to undermine it while warning his workers that no-one who left to take a job with the new firm would be re-employed at N&C. The company never grew into a serious threat and was later consolidated by Nettlefolds.

In 1874, he decided to make a full-time career of politics and he and his two brothers sold their half of the partnership for about £600,000. Chamberlain emerged with about £120,000, more than enough to support a varied political career in which he became President of the Board of Trade under Gladstone's Liberals and Colonial Secretary under the Conservative Lord Salisbury.

As with Sir John Guest, his life highlights the cross-fertilisation between industry and national politics that existed in the Victorian age but was lost in Britain during the following century. The Chamberlains went out in style – they organised a works outing in which almost 1000 employees and their wives travelled by special train to see the Crystal Palace in London, where they were given tea and a three-course dinner.

N&C was now Nettlefolds, and Joseph Nettlefold became chairman. He planned a new wave of acquisitions to mop up rivals and, needing to access the capital markets, took the company public in 1880. The wave of acquisitions secured for it a virtual monopoly of the home wood screw market, but it also created problems, turning the initially compact Heath Street works into an increasingly inefficient warren of mills, packaging rooms and warehouses.

Joseph died young, aged 54, in 1881 and was succeeded as chairman by his younger brother, Frederick. During his 10-year tenure, the company built a steelworks at Rogerstone, South Wales, to provide the raw material

for some of its fasteners. As Europe's largest fastener manufacturer, Nettlefolds also played a formative role in creating
a European wood screw cartel, the International Woodscrew
Union, whose members – British, French, German and
Belgian – agreed not to export into other members' countries and attempted to ensure that each sold at the same
price into non-member territories.

Such was the world before UK restrictive practices
legislation and the advent of the European Economic
Community. However, it did not save Nettlefolds from
being pressured by American and German competition in
neutral, non-colonial markets where the company consequently made little headway.

Nettlefolds' underlying pre-tax profits passed £100,000
for the first time in 1889, doubled to more than £200,000
three years later, then fell back to just under £140,000 in
1900 and 1901. Some of the profit fall was probably due
to transfers to reserves, but it may also have reflected a
waning of the dynastic dynamism that had established the
company's supremacy in its home market.

Arthur Keen, Nettlefolds' long-time suitor, sensed that
his chance had come at last. As the relatively small PNB,
he had found his advances easily spurned by his neighbour.
But now, with the might of the newly-created Guest, Keen
behind him, he constituted an altogether more compelling
proposition.

With characteristic dexterity, Keen employed a carrot-
and-stick approach. In September 1901, he asked Edward
Nettlefold for a meeting. At the meeting, he played the
vertical integration card. Keen said later: "I explained the
principal advantages [of a deal] that would accrue to

Nettlefolds, which were that it would make them practically self-contained, which at the present they were not, as they had to commence with the manufacture of their products from all bought raw materials, whereas we should enable them to commence at the base, which referred to our iron ore, coal, limestone and all other materials necessary for the manufacture of pig iron."

Keen was not entirely convinced that Nettlefolds would accept this argument. So he set out to concentrate his prey's mind further by buying modern American wood-screw-making machines and transporting them, amid considerable publicity, to the London Works. Joseph Chamberlain would no doubt have ruefully approved of these tactics.

Keen also had an inside track. Guest, Keen's auditor was the Birmingham chartered accountancy firm Carter & Co, which had been Keen's auditor at PNB. Edward Carter, one of the firm's leading lights, had even been a non-executive director of PNB although he resigned following the Dowlais merger. Coincidentally, Carter & Co. were also Nettlefolds' auditors. Eric Carter, one of the partners, now acted as a matchmaker to the Guest, Keen–Nettlefolds deal. Secret discussions between Arthur Keen and Nettlefolds took place in his dining room. When the marriage was consummated, it was natural that Carter & Co. should be elected as auditor to the enlarged group.

Threatened by further competition on their doorstep at a time when profits were already declining from historic highs, Nettlefolds duly succumbed. In 1902, it agreed a takeover by Guest, Keen for £630,000 [about £56 m at 2009 prices]. Four Nettlefolds directors, including Edward, joined the board of the group that was henceforth called Guest, Keen & Nettlefolds (GKN). As was indeed his wont, Arthur Keen had got his way.

The new company was the 15th largest in Britain, with assets of £4.54 m and pre-tax profits of almost £800,000, and was the country's leading iron, steel and coal business. The only larger industrial groups were Vickers and Armstrong, Whitworth. Keen liked to present the deal as a rationalisation move caused by the overlap of the two companies' product lines. This, however, was a smoke-screen because the degree of duplication was in fact very limited. In truth, it was the final major act of empire-building by this formidable man, now aged 67 but still far from retirement.

No matter the profusion of directors on what was effectively a three-company board, Arthur Keen dominated the group. With his bald pate and neatly trimmed white beard and moustache, he cut the figure of an archetypal Victorian patriarch. "He had difficulty in devolving respon-sibility and power, and his appetite for work appeared to be insatiable," wrote Jones.

However, his health began to decline. In 1908, he retired from the Midland Bank board. In July 1912, when Dowlais received royal recognition through a visit by King George V, Keen could not travel to Merthyr to meet His Majesty. By then, GKN's profits had declined to just over £600,000.

The former Guest and Keen businesses remained powers in their homeland, but overseas they were hard hit by rivals, particularly from the newer industrialised countries. Only Nettlefolds, with its hammerlock on the home market, continued to prosper. At the time GKN was formed, it contributed a quarter of group profits; a decade later, it accounted for half the surplus.

The high tide of British industrial success in the century from 1750 was now ebbing fast. One English bolt maker reported in 1909: "Our manufacturers are gradually being pushed out [of export markets] through low prices of German, French and American goods." Dowlais followed Nettlefolds in seeking protection through a cartel – it formed one with German and Belgian rollers of steel rails. UK steel rail output peaked at 1.235 m tons in 1882 and more than halved in the next decade, overtaken by America and matched by Germany.

A rather larger and more deadly political challenge from Germany loomed increasingly large. On 4 August 1914, Britain declared war. Because of the widespread view that the First World War would be over by Christmas, the British government initially took no special measures to direct and control industrial production. Indeed, a week after the outbreak of hostilities, the government-inspired phrase "Business as Usual" appeared for the first time, in the *Daily Chronicle*. The only GKN works affected in this first, somewhat unreal, phase was Cwmbran, because the government asked the GKN board to authorise a plant to make benzol for explosives from the by-products of the coke ovens there.

On 8 February 1915, Arthur Keen died of a heart attack. He was aged 80 and had been GKN's master-builder. Like many another industrial tycoon before and since, Keen's forte was making the deal rather than managing what he had made. As a result, GKN had plateaued after 1902 and it was only Nettlefolds' intrinsic strength that saved the group from a greater decline.

Keen's personal financial legacy was an estate worth more than £1 m – £74 m in 2009 terms. But he also left a huge vacuum at the top of GKN. Like other dominant figures, he had no obvious successor of the calibre required to direct, streamline and re-energise the agglomeration that was GKN. His son, Arthur T. Keen, succeeded him, but he died in July 1918 and was in turn succeeded by Edward Ponsonby, Earl of Bessborough – husband of John and Charlotte Guest's youngest daughter, Blanche, and who had advised Wimborne on the sale of Dowlais to Keen.

By then, Britain's war – and GKN's – was nearly done and won. During it, the internal direction that GKN lacked was temporarily covered by government control. In May 1915, when it became obvious that hopes of an early end to the conflict were fanciful, the future Prime Minister Lloyd George created a Ministry of Munitions to ensure armaments supply.

Such an initiative was sorely needed. In 1914, Britain's total munitions supply could not support a single major offensive. The Munitions Ministry took command of the industrial supply chain, buying, supplying and distributing the raw materials required by factories which it variously directed to make ammunition, weapons, vehicles, other equipment and uniforms. It reorganised the labour force to maximise output and used an army of accountants to ensure that costs were kept under control and to prevent profiteering.

In November 1915, the Ministry designated hundreds of factories as Controlled Establishments under the new Munitions of War Act. Profits of Controlled Establishments were indeed controlled: the government established a standard profit level based on an average of profits in 1913–14. Any profit earned over and above this amount was taxed at 80%.

In all, 24 GKN works were included in the Controlled Establishments list, from the London Works and Heath Street to East Moors and Dowlais. Steel was critical to the war effort and Britain was particularly inferior to Germany in the production of high-grade alloy steels. Shell steels were also in short supply. A huge effort was made by the government to expand capacity.

East Moors, which supplied plate for warships, underwent a significant and fundamental transformation as a result of the war demands. It suffered severe supply difficulties as merchant vessels bringing its iron ore from Spain were repeatedly torpedoed by German U-boats. In January 1916, supplies for Dowlais had to be diverted to Cardiff because ore stocks there were so low. As a result, the Ministry proposed the conversion of steel-making at East Moors to basic open-hearth furnaces, thereby not only allowing it to access UK ore supplies for the first time but also enabling it to mix pig iron with scrap, which could not be used in the acid process. Officials also asked GKN to consider converting Dowlais to the basic method, although this never happened. However, East Moors further increased capacity in 1917 by installing two new open-hearth blast furnaces to make more special and shell steels.

GKN's biggest problem in the early years of the war, in common with its peers, was the shortage of male workers. Thousands of the company's employees answered the call of the "Your Country Needs You" campaign. By July 1915, almost 5000 employees had volunteered. Conscription was introduced in 1916, and a system of "certified occupations" was introduced to ensure that specialist skilled men did not join up. Even so, output was being affected.

As a result, factories increasingly turned to women workers. In munitions, women aged from 14 to middle-age entered the labour force, working 12 hours a day, seven days a week. Their punctuality was good and their productivity was high – higher, some reports estimated, than pre-war male-dominated levels. In the Cwmbran nut and bolt works, the women workers were nicknamed "Makepiece's Angels" because the foreman was called Makepiece.

At Dowlais, women worked in the brickyards as machine hands, moulders and clay grinders and in a host of other departments. Women had always been employed in Heath Street, and their numbers now increased exponentially. Across the country, there had been less than six million women in paid employment immediately before the war. By 1918, the total had increased to 7.5 million.

In pure financial terms, GKN did not benefit from the war. Profits in each year of the war were lower than in 1913. The disruption to export markets and the additional costs of production, including wage rises, outweighed the increase in output volumes. By 1918, Dowlais and East Moors were making a substantial loss and the group was being kept afloat by Nettlefolds' profits and interest payments on GKN's bank deposits. However, the group did gain from the government-financed capacity modernisation and expansion at many of its works.

But for Britain, as for the war's other main protagonists, there could be no compensation for the biggest loss of all: the millions of men, many of whom would have been the young managers and skilled workers of the next business generation, who died in the Great War.

Of the 10 million killed, Britain lost 750,000, France almost twice that number and Germany almost two million. Those countries' economies carried the losses through the next decade and more. More than 100 men from GKN's Fasteners factories were killed. One Dowlais worker, Sergeant John Collins, won the Victoria Cross (VC) as a Private for gallantry in action in spring 1918 at Beersheba, Palestine.

Collins became the second GKN employee to be awarded the VC. Private John Williams was also awarded the honour. It was made following an action in 1879 at Rorke's Drift in the Zulu War when, as part of a contingent of 150 soldiers, he helped defend a supply station against 4000 Zulu warriors. The action – immortalised in the film "Zulu" – was particularly noted for the granting of 11 Victoria Crosses, the most awarded in a single action to that date and since. Williams worked for nearly 40 years at the GKN Bolt and Nut factory in Cwmbran until his retirement in 1922. When he died in 1932, he was the oldest Rorke's Drift VC survivor.

The company did write its own postscript to the mistakenly entitled "war to end all wars". Near the conflict's end, the Ministry of Munitions came up with the idea of honouring some of those who had remained in the factories, doing invaluable work. They asked GKN to nominate employees for the Order of the British Empire.

The GKN directors considered this request, and politely declined it. Such a selection, they believed, would "make differences which would be likely to cause jealousy". They thought it would be invidious to select a handful of factory workers for honours when so many GKN people – whether working at home or fighting and suffering overseas – had given their all for their country.

CHAPTER 5

# The Empire-
# Builder from Merthyr

The British economy enjoyed a post-war boom in the two years following 11 November 1918, but GKN did not share in the upswing.

Although Nettlefolds remained in good shape, the former PNB businesses were suffering from years of under-investment. James Jolly, who joined the group as company secretary in August 1918, remarked that Arthur Keen had preferred to invest in gilts [government securities] rather than machinery.

The board was also aware of its weakness in top management. Lord Bessborough was the first official non-executive chairman in GKN's history (although Lord Wimborne had also been effectively non-executive) and his fellow directors included no outstanding executives.

To plug both the competitiveness and the personnel gap, GKN therefore took a short cut: in August 1919, it acquired the nut and bolt maker F.W.Cotterill, a competitor whose managing director, Tom Peacock, was widely respected in the industry. Peacock was immediately installed on the GKN board. The following year, the group further consolidated its leadership in fasteners by acquiring Bayliss, Jones & Bayliss.

Even GKN's quickfire deal-making paled by comparison with that of another management team which now entered the group's orbit. H. Seymour Berry and David Llewellyn were a duo of Welsh entrepreneurs who had built a substantial coal and engineering business through a whirlwind of acquisitions.

Appropriately enough for someone who was to exert a very significant influence on GKN, Berry was born and raised in Merthyr Tydfil. He qualified as a teacher but then left the profession and became a (real) estate agent. During the war, he secured a position with Cambrian Trust, one of the leading South Wales mining companies. Berry rose to run the business before meeting by chance with Llewellyn on a rail journey from Porthcawl to Cardiff, happening to sit in the same carriage. The ensuing conversation transformed both their lives.

The pair complemented each other perfectly. Berry was an entrepreneurial financier who could read a balance sheet at a glance, while Llewellyn, a mining engineer, knew the coal industry inside out. They embarked on a wave of takeovers in the sector, so that by 1919 Berry was a director of no fewer than 66 companies, most of them in coal. He had also moved into local newspapers – a small step which anticipated the later acquisition by fellow Berry family members of *The Daily Telegraph*. Llewellyn also had a distinguished heir – his son Harry became an Olympic show-jumper.

Berry and Llewellyn had – at least for the moment – had their fill of black gold. They were ready to diversify. As with Arthur Keen, opportunism was the name of Berry's game, and an opportunity soon presented itself. Again, the Great Western Railway played a pivotal role.

On a train journey in 1919, William Trimmer, managing director of Uskside Engineering and a friend of Berry's, met H. G. Hill, a director of the family-controlled steel company John Lysaght, which had been founded in 1857. Lysaght had good assets in the shape of a steelworks at Scunthorpe, modern rolling mills at Newport and a flourishing export market in sales of galvanised steel to Australia. But Trimmer learned from Hill that the board was very concerned about the damage that a post-war slump could do.

Trimmer passed this information on to Berry and Llewellyn. The pair saw their chance. They persuaded Viscountess Rhondda, daughter of Berry's former boss at Cambrian, to back them. With her support, they bid £5 m for Lysaght and won over the board.

Berry and Llewellyn did not stop there. Within months, they agreed the takeover of Joseph Sankey & Sons, originally a maker of "hollow-ware" such as trays and kettles, which had diversified into two new growth industries: electrical laminations and, latterly, components for the nascent motor industry.

Sankey's first involvement with the motor car was a personal one. George Sankey, one of Joseph's four sons, bought an Oldsmobile in 1902, but decided that he wanted to increase its passenger capacity. So he extended the car body, only to find that the six horsepower engine could not cope. He eventually exchanged the Oldsmobile for a De Dion four-seater.

Two years later, George Sankey was approached by a friend who had worked for the Wolseley Sheep Shearing Machine company, based in Birmingham. The friend had diversified into motor car production, setting up the Wolseley Tool & Motor Co. in 1901. Now he was looking for a company to press metal body shells for wooden car frames. Would Sankey be interested? Yes, we would, George told Herbert Austin.

On the back of Austin's success, Sankey was able to expand into supplying body panels to other car-makers – Daimler, Humber, Rover and Argyle. It sold into France and the US. Then, in 1908, it developed and patented the first pressed and welded, detachable car wheel. With a certain foresight, and a degree of understatement, the Sankey board reported: "The increase in our business is largely due to motor car stampings, the manufacture of which ... promises to be a permanent and remunerative branch of business."

Sankey outgrew its Birmingham works and, in 1909, found a disused tramcar factory at Hadley Castle, near Wellington in Shropshire. It was a good location, on an arm of the Shropshire Union Canal and a branch line of the London and North-Western Railway. Coincidentally, the plant had previously been a steelworks owned by Nettlefold & Chamberlain who had sold it when they opened the Rogerstone steelworks in 1886.

One of Hadley Castle's star products was the Sankey wheel, which soon added William Morris – with Austin, the greatest of Britain's car tsars – to its customer list. Its other major innovation was a system of car and charabanc body design pressed from sheet steel, which was developed by George Sankey and a colleague, and which remained in use until well into the 1950s. As a result of these technical breakthroughs, by 1913 Sankey was producing 30,000 wheels a year and 3000 bodies.

During the First World War, Sankey produced a variety of armaments but its main achievement was the manufacture of the steel helmet. At the war's outset, soldiers lacked protective headgear – all they had was a cloth cap. Sheffield steel companies told the War Office that it was impossible to produce a pressed steel helmet strong enough to withstand a revolver bullet fired at close range. As a result, the government specified a mild steel hat which offered little more protection than the cap.

George Sankey was having none of this. Harold, his eldest son, was in the trenches on the Western Front and his nephew, Sidney, was killed there in 1915. He persevered in trying to develop a strong manganese steel helmet and, eventually, he succeeded. During the remainder of the war, Sankey supplied 5.5 million of them – almost the whole requirement of the British Army.

Sankey emerged from the war making good profits, and in no desperate need of consolidation. But Berry's powers of persuasion, aided by long-standing supply links between Lysaght and Sankey, convinced George and his colleagues. On 19 November 1919, they announced that Berry had made a firm offer for the business, which they were recommending to shareholders. A fortnight later, with the offer done and dusted, Sankey vacated the chair and Berry took it.

The wheeler-dealers had still not finished. Berry and Llewellyn had one more company in their sights. For a Merthyr man who had built an industrial empire made of steel, coal and engineering, it was a natural target: Guest, Keen & Nettlefolds. On 20 February 1920, the pair pressed their case on Lord Bessborough at a meeting in Birmingham's Queen's Hotel.

Bessborough successfully resisted the swashbuckling duo's aggressive takeover bid, under which GKN would have been swallowed up into Berry's industrial combine. But Bessborough and GKN were not strong enough to repel the boarders. They agreed that Berry's two companies, Lysaght and Sankey, would be merged into an enlarged GKN, with Berry becoming joint deputy chairman.

Bessborough died suddenly 10 months later, and was succeeded by the former Nettlefolds director Edward Steer. But Berry and Llewellyn were the twin driving forces of the new GKN. They faced an immediate challenge, as the post-war slump feared by both the Lysaght and the Sankey families at last became reality.

Lysaght was forced to accept orders at a loss merely to provide work for its labour force; its Scunthorpe steel works and the Welsh rolling mills were temporarily closed. Dowlais and East Moors were equally hard hit. The price of plate and heavy rails collapsed: from £25 a ton in January 1921 to less than £9 a ton in October 1922. Unemployment soared: by January 1922, more than one-third of the pre-recession UK steel workforce had been made redundant.

As the upturn started in early 1923, Berry and Llewellyn launched what proved to be the final thrust of their extraordinary acquisition spree. They plunged back into coal, gobbling up Welsh colliery companies to the point where GKN's output was more than doubled to 6.5 m tons a year, more than 11% of the total South Wales coalfield.

For a time, this strategy paid off handsomely: 1922–24 were boom years for the British mining industry. UK output increased from over 163 m tons in 1921 to 276 m in 1923, with exports surging from 24.7 m tons to 79.5 m tons over the period. Much of this advance, however, was due to exceptional and temporary factors – a four-month strike by American miners and the Allies' occupation of the Ruhr which halted coal output there.

But in 1924, the British economy declined again, cutting domestic coal demand. At the same time, export markets closed up: the US strike was over and Ruhr coal production resumed. The UK coal industry was devastated: unemployment climbed 10-fold from 2.1% in March 1924 to 25% 15 months later. The whole industry operated at a loss. South Wales, which depended on export markets for almost half its sales, more than double the UK industry average, suffered most of all.

After their breakneck expansion, Berry and Llewellyn went into sharp reverse. They closed pits and let mining leases lapse. Development plans were abandoned. The Dowlais group of collieries, once a mainstay of GKN, was effectively wound up. And, since wages accounted for more than two-thirds of total costs, the company and its fellow mining groups demanded pay cuts throughout the industry.

After the miners rejected the proposals, they were locked out on 1 May 1926. Three days later, at midnight, the Trades Union Congress began the first national strike by all union members in British history – the General Strike. The dispute barely lasted a week, although the miners held out for another six months. When they returned to work, they found their former export markets had been undermined by a combination of more efficient industries and severe import controls in mainland Europe.

Berry, who was made a peer in 1926 and became GKN's chairman a year later after Steer stepped down, was still wrestling with the downturn when, on 23 May 1928, he was killed in a riding accident. He was only 51, but had certainly lived up to his motto: "The labourer is worthy of his hire, but so is capital." His home was the 2600-acre Buckland Estate in Breconshire – hence his title, Lord Buckland – which included five miles of trout and salmon fishing on the Usk and fine shooting grounds. The house itself featured a 70-foot hall. He left an estate worth more than £1.1 m. Not bad for a teacher-turned-estate agent.

But Berry also paid his dues and honoured his roots. In life, he was a great philanthropist – he established a technical institute in Merthyr with a £25,000 grant and gave £20,000 for a new hospital in nearby Pontsarn. There were a host of other donations. His will set up a trust to provide relief for Merthyr's poor, funded by £50,000-worth of GKN shares. Other GKN shares were allocated to provide prizes at local schools and support a non-conformist chapel in the town.

He was, in fact, a classic entrepreneur with a great sense of humour: "He loved a great joke as hugely as a great stroke of business," said a friend, T. P. O'Connor, then Father (senior MP) of the House of Commons. "He never took himself with any pretentious seriousness."

In 1928, amid GKN's headlong retreat from coal, he agreed to sell one of the largest anthracite mines in Wales to Sir Alfred Mond, one of the founders of Imperial Chemical Industries. When Mond refused to pay another £10,000 for the business, Berry – who was desperate to sell – nevertheless suggested that they toss a coin for the extra sum. He won. Mond paid up.

Despite leading GKN down a coal-de-sac, Berry left a deep imprint on the group. His two major acquisitions, Lysaght and Sankey, made major contributions for more than half a century – in Sankey's case, for a good deal longer. In one respect, however, Berry's premature passing marked the end of an age for GKN. After him, GKN was never again dominated by an independently wealthy, free-wheeling entrepreneur. Henry Seymour Berry was GKN's last tycoon.

CHAPTER 6

# Depression and Rearmament

For the best part of the two decades following Berry's death, GKN was headed by chairmen who were essentially non-executive: Sir John Field Beale, a lawyer, and his younger brother Sir Samuel Beale. The executive powers in the group were Tom Peacock, joint managing director from 1920, and, latterly, James Jolly, who became joint MD in 1934.

Peacock was a details man rather than a visionary. But that focus was precisely what GKN needed as it began to confront the biggest trading challenge it had ever faced: national economic decline in the late 1920s which accelerated into the depression of the early 1930s after the stock market crash which started on Wall Street on 24 October 1929.

The nut and bolt business, where Peacock had made his name at Cotterill, struggled in the late 1920s as demand fell. But its problems were comparatively minor set against those of the steel operations in general, and Dowlais in particular. The old works was now suffering severely from its obsolescent acid technology and sustained lack of investment.

Not surprisingly, Dowlais was struggling to compete in the manufacture of steel rails, its staple product, with better-equipped manufacturers such as Baldwins' Margam and Port Talbot works, part of which had only opened in 1922. In 1928, for the first time in half a century, Dowlais failed to secure a single order from a UK railway company. It did have a substantial contract to supply rails to the Egyptian government, but this turned into a nightmare when Dowlais could not produce rails to the required standard, and the Egyptians exercised their right to re-order from elsewhere.

With the onset of the Depression, Dowlais's situation became desperate. East Moors was also stuttering, as ship-building slumped and plate orders fell. As a result, GKN was highly receptive to an approach made by Baldwins just before Christmas 1929 for a merger of their steel interests. The deal was agreed within three days, and on 2 January the new Guest Keen Baldwins (GKB) Iron & Steel company came into existence.

The Baldwins merger sounded the death knell for Dowlais. Already starved of work by the Depression, the loss of the Egyptian order was the straw that broke the camel's back. On 4 October 1930, 171 years after it opened, Dowlais ended steel production. This time, unlike 1848, there was no last-ditch reprieve. The blast furnaces were blown out, the Bessemer converters de-commissioned, the main mill shut down. Some plant and machinery was moved to Cardiff or Port Talbot.

The impact of the closure on the local community was devastating. It was, in many respects, the precursor of all the closures that followed later in the century, as the once world-leading British steel industry belatedly came to terms with its fall from pre-eminence.

About 3000 people lost their jobs. Five years later, when a Royal Commission investigated Merthyr's economic situation, it found that almost 64% of the eligible-for-work population was unemployed. In November 1936, the new King Edward VII visited the area and was shocked by the deprivation. "These works brought all these people here. Something ought to be done to find them employment," he said.

Dowlais's coke ovens were reopened in 1935 as the steel trade recovered but they were a feeble phoenix, providing work for only 200. A foundry continued to operate on the site, and was expanded in 1958. But Dowlais's days as a steel-maker were done.

In truth, the business had been struggling long before the Depression. It had reaped the early benefits of the pioneer, but it had never been modernised to match the new competitors, at home and overseas, that entered the industry with their purpose-built basic steelworks. Ironically, it was a GKN man – A. J. Reese, who became general manager of East Moors – who identified the threat to older British works such as Dowlais as early as 1916.

Reese had visited the US to study American steel-making and contrasted what he saw there with the UK scene: "I have observed in this country that there are a great many very antiquated ironworks in existence and operation: they are plants the design of which represents a period many years out of date," he told a government inquiry into the steel industry.

"There are blast furnaces which in the United States would have been done away with years ago as being absolutely inefficient and not suitable for operation in competition even at that time. Those furnaces are all much too small. The outputs are really ridiculous." He was speaking generally. But he might have been pronouncing Dowlais's epitaph.

The GKB management was not going to make the same mistake of underinvestment at Cardiff. As the Depression eased, and the steel industry picked up, they completely rebuilt East Moors. The reconstruction took two years, at the astronomical cost of £3 m. But when it was over, the company had a modern works that could at least stand muster with the Americans and the Germans. The investment was made even more timely by the world events that were about to unfold.

As in later recessions, the Depression triggered a transformational restructuring by GKN. The Baldwins merger and Dowlais's closure were only two elements in this. Three weeks after the creation of GKB, the group merged its struggling mining businesses into a new combine, Welsh Associated Collieries, which embraced companies comprising about 60 pits, representing a quarter of the South Welsh coalfield.

GKN held a majority, but the merger clearly marked the beginning of the end of the Berry-Llewellyn coal expansion strategy. The group was turning its back on the industry, never to return. In 1934, it merged WAC into

Powell Duffryn, a large and committed mining concern. GKN temporarily retained a minority stake which it subsequently sold.

Despite the slump, the group's management also continued to expand core businesses. Within days of the Baldwins merger, GKN bought Exors of James Mills (named after the executors of its founder, James Mills), a Cotterill and PNB competitor which supplied railways chains, spikes, bolts and other equipment and had developed a significant market in India.

Then GKN took its first big step into continental Europe by acquiring Aug.Stenman AB, a Swedish rival of Nettlefolds which, along with other Swedish screw-makers, had made successful incursions into the UK market and had refused to join the international cartel that Nettlefolds had organised.

The group's reaction to the Scandinavian raiders was straightforward: it was having difficulty beating them, so it decided to buy the biggest of them. The deal took two years to negotiate, and even then GKN had to allow Stenman a high degree of autonomous operation. However, it served its purpose: Stenman was now, more or less, in the (Nettle)fold.

As the Stenman deal was put to bed, GKN began to look further afield for its next significant move. In 1931, it was approached by Owen Williams, chairman of the fasteners and railway fittings business Henry Williams India. Williams, based in Andul Road, Calcutta, had found itself in increasing competition with exports from GKN's former Cotterill and Bayliss subsidiaries, and the Exors of James Mills acquisition further expanded the group's

challenge to Williams' home market. Owen Williams suggested that GKN might like to buy a stake in his company.

Tom Peacock and his colleagues saw the logic of such
a step. The Indian government was starting to build trade
barriers to protect its domestic producers, and the GKN
board concluded that it would be cheaper and quicker to
buy into an established business than to set up their own
operation from scratch.

The talks were protracted, but eventually – in May
1934 – GKN agreed to buy a 51% majority stake in Henry
Williams and the company's name was duly changed to
Guest, Keen, Williams. The group was now firmly established on the subcontinent. Despite the extreme volatility
of GKW's performance in the tempestuous decades that
followed, GKN was in India to stay.

Peacock and his colleagues could conclude the GKW
deal with confidence in the group's future, because GKN
had by now successfully weathered the Depression. In
modern recession parlance, the slump was a U-shape with
characteristics of a "V" because of the speed with which
it took hold and – eventually – receded. Unemployment
in Britain doubled in just over a year to 2 m by August
1930, while demand plummeted to a trough in 1933
before beginning a rapid upturn.

GKN's profits tracked the downturn, falling from
almost £1 m in 1930 to less than £222,000 at the nadir.
Three businesses kept the group afloat: Sankeys' involvement in the growth sectors of automotive and electrical
meant that it was able to hold profits at immediate pre-
Depression levels; Nettlefolds' profits halved during the
slump but the business still made more than £146,000 at

the height of the downturn. Best performer of all was Lysaghts, whose profits reached almost £200,000 even in 1933.

A modest cyclical upturn helped the British economy off the bottom, but the main catalyst for recovery was the government's decision in November 1933 to rearm. Although Adolf Hitler was consolidating his power in Germany, he had not yet launched the massive expansion of the country's armed forces that followed. But Britain had fallen well behind many of its peers in its spending. As a result, first the Royal Navy and then the RAF announced major increases in their budgets.

GKN's steel-related businesses, both upstream and downstream, benefited increasingly from rearmament as the 1930s wore on and the likelihood of a second world war intensified. Within the company, however, the balance of power had shifted irreversibly from Welsh steel and coal to West Midlands engineering.

The group was more international now – apart from the Swedish and Indian acquisitions, Lysaght had developed extensive steel mills and finishing operations in Australia – and it was highly devolved, but its centre was Smethwick, where Tom Peacock and Jolly were based.

Peacock could be "very tough and yet very generous; he was very unpredictable," said Sir Anthony (Tony) Bowlby, who ran Nettlefolds under him. He was known to fire an employee, order the individual to report to his home near the Smethwick head office, offer the man his job back, take him round the garden, buy him a beer and send him back to his factory.

Peacock also put down roots in a way that Arthur Keen had never managed. His son Kenneth, who ran sales and marketing at Nettlefolds, became the youngest director in GKN's history when he joined the board in 1933, aged 32, and was promoted to joint managing director three years later.

In 1938, the group made its record inter-war year profit – almost £1.1 m. By then, group companies were churning out materials for war – steel for shells and air raid shelters, for aircraft and aero-engines, bombs, bullets, armoured vehicles, helmets (Sankey again) and ships. A Lancaster bomber contained about four tons of steel. An aircraft factory needed up to 40 types of tool steel before it could start production.

GKN established its own war cabinet – Samuel Beale, the Peacocks and Jolly – to oversee matters in the first months of the war. In 1940, after the fall of France and the Dunkirk evacuation, the Ministry of Supply (heir to the First World War Ministry of Munitions) declared GKN and most of its subsidiaries "controlled undertakings". As Samuel Beale explained to shareholders, "war meant control – control of supplies, control of production, control of the destination of products and of the price at which they were sold."

The Ministry of Supply promoted consolidation to achieve economies of scale, so GKN was able to acquire 40% of the Somerset Wire company which then promised to buy all its wire and rod supplies from the Cardiff mill. GKN acquired full control of Somerset after the war. Lysaght and the fasteners businesses were also able to complete takeovers on the same principle. Less constructively, the Ministry of Information also intervened in GKN's affairs – it censored the company's annual reports.

Group companies quickly graduated from simply increasing output of products they had made pre-war to the manufacture of material that they would never have imagined. Sankey entered the aerospace business: first by making spinners for Mosquito and Spitfire aircraft, then – at Hadley Castle – by producing Spitfires themselves. Near the war's end, a secret factory was established at Sankey to make parts for jet engines. As D-Day approached, Sankey was making sections for Bailey Bridges while Lysaght assembled a specialised tank.

Numerous GKN factories were bombed, although few were seriously damaged. Profits were strictly controlled under the revived Excess Profits Tax. What the war did breed, in some plants at least, was a camaraderie between manager and workforce which had not previously existed.

The government needed to raise output, and GKN benefited accordingly. Nettlefolds' Cardiff rod and wire mill – which had been moved from Rogerstone in the 1930s – got government investment to expand. Garringtons was selected for significant investment to increase its production of shells and bullets.

In total, the government spent more than £500,000 to expand capacity there through a new drop forge – itself larger than the whole Garringtons operation at that time – and a forge to make shells by a completely new process designed to save 30% of the steel that was normally required to produce a shell. These large schemes had one overwhelming benefit for GKN – they brought Raymond Brookes to work for the group.

Brookes, who had been working at another Black Country forging company, was hired by an entrepreneur called Jack Bean. Bean had himself tried to buy Garringtons before the war as part of an attempt to build a significant forgings group out of several businesses. GKN had rejected his approach, but had asked him to become Garringtons' chairman.

One day in 1941, Bean called Brookes out of the blue and asked him to meet the next day at 12.55 pm precisely at Wolverhampton's Star & Garter hotel. "He knew all about me," recalled Brookes. "He had got big government expansion schemes which he believed the then management of the company would not be able to handle." Bean asked Brookes to run the new forging projects. Brookes agreed. It was 1.30 pm and the whole conversation had taken 35 minutes. "I did not know what my salary was going to be; I didn't even know what my status was going to be," Brookes said.

Garringtons employed 250 people and its managing director was Albert Beech. He did not intend to retire and his son, Jack, had been appointed general manager. Brookes agreed with Jack that they would be joint general managers. During this period, the two never went home to sleep: "We were required to stay at the plant 24 hours a day," Brookes said.

By the end of 1941, the drop forge was producing 2.5 times its rated output. The shell forge was the tricky bit. The material savings it promised would be gold dust in a war economy where every ounce of steel counted. Realising them was another matter. The new process called for a machining tolerance at least four times lower than in conventional shell production. "It took us a year to make a good shell," said Brookes.

"We had four basic producing units. We knew how to make the shells but the practitioners and supervisors around us would never stick to a process formula. They all introduced their own variance. So finally, I pulled in a chap who had got a very precise and meticulous approach to life and had been in the animal medicine business, and knew nothing about forging. We gave him an operational chart and the check frequencies and everything else, and put him to work."

One midnight, Jack Beech and Brookes were having supper when the man came up to them and said: "All four machines are producing shells. The overhead conveyor is full of hot shells and they are going to get down the other end of the factory within about 20 minutes. What do we do when we get them there?" Brookes and Beech scoured the factory for workers and came up two short. "So we manhandled shells all that night."

The process marked a technical breakthrough. Brookes later took a British team to the US to advise on the adoption of the same process in an American forging plant. Equally instructive, though, was the team spirit that the Darlaston experience embodied. It epitomised the wartime ethos that prevailed in numerous British factories.

Brookes and Beech used to hold midnight gatherings with the workforce – dinners, concerts and the like. At one of the dinners, when he had consumed a significant quantity of whisky, Brookes became somewhat Churchillian. "You are such a magnificent bunch, you work so tremendously," Brookes told the men. "The whole damned industry in terms of what it does to people mentally and physically is a disgrace. We ought to do something about that. After the war, we will have a forge which will be like a dairy, which will be three-quarters glass, which will have no flames, no bangs, no sweat."

Much later, when he was chairman of GKN, Brookes reflected on that night at Darlaston: "I sometimes think that when you speak emotively, you do not speak from the top of your mind, you really speak from the depth of your mind," he said. "Alcohol, if it loosens your tongue, it sometimes can bring out the best in you as well as the worst. I remembered those words and I wrote them down." And he kept his promise.

CHAPTER 7

# The Fight for Steel

As Britain's war ended, another began for GKN. On 26 July 1945, an astonished world heard the news that Sir Winston Churchill's Conservatives had been defeated in the General Election by the Labour party led by Clement Attlee.

Attlee did not just win – he overwhelmed his opponents with a majority of 146 seats. By any stretch of the imagination, this was a mandate for massive change. The government duly delivered. It introduced the National Health Service and the Welfare State. In the process, it laid the foundations for a new post-war order which marked the single sharpest break with established principle and practice since the Industrial Revolution consigned Britain's agrarian-dominated economy to history.

New Labour had an industrial agenda too, and a vocabulary to describe it. In its quest to build a New Jerusalem, it did not mean to demolish Britain's dark, satanic mills – it planned to take them over. The operative word was Nationalisation, which in those heady days was supposed to mean that the pillars of British industry were now owned by and for the people instead of by a fragmented bunch of private individuals, allegedly motivated by self-interest and self-aggrandisement.

The Attlee government nationalised the Bank of England, the gas and electricity industries, the railways and the coal mines. Then it turned its attention to steel. For its supporters, the polluted, post-war air reverberated with the lines of great British poets, and not just William Blake. Almost 140 years after William Wordsworth had described the impact on contemporaries of the French Revolution; Labour supporters could echo his evocation: "Bliss was it in that dawn to be alive/But to be young was very heaven."

At his office in Smethwick, James Jolly was somewhat less lyrical. Jolly, a very tidy, very objective, very precise man – "It wasn't a question of asking his chauffeur to be there at quarter to four; it was twenty minutes to four on the dot," a colleague said – must have been personally as well as professionally offended by the political dogma driving Labour policy.

Jolly had succeeded Samuel Beale as chairman in 1947. Now he led the fight against nationalisation. "Your board are firmly convinced," he told shareholders in 1948, "that, from the country's point of view, it would be a national disaster if the state with its cumbersome, slow-moving and doctrinaire methods attempted to control by nationalisation that highly complex industry known as the Iron and Steel Trade." It was a declaration of war.

GKN had long since ceased to depend on steel-making for its profits, which increased from less than £4.5 m to a record £6.1 m in the financial year to March 1948. But steel-making was the feedstock for its engineering operations and it remained a vertically-integrated steel-based company – the largest of its kind in Britain.

Even though Labour was barely two years into its nationalisation programme, Jolly had a target to aim at. Some of the new public enterprises – notably the National Coal Board – had not exactly lived up to the promise of the new Socialist dawn.

Jolly said: "It's a striking fact that nationalisation of industry has not shown any great efficiency, any lowering of prices, any improvement of quality or service, or contributed anything more to the competitive power of Great Britain in export markets than when operating under private enterprise. Rather the reverse."

Jolly had more than enough on his plate. Apart from the steel nationalisation campaign, he had to contend with the disruption to GKN's extensive Indian operations caused by the tumultuous events following its Independence on 15 August 1947.

The division of the subcontinent and the consequent conflict between Hindu and Muslim threw normal industrial life into abeyance. "The disturbed and at times chaotic political situation in India militated against trading conditions, with labour unrest and steel supply difficulties," Jolly reported to shareholders with a matter-of-factness which belied the extreme turmoil.

But he and his colleagues had no intention of following the British government out of India. Indeed, India would need GKW as much as GKW needed India: "The economic well-being of India cannot be accomplished without such undertakings as Guest Keen Williams," Jolly declared.

At home, despite the steel nationalisation threat, Jolly and his board pushed ahead with expansion plans. The most spectacular organic investment was to fulfil Raymond Brookes' wartime pledge to the Garringtons workforce – to build "the forge like a dairy".

Here, too, GKN encountered government intervention. It was pressured into siting the new forging plant at a derelict government-owned site in Bromsgrove, Worcestershire which had been used as a shadow factory during the war. Apart from the bombed-out plant, there was one other small problem: "There wasn't a die-sinker or tool-maker in the whole of Bromsgrove," Brookes recalled. "Every skill had to be brought in."

GKN raided the Scottish forgings company Scottish Stampings (which it later acquired). It established a nearby country house as its headquarters, built houses for the workers through a local housing association and hired special trains to bring the Scots down from the north. Then it faced up to the next problem – the showpiece factory had no work.

"Sometimes in life, you get a bit of luck," said Brookes. He remembered a conversation with Garringtons' chairman, Jack Bean, during the war. Bean had come across a product called the Ferguson Agricultural System – a small tractor, with implements articulated to the tractor rather than trailed to it, and with hydraulic depth control for all forms of cultivation.

As its name suggested, the system had been invented by Harry Ferguson, an American who, in the great tradition of inventors, had come up with the idea while sitting on a farmyard gate. Ferguson, an old friend of Bean's, had licensed Ford to make the tractor in the US.

Brookes, with an introduction from Bean in his pocket, travelled to the US and proposed that GKN make the tractor implements for the UK market in the new Bromsgrove facility. Brookes had identified a nearby factory which could make the tractors. Ferguson would not commit himself, but he sent Brookes away with hope in the GKN man's heart and some encouraging words in his ear: "Well, young man, I do not know if I will do this or not, but if I do come to England, you will deserve to be seen."

Ferguson did indeed come to England, and he did see Brookes. The consequence was that, in 1947, Bromsgrove started producing forgings for all the Ferguson tractor implements. Soon, it won the tractor forgings too. It was the start of a long supplier–customer relationship, which continued after Ferguson sold his business to Massey, creating Massey-Ferguson. It was also the real start of what, with other factories in other countries, became GKN's OffHighway division.

At almost the same time, and even more audaciously in face of the nationalisation threat, Jolly expanded GKN's upstream steel interests. In February 1948, he bought the Brymbo steel works near Wrexham in North Wales: "Their production of special steels is especially valuable to certain members of the group for their fabrication needs," Jolly said.

Brymbo came to symbolise the group's determination to retain its steel heritage despite the best efforts of successive Labour governments to deprive the company of that legacy. In truth, Brymbo's significance for GKN did not lie in its longevity – it had been founded as an ironworks in the mid-1790s – nor its pioneering role in steel's development – John Henry Darby had built the first basic open-hearth furnace there in 1884–85. As Jolly noted, Brymbo's real importance was as a supplier of value-added steels to GKN companies such as Sankey, with which it had worked since the early 1900s. Not that Brymbo, immediately post-war, was in the best of health. Brookes recalled how it had lain "idle and empty". But Jolly was prepared to buy its potential, even though nationalisation threatened to ensure that GKN would never benefit from it.

The political wheels ground slowly on towards the fateful moment, although a fair amount of grit got into those wheels. Steel nationalisation met strong resistance from the industry and its parliamentary allies, and did not enjoy overwhelming public support.

The government's authority was compromised, not just by the less-than-stunning results of earlier nationalisations, but by the huge and unexpected devaluation of the pound in September 1949, when its value was cut by 30.5% from \$4.03 to \$2.80. The devaluation both symbolised and gave profound effect to Britain's post-war decline and the rise of the United States. The American half-century was beginning while the sun set on the British Empire.

Aware of the government's weakened mandate, Jolly turned up the volume of GKN's protests as the nationalisation vote neared. He did not flinch from making increasingly political statements: "It would seem that the present government has not the courage to withstand the pressure of its doctrinaires and malcontents. The only solution therefore will be for this government not to be re-elected to office."

By "doctrinaires and malcontents", Jolly might have been thinking of Labour's firebrand Chancellor of the Exchequer, Sir Stafford Cripps. Cripps, who had presided over the devaluation after denying nine times that it was on the agenda, told the House of Commons: "If we cannot get nationalisation of steel by legal means, we must resort to violent methods."

This kind of left-wing rhetoric overcame a compromise proposal, favoured by more moderate members of the Cabinet, to take shares in individual steel companies through the British Iron and Steel Federation, the industry's trade association. The Conservative-dominated House of Lords resisted the Iron and Steel Bill fiercely, but it was enacted on 24 November 1949. Nationalisation took effect on 15 February 1951.

Four GKN steelworks – the East Moors works owned by the Guest Keen Baldwins joint venture, the Cardiff rolling mills, the former John Lysaght works at Scunthorpe and Brymbo – became part of the new Iron and Steel Corporation of Great Britain. Jolly delivered the GKN board's judgment on the decision: "It is our definite and unanimous opinion that nationalisation will not lead to greater production, cheaper production, or better quality." GKN received total compensation of £18.7 m in Iron and Steel Corporation stock, of which the board promptly and wisely sold £15.5 m-worth.

The Corporation's days were numbered almost as soon as it came into existence. By then, Labour was clinging to power by its fingernails: its majority had been cut to five in the previous year's General Election. Eight months after Steel Nationalisation took effect, Churchill was returned to power with a majority of 26. His Conservative government quickly established the Iron and Steel Holding and Realisation Agency to implement Steel Denationalisation.

Jolly did not remain to lead GKN's triumphant return to steel-making; he retired as chairman in 1953, 35 momentous years after joining the group. No GKN leader has spanned such an epoch – from the immediate aftermath of the Great War, through the Wall Street Crash and the Depression, rearmament and the Second World War to the new world of post-war Britain. An austere and immensely modest man, he described his life's work with typical self-effacement: he thought that he would perhaps go down as someone "who had created a certain amount of order out of chaos".

Raymond Brookes, whose first forays into the automotive industry at Garringtons were sponsored by Jolly, thought his former chairman had achieved rather more than that. Jolly, Brookes believed, created a bridge to the future for a later generation to cross. "He was a steadfast friend of the maverick," Brookes said in 1972. "He was a financial man, who had his roots in Railways or Railway equipment and indirectly in steel. He was steeped in cartels and monopolies in steel and its re-rolling, in fasteners and so on. That was the guts of the Guest Keen that I joined in 1941 – the rest didn't matter.

"And yet I think he always saw the weakness in the narrowness of that base and its vulnerability to social and political trades and pressures. I think he was long-headed enough to see in this [the Garringtons initiative] a wide-riding automotive area … On his part, it had to be a great act of faith, because there was nothing in his background to give him the dimensions for judgement, other than belief in people. Although he was a dry-as-dust financial man and a very orthodox one in many ways, there was this completely opposite side to his character."

Jolly also had the human touch: "Particularly in a time of stress and trouble when you would think he wasn't in a position to know how one felt, he would ring me up and say that he'd like me to come and have a cup of tea with him. And he would let you get rid of all your tensions and anxieties first, then get you talking on where you wanted to go and what you wanted to do," Brookes said.

"If Jolly had not had the breadth of mind and vision and integrity, I very much doubt that GKN would be in its present position. He didn't create all the newish things in GKN, he didn't even see them, but he had time for the people who wanted to go that way. The GKN Board was dragged into lots of these new activities and never wanted to go."

If Jolly was a reformer despite himself, then Ken Peacock, his successor, was something of a throwback to GKN's past. Not because he was the son of a GKN managing director – he was neither the first nor the last senior GKN executive to follow his father into the company's upper echelons – but because of his career background and the way he managed the expanding group.

Jim Parsons, GKN's first post-war graduate recruit who became the group's first Personnel director, worked with Peacock throughout the latter's chairmanship. "He was a very gifted amateur," Parsons said. "He was very well-liked throughout the company." Sir Anthony Bowlby, who was hired into GKN by Peacock and who later ran the Fasteners business under him, said: "He had an extraordinary kind of charm, great ability and an elephantine memory."

This was the last decade of the "Gentlemen versus Players" annual cricket match at Lord's, between the English county cricketers who were amateurs and those who had turned professional. Peacock was no amateur in the strict definition of the term, but in spirit he fitted Parsons' description to a tee, or rather, a stump.

He loved motor racing, and was very good at it – he competed in the RAC TT in Ireland (every year from 1929 to 1934) and at Le Mans, as a member, variously, of the Lea-Francis, Riley and Aston Martin teams. The climax of his racing career came in 1934, when he was awarded the "Index of Performance" at Le Mans, which placed him as a top performer in the event, regardless of race class. He was also a great country pursuits enthusiast, riding with several groups of hounds in the Cotswolds and West Country and living on a large farming estate.

In a sense, Peacock personified GKN's roots – he served a kind of apprenticeship at Nettlefolds in Heath Street but also became very close to the South Welsh steel operations. He also reflected the predominance in mid-20th century British boardrooms of the generalist, a strain which disadvantaged UK plc against its main competitors, where professional managers, finance specialists or engineers ruled the corporate roost.

Peacock did not go to university, and had no professional or technical training. He managed by a combination of humanity and instinct: "He thought that if you treated people properly and gave them responsibility, they would react," recalled Bill Nicol, the company secretary. This concern for people left a lasting imprint on GKN in at least one important way.

In April 1936, Peacock and Thomas Zachary Lloyd, Heath Street's general manager, persuaded the GKN board to introduce a contributory pension scheme, which could be adopted by any works or subsidiary in the group. It was arranged with the Prudential, and male workers (the scheme was closed to women for many years) were asked to contribute one shilling [5p] a week, while white-collar staff paid 5% of their pensionable salary.

At Heath Street, take-up was huge – around 90% of those eligible joined the scheme, which was subsequently extended throughout the group. The tradition endured into the 21st century – by 2009, GKN was one of the last major employers in the UK to maintain a Defined Benefit pension scheme for all UK employees.

Peacock's management by instinct had more mixed benefits for the group. Nicol said: "His great expression was, 'You have got to have the feeling in the water.'" One of many areas to which Peacock applied this approach was acquisitions. During his 12 years at the helm, GKN bought a large number of companies as the long-standing, vertical integration strategy became extended – and, ultimately, distended – across a motley assortment of steel-using businesses.

Jim Parsons remembered the acquisition of a specialist fasteners company in Leicester, run by a man called Ted Parsons (no relation), which made screws for watches and other intricate equipment. "Ted Parsons was reluctant to sell to GKN, but he eventually said to Peacock, 'Sir Ken, I'll sell on two conditions. First, you leave me to run the business'. Ken Peacock said, 'Fine, that's exactly what we want.'"

"'The second condition,' stipulated Ted Parsons, 'is that I get a new Rolls-Royce every January.' This was a ridiculous request, given the longevity of a Rolls. 'Done,' Peacock said immediately." Ted Parsons may of course have been aware of his prospective new boss's fondness for motor cars.

This scene unfolded late in Peacock's tenure. By contrast, there was no question about the logic of his first major acquisition. On 12 October 1953, GKN announced that it was in talks with the Iron and Steel Holding and Realisation Agency about buying back its nationalised steel works.

CHAPTER 8

# Metal Bashing

The deal was eventually done in two parts over 18 months, because GKN drove a hard bargain: "There have been considerable difficulties in arriving at a settlement in any form," Peacock reported to shareholders. "The terms for the buy-back had to be commercial and equitable."

In May 1954, the group reached agreement to buy back the South Wales operations, for £8.27 m. In the process, GKN acquired full control of Guest Keen Baldwins. And on 1 December 1955, GKN re-acquired Brymbo and Scunthorpe for almost £3.6 m – making a total price of just under £11.9 m [about £225 m in 2009 money]. Peacock's rationale was straightforward: over 80% of the billets, bars, slabs and strip produced by the works were either consumed within the businesses or were supplied to other GKN companies.

Steel was back home in GKN. With the cornerstone restored, the way was clear to build a vertically-integrated combine. By the late 1950s, the company was declaring, in a book designed to publicise its activities: "There is virtually nothing in steel that GKN does not – or cannot – make." Its product range comprised a veritable encyclopaedia, an A–Z, of metallic bits and pieces, from agricultural silos and sheds to zinc die castings. GKN was the epitome of a modern metal-basher.

On the face of things, the strategy was paying off handsomely. Return on net assets (RoNA) fell below 15% in only one year during the decade. In 1956, it hit a decade-peak of 19%. Profits advanced with ostensible smoothness. In 1953, trading profits had fallen under the weight of steel nationalisation from £9.4m to £7.4m. By 1959, they stood at £25.8m. The workforce that produced those profits had climbed to 76,000, three-quarters of them in the UK. Peacock celebrated "a decade of growth". He would no doubt have echoed Prime Minister Harold Macmillan's famous declaration in July 1957: "Let's be frank about it; most of our people have never had it so good."

For the country, certainly, the late 1950s was a time of remarkable affluence when compared with the post-war years of austerity barely a decade earlier. And for a big group like GKN, feeding into so many products benefiting from rising domestic consumption, growth appeared assured. Under the surface, however, the situation of both the country and the company was considerably less rosy.

In truth, the 1950s was an increasingly complacent decade, and the apparently effortless national growth, full employment and rising demand concealed a growing multitude of sins: sins of rising inflation, increasing labour problems, falling UK competitiveness. The cycle was not yet vicious, but the ingredients for Britain's subsequent downward spiral were congealing: rising union militancy prompted increasingly high wage claims which were usually conceded by employers, both public and private sector, who passed through the costs of exorbitant settlements in higher prices that were, at the time, swallowed up by rising demand.

For the country, these weaknesses translated into a rising balance of payments deficit and, consequently, intensifying pressure on the pound as the spectre of devaluation reared its ugly head. But generally speaking, the spreading "British disease" was a silent enemy, all the more lethal because it was so insidious.

Peacock noted that "in terms of days lost as a result of industrial disputes – both official and unofficial – 1959 was one of the two worst years for British industry since the war", although GKN itself did not suffer directly from strike action. So the company could continue to report apparently healthy numbers even while the competitiveness of Fasteners, its most consistent performer since the Depression, was being undermined by a combination of lack of investment and cheaper, better products from the sunrise economies of Japan and South-East Asia. There, screws were called "Nettlefolds" – but that did not deter ambitious Asian manufacturers from trying to compete with the British. Quite the opposite.

Fasteners had long since surpassed steel as the heart of GKN. Not for nothing was the group's tiny head office located in Smethwick, in a building that had formerly housed one of Keen's nut and bolt factories. But the long years of religiously-applied monopoly over the British screw industry had corroded the once-dynamic screws operation. Heath Street might be the ancestral home of the international screw industry, its price list the Bible and tome of reference for all Fastener manufacturers throughout the UK and Western Europe, but it was verging on obsolescence.

It had been bad enough in 1946, when Jim Parsons arrived fresh from the Air Ministry. Anthony Bowlby, an old friend of Parsons, invited him into Heath Street and promised to train him up. "They certainly did that," Parsons said. "It was on-the-job training. They took me down into a basement. I'm 5 ft 10 ins tall; there, six-and-a-half feet high, was a pile of trade union agreements. My first job after I had been trained was to summarise this huge pile. When I arrived at Heath Street, they had only just stopped delivering screws in dog carts. In the company budget, there was a number in respect of 'steak for dogs'."

The dogs might have been removed by 1946, but a decade later the company was going in their direction. Claude Birch, who joined GKN in 1954 from being the youngest works director in the history of Rolls-Royce's Derby aero-engine factory, could not believe how outdated the Heath Street production methods were. The factory was turning out 50 m gross of screws a year in 17,000 varieties. But some of the machines producing them dated from the 1880s, the belts for the steam engines ran underneath the floor and the works had not been painted in years.

Birch described Heath Street as being "straight out of Dickens". He asked a former Rolls colleague, Freddie Morley, to look at the plant. Parsons recalled: "Freddie

Morley was a rough, tough production man. He came over and walked through Heath Street, and said, 'This whole operation is like something out of the Industrial Revolution. You need to blow it up and start from scratch.'"

Equally obsolescent was GKN's management structure, which with the wave of expansion during the 1950s had now reached saturation point. The group was highly decentralised in all but one respect – Peacock, its chairman, sat on the board of each and every one of the 75 subsidiaries that by 1959 comprised Guest, Keen and Nettlefolds.

Each weekend, Peacock took two briefcases stuffed with papers home to his country estate. In all, he now had 90 direct reports. Even his elephantine memory was being stretched to the limit by this incredible commitment. He was literally working himself into the ground.

Despite these increasing strains, 1960 was another year of great success for GKN. Sales exceeded £250m for the first time; trading profits reached a new high of £31m. Peacock could report "a high rate of activity" virtually across the group. But he also turned his eyes to a more distant horizon, where he identified with some prescience increasing challenges ahead.

"It will be difficult in the present decade to maintain the rate of growth achieved in the 10 years to 1960," Peacock told shareholders in May 1961. "Our sales in the home market and as exports from the UK will be subject to strong competitive influences from the Common Market countries and elsewhere, notably Japan."

Peacock was worried about the impact on GKN of Britain's exclusion from the European Economic Community (EEC). "As direct exporters, we have already begun to suffer from the raising of the tariffs of some members of the Community ... purchases formerly made from us are, in consequence, being diverted to suppliers from within the Community. As exporters, and particularly as indirect exporters, we cannot but regard the exclusion of this country from the large and prosperous market represented by the Community as an impediment to the long-term growth of the industries which we serve."

But no relief was to be forthcoming on this front for a decade – later in 1961, and again in 1962, France's president General Charles de Gaulle repeatedly refused to let Britain join the EEC. GKN was going to have to live with the handicap of non-membership for the time being.

Peacock was also critical of the Conservative government's "stop-go" economic policies. Stop-go was the phrase coined for the Macmillan government's attempts to regulate the domestic economy through measures aimed at turning domestic demand on and off like a tap. Purchase tax would be raised, or lowered; credit restrictions eased or tightened.

"Repeatedly, the Government has tried to encourage exports by taking measures to restrict home demand," lamented Peacock."In the short term, such measures may indeed have a beneficial effect on exports ... [but] the long-term result must be to diminish investment and therefore to limit the capacity available to accommodate both a rising home demand and a large volume of exports. What is helpful to exports in the short term is thus inimical to them in the long term."

His words fell on deaf ears. Indeed, the government stepped up its attempted micro-management of the economy by resorting to the kind of expedients that were to become all too familiar in subsequent years. 1961 brought both a "pay pause" – a freeze on pay increases in a bid to bring down inflation – and a "little Budget", a device later re-christened "mini-Budget".

Neither these nor other measures were able to galvanise the economy. In 1961, GKN's steel profits, hit by rising energy and wage costs, almost halved to £6.4 m. The UK engineering and distribution operations held up better, but their profits still went down. Overall margins slumped by more than three percentage points from 12.2% to 9%. RoNA fell back to 11.3%, its lowest level for 10 years.

Under Peacock, GKN had consistently maintained a high level of capital spending, but now it cancelled or postponed several investments. This despite its growing awareness of the need to develop higher-value products against the increasing competitive threat from emerging economies.

Profits slipped further in 1962, and British Railways took the manufacture of permanent way (track) castings in-house, ending 60 years of supply from the Cwmbran works. As a result, much of Cwmbran had to be shut down. The following year, trading profits recovered slightly, but only because of acquisitions. Peacock called 1961–63 "the lean years".

Behind these gloomy scenes, however, the company had laid several critical foundations for long-term future growth. In 1961, Sankey won a large order from the Ministry of Defence for a new Armoured Personnel Carrier. This vehicle became the Saxon, which not only proved a notable commercial success in its own right but led to the establishment of a GKN Defence business with very significant ramifications for the group.

Structurally, GKN re-organised its sprawl of subsidiaries into eight "subgroups" – effectively divisions – starting with Iron and Steel-making, then Rolled and Drawn Steel Products; Fasteners, General Engineering and so on. This had the immediate benefit of reducing the number of direct reports to the chairman from 90 to eight, although it did not provide an overnight solution to all GKN's issues of control and coordination.

There was also a Forgings, Pressings and Castings subgroup, which contained Garringtons, Scottish Stampings and a number of other companies – including a small business called BRD, based in Aldridge near Birmingham.

Its initials stood for The Blade Research and Development Company, reflecting what had been its main business line, aero-engine turbine blade manufacture. BRD was built up very rapidly to meet demand for military aero-engines after the Korean War broke out in 1950. It devised a method of mass-producing forged and pressed blades – making them at the rate of hundreds per hour, rendering obsolete conventional precision-forging techniques which could only produce five or six an hour. It also established a facility for machining aerofoil forms in very large numbers.

BRD was highly successful. It produced blades for every stage of the Rolls-Royce Avon engine, which powered the Canberra bomber and Hawker Hunter fighter, and the Armstrong-Siddeley Sapphire engine, also used in the Hunter. However, when the Korean War ended in 1953 and demand slumped, the aero-engine makers took almost all blade manufacture back in-house, leaving BRD with ranks of idle machines and a massive hole in its order book.

Raymond Brookes, who had management responsibility for BRD and had been closely involved with its development, identified con-rod manufacture for Britain's burgeoning motor industry as one new opportunity, and BRD moved successfully into it. But con-rods alone were nowhere near enough to plug the gap left by turbine blades, and Brookes came under intense pressure from the GKN board to close BRD down.

Brookes resisted equally strongly. The demands severely offended one of his core management principles: "Here we had a company with a very short life, built up from scratch with people from all over Britain and with all the pain and grief you get from quickly welding together a force like that. And this was finally a magnificent force.

"In my opinion, it is the team of men you have that comes first. Oddly enough, I think the product comes after. I do believe that it is possible to get a team of men together, particularly if you can test them out on something, and once you decide that they are good enough, I think you can make anything with that team."

Some directors wanted to fire him. But he was backed by his mentor Jack Bean, a main board director. "Jack Bean said to the powers that be, 'If you sack him, then you sack me and that means you are sacking a Director and that makes it a Board matter. And if he resigns, I resign and that still makes it a Board matter.'"

The directors backed down and Brookes came up with an idea: he put in a crankshaft machining line, which could work with Scottish Stampings where GKN was making crankshaft forgings. But that wasn't enough to make BRD profitable either – Brookes needed something else. He sat down with Leslie Maxwell-Holroyd, a tough and dynamic figure on the GKN board, and they went through a list of what BRD might make, which were the most promising products and markets to attack.

"First of all, it could not be offensive to any existing GKN customer and it could not be offensive to any existing company in GKN," Brookes said. "Desirably, it had to have virtues of vertical integration built into it. Furthermore, the market needed to be a monopoly which could be assaulted." Brookes appreciated the irony in this, since as he noted, "GKN were always instinctive monopolists".

Two products emerged at the top of Brookes' and Maxwell-Holroyd's list. One was medium and large outboard motors, but the board would not commit the large-scale marketing resources BRD needed to break America's monopoly of this business.

The other potential product area had a high forging content and was produced in vast numbers. Brookes won the backing of Peacock and the board to go for it. "It" was automotive transmissions: propeller shafts, universal joints, and driveshafts.

CHAPTER 9

# Constant Velocity

Trevor Holdsworth arrived at the Smethwick head office in 1963 from the sixties-style Knightsbridge premises of Bowater, the paper and packaging giant where he had been financial controller of the UK paper mills. It wasn't just the drabness of the head office that surprised Holdsworth. "GKN struck me as rather an old-fashioned business in management style, systems and structure," he said. "So many individual companies all reporting in separately. Overseas businesses only in the Commonwealth countries – nothing on mainland Europe or in America."

As a bright young brain, Holdsworth was set to work analysing the GKN companies' development strategies. He rapidly came to the same conclusion that Raymond Brookes had reached – the group must expand in the motor industry, because it was a growth business and, importantly, because it presented the opportunity to move GKN upmarket into more sophisticated products.

Now, more than ever, that strategy made every sense. In 1950, passenger car and light commercial vehicle ownership in the UK had stood at 2.3 m vehicles. By the early 1960s, ownership had more than trebled and in 1964 it reached about 8 m vehicles. By any standard, this was a high-growth market. Almost all of these vehicles were made in Britain; imports represented a single-digit fraction of the UK market. In 1960, UK output reached a record 1.35 m cars, of which 42% were exported. In 1963, output hit a new peak of 1.6 m vehicles.

Almost all of these cars and vans were rear wheel drive vehicles. They were steered through the front wheels but needed longitudinal propeller shafts to transmit the power from the engine at the front through a differential gear to the axle and driven wheels at the back. A company called Birfield dominated the manufacture of propshafts in the UK through its Birmingham-based subsidiary, Hardy Spicer. With BRD, Brookes now set out to challenge Birfield and its entrepreneurial chairman, Herbert Hill.

Privately, he sounded out the main car makers on whether they would be interested in an alternative source of supply. Ford was very receptive; Jaguar and Rootes were interested; but the British Motor Company (BMC), the product of the 1952 merger of (Herbert) Austin and (William) Morris and which was the UK market leader by some distance, said no.

"Secrecy had to be the order of the day," Brookes said. "So we arranged to do our own design work secretly. We took the team away from BRD. We ordered our plant through third parties on an export basis so that our name was never connected with it, and we had 18 months to get the project rolling."

The secret held for less than seven months. Then Hill heard about the upstart challenger to his supremacy and immediately launched a counteroffensive: "He literally went round the motor industry, asking the companies 'Where do you stand? Are you going to back this new GKN project to my detriment, or are you going to withdraw from it? If you do the latter, we will continue to invest in new plant and if you don't, we can't be sure that your supply position will be secured,'" Brookes recounted.

That implied threat was enough to put off most of Brookes' potential customers: "My supporters folded like ice in the midday sun," he said. Only Ford stood solid. But they had to start getting the GKN shafts in three months – and BRD hadn't planned to make any shafts for another nine months. It had an empty shop and no machines.

"To cut a long story short, as one little team we made them, but God knows what they cost," Brookes said. "We did not have any machinery worth speaking of – we had to make them virtually with knives and forks. We collected some old junk from here, there and everywhere, any old machines from wherever we could get them. Then we made those propshafts by all the wrong means. I would think on a product that was worth about 40 shillings [£2] when it went to Ford, we probably spent at least about a £25 note with every one that went out. But the main thing was that we did it."

When Brookes was called back by Ford a year later to talk about further supply, the notoriously hard-nosed, numbers-driven Blue Oval executives remarked that it must have cost BRD a lot of money to produce the shafts. Ford was not minded to pay the full cost, whatever that was, but it did want to pay something more. GKN companies had of course supplied Ford for years, but this episode sealed a supplier–customer relationship which became one of GKN's most important for decades to come.

Brookes had broken Hardy Spicer's lock on the prop-shaft business. But Hardy Spicer's hold on the UK market for constant velocity joints (CVJs) was tougher to crack. Demand for CVJs was small, but growing fast. It was one of the less conspicuous, but most far-reaching results of the Mini revolution.

The impulse for what became the Mini was the Suez crisis of 1956. Suez was the first of the three great Middle Eastern crises of the second half of the 20th century to trigger an oil price surge which led to petrol rationing in the West. Like the subsequent oil price shocks of 1973–74 and 1979, Suez was in the longer term beneficial for the motor industry. The petrol shortages caused a surge in demand for low-consumption ultra-small cars. British manufacturers did not produce any such models, so people rushed to import German bubble-cars, which could carry only one or two people. However, the marketing of these cars was fairly primitive: vehicles named Heinkel and Messerschmitt were unlikely to win British customer loyalty.

BMC spotted the opportunity and asked its top designer Alec Issigonis – who had conceived the Morris Minor a decade before – to develop a mini-car to meet the demand. The only instruction to Issigonis was that the car had to use an existing engine. Where Issigonis put that engine was up to him.

In the greatest of several strokes of genius, Issigonis mounted the engine in transverse mode rather than longitudinally. That saved space, but what made the package really small – miniature, even – was that Issigonis drove the car as well as steered it through the front wheels, thereby eliminating the need for a propshaft. To do that, he had to have a new kind of joint for the driveline, the means by which torque was transmitted from engine and gearbox to the front wheels. The Constant Velocity Joint (CVJ) was born.

Or, to be strictly accurate, reborn. The CVJ actually dated from the early 20th century. It belonged to the established engineering family of "Universal" joints, which transmitted torque while enabling relative movement between the wheels and therefore "articulation" of the drive.

There was an older type of universal joint, called the Hookes joint, which BRD began to make when it entered the propshaft market: Hookes joints were an important component of the propshaft for rear wheel drive vehicles, although they owed their name to one Robert Hooke who predated the motor car by about 250 years, having lived from 1635 to 1702. Hooke produced a working Universal [Hooke's] joint in 1676. He was also noted for laying out the street structure of London following the Great Fire in 1666. However, Hookes joints were not suitable for front-wheel drive cars, where driveshafts transmit the torque between the gearbox and the front wheels and steering causes considerable articulation in the joints. Hookes joints could cause considerable vibration because of these large angles of articulation and their inability to deliver constant velocity in the driven shaft.

Joe Robertson, who was brought into GKN as head of the patent department by Geoffrey Hughes, GKN's first General Counsel, said: "A Constant Velocity Joint, as its name describes, eliminates any variation in angular velocity between the input and output of the joint, and therefore minimises vibration." Moreover, because it allowed front-wheel drive, the CVJ saved both cost and space. Brookes saw quickly that it was a product for the future.

Brookes' problem was that Hardy Spicer was the sole UK supplier of CVJs, making them under licence from the American company Dana Corporation which owned the original CVJ patent. Hardy Spicer had taken out numerous patents to protect its position. Brookes needed to find a way through the patents.

"Maxwell-Holroyd, then a director, got some advice from a patent agent about the Hardy Spicer patents," said Geoffrey Hughes. "This agent said that we could make CVJs without infringing the patents, but I wasn't so sure." Brookes gave him the papers. Hughes, who knew a thing or two about patents, studied them and found his first impressions confirmed. "I wrote a note to Brookes that, although there might be a chink in the patents, if we tried to make CVJs, we would be involved in a legal dispute for 10 years."

Brookes responded with what Hughes could justifiably regard as a deliberate hospital pass. "He said, 'That's a very good note, Geoff' – he always called me Geoff when he had something unpleasant in mind – 'You know Maxwell-

Holroyd – would you like to explain it to him?'" Maxwell-Holroyd's refusal to take no for an answer was legendary. Hughes duly trooped off to see him. "It can be quite difficult being an in-house lawyer," he reflected years later, memories of the bruises from that encounter resurfacing. "I spent hours with Maxwell-Holroyd and in the end, he said: 'OK, you'd better come and have a drink', which was certainly a welcome invitation."

For Brookes, it was back to the drawing board to plan how to break into the CVJ market. Expansion in automotive was all the more critical because GKN was on the point of losing its steel-making interests for the second time to nationalisation by a Labour government. And he was now perfectly placed to lead the group into that expansion. On 13 August 1965, Sir Kenneth Peacock, suffering from poor health, stepped down as chairman. The Board appointed Brookes, who had been made managing director the previous year, to succeed him.

GKN's appointment of Raymond Brookes was a landmark in the evolution of the company. During his eight years in charge, he modernised the group, transforming both its ethos and its business base out of all recognition from what it had been before.

His appointment was also a landmark on a personal level, because it reflected the revolution in British society that was taking place in the world outside GKN. The mould that had been filled for decades by a narrow social, political and industrial establishment, the ruling class structure that had stood unchanged since the late Victorian age, was being broken by a new, upwardly-mobile generation.

Brookes was the epitome of this new mobility. He had left school in West Bromwich, heart of the West Midlands Black Country, in 1923 at the age of 14. There was only one engineering apprenticeship available in the whole area. Brookes and his best friend both desperately wanted it and couldn't agree on which one should go for it. So, more than half a century before the Conservative Employment Secretary Norman Tebbit told people to "get on their bikes" in order to find work, Brookes said to his friend: "I'll race you there". Brookes won the race and landed the apprenticeship.

He then embarked on a determined drive for self-improvement. He renegotiated the terms of the apprenticeship so that it combined mechanical engineering, accountancy and law, including five nights a week at West Bromwich Technical College. He got a part-time job selling programmes at the local theatre so that he could see plays and develop his cultural knowledge. He took elocution lessons to revise his Black Country English, although to the end of his life he could tell Black Country jokes in that accent. "He was absolutely a self-made man," said Jim Parsons.

Despite his achievements, Brookes remained sensitive to his humble background. Parsons had lunch with him one day in the executive dining room at Smethwick and the two men started talking about education. "You don't list your school in your *Who's Who* entry. Why not?" Parsons asked his chairman. "I left school at 14 and was educated at West Brom Tech College," Brookes replied. "That's why I don't put it in." "But wouldn't it be rather good to say that?" asked Parsons. "I'm not sure," Brookes thought. When the next edition of *Who's Who* came out, Parsons turned to Brookes' entry. There, under Educ. was listed "West Bromwich Technical College".

When Brookes became chairman, the 20-strong GKN board included six knights of the realm together with a battery of public school-educated GKN veterans, two of them Oxbridge Classics scholars. Brookes more than held his own with any and all of them. "He was brilliant at board meetings," said Parsons. "He was like a chess player – he knew what was going to happen three or four jumps ahead. He was also a brilliant analyst – he could tear a flawed piece of analysis to pieces."

Brookes was critical, but never for destructive purposes: "If someone didn't meet their budget, he wanted to know why and what that person was going to do about it. If someone beat their budget by a large margin, he was also rebuked for setting it too low, and told to raise it." Across the company, Brookes set standards of behaviour and achievement. "He introduced discipline and a strict adherence to standards. If you didn't meet those standards, you were in for a very big rocket and people knew it," said Parsons.

Because he was approachable, he was often addressed in matey fashion by executives or senior managers. "Brookes didn't mind people calling him Ray, so long as they did exactly what he told them," said Geoffrey Hughes. "Many's the time I saw people waiting outside his office, saying 'I'm going to tell him what for' who came out three minutes later having agreed to do the opposite of what they wanted. He would come into steel-related meetings and launch a disquisition on this or that. We wouldn't understand what he was getting at for a long time, but in the end you realised that he had thought the subject through completely, much better than the lawyers, accountants or steelmen, and understood everything about it. He was a most devastating businessman."

Brookes needed all his abilities to meet the challenges and take the opportunities now facing GKN. Peacock homed in on the central problem in his final message to shareholders, describing the year as "one of the most inflationary periods since the war, with steep rises in both wages and prices." The new Labour government under Harold Wilson established a Prices and Incomes Board to try to regulate both sets of costs. Pressure was building on the economy, and with the pound in recurrent difficulty an inflationary devaluation was a persistent possibility.

For GKN, overwhelmingly dependent on its UK manufacturing base, the continued competitiveness of UK plc was critical. In the year that Brookes took the reins, GKN's total workforce passed the 100,000 mark. Just over three-quarters of the total was in Britain, and of that 76,000 almost 63,000 were now employed outside steel-making.

The UK operations generated about two-thirds of GKN's sales and trading profit – just over £350 m and £30 m respectively in 1965 – with India and Australia, by far the largest overseas businesses, making consistently decent contributions. About a third of the UK sales went for export, either directly – as in the 450 tons of wire from Rolled and Bright Steel for pre-stressing the concrete structures of the new Sydney Opera House – or indirectly, through avenues such as vehicle exports.

Ominously, Brookes noted that the Forgings and Castings business was affected in 1965 by "alterations to vehicle production schedules caused by the greatly-increased number of strikes in the plants of some of our main customers". The UK trend line for days lost due to industrial disputes had been edging up since the mid-1950s. In 1965, according to official figures, days lost spiked to 1 m, by far the highest total ever recorded. Yet the official figures told only a fraction of the story: it was the unofficial strikes that did most of the damage. Because of these wildcat strikes, the total number of days lost in the motor industry in 1965 soared to 6 m. At one plant alone – Rover's Solihull factory – there were 101 unofficial stoppages in a year. As a result of the strikes, UK car production, which had hit a post-war peak of almost 1.9 m units in 1964, dropped 8% to 1.72 m in 1965.

Brookes did not allow such factors, however great and however disadvantageous, to deflect him from his central focus on taking GKN higher up the technological value chain. Harold Wilson, whose premiership was confirmed in early 1966 by a landslide election victory, had declaimed back in 1963 about a new age of science and "The Britain that is going to be forged in the white heat of this revolution". The national reality fell far short of Wilson's rhetoric, but the changes engineered by Brookes ensured that GKN at least achieved technical self-advancement.

With steel-making on the point of renationalisation and Fasteners losing more ground to its Asian rivals, the group had to evolve rapidly or face decline to the point of extinction. Even without renationalisation, steel-making was a fast-waning power inside GKN. Its 1966 RoNA plummeted to 3.3%, "bedevilled by politics, world surplus, dumped imports, intensified domestic competition and serious under loading of plant," as Brookes enumerated the forces assailing it.

The cumulative effect of these pressures was to heighten still further the importance of GKN's strategy to expand in automotive. Speed was of the essence, so GKN could not just rely on organic growth. Brookes had no intention of doing that anyway. He already had a target in his sights, one that was both natural and obvious – Herbert Hill's Birfield.

Surprisingly, the first move was made not by him, but by Hill. "After we were well-established with BRD, Herbert Hill used to make noises to me about getting together, but I did not express too much interest," Brookes recounted. "Ultimately, our strength reached the point when I thought it became necessary for them to want a merger."

The ritual M&A dance ensued, with Hill trying to entice Brookes to put GKN's name to a very high price, and Brookes resisting. Eventually, they reached a verbal agreement – whereupon news of the hitherto confidential negotiations leaked. Birfield's share price duly went into orbit. Brookes had no doubt that Birfield was responsible for the leak, and that it was attempting to drive the price out of GKN's reach because it had never intended to be taken over.

The GKN chairman was not going to let such machinations deflect him from his objective. For the first time in its history, GKN launched a hostile bid, which soon became its first successful hostile bid, as Birfield – no doubt surprised by GKN's aggression – finally caved in. "It was hotly contested," said Geoffrey Hughes. "I still have the solid silver beer tankard that GKN gave those involved in 'The Battle of Birfield', as it says on the side."

Much to Brookes' frustration, the deal was referred to the Monopolies Commission, which did not approve it until January 1967. But it was worth the wait. Birfield was a valuable prize. GKN paid £27.6 m in cash and loan stock – £370.5 m at 2009 prices – for a profitable business with net assets of £32.4 m and current annual sales of £40 m. Moreover, Birfield was an excellent fit: "Their predominating activities in transmission equipment, hot forgings, cold extrusions, malleable iron castings etc integrate naturally with existing GKN operations," Brookes told shareholders. [One interest which GKN chose not to retain was a stake Hill had taken in a start-up information technology business called Hoskyns, after its founder John Hoskyns. Years later, after he had built his firm into one of the foremost UK IT services companies, Hoskyns was a key behind-the-scenes figure in Margaret Thatcher's government. Later still, he became Sir John Hoskyns, head of Britain's Institute of Directors.]

Birfield significantly extended GKN's interests in UK motor components by bringing in Hardy Spicer's propshafts – which made GKN the undisputed UK market leader – and, of course, its much-desired CVJs. Birfield also owned Laycock, maker of automotive clutches. Apart from the relatively modest BRD start-up in propshafts, the acquisition was the first real move by GKN into proprietary automotive parts, as opposed to the commodity forgings and castings that had long been part of its portfolio.

But there was more – as things turned out, much more. Hill had always had an eye for overseas interests, and had acquired a number of minority stakes in mainland European businesses. "It was very unlike GKN," said Hughes. "We wanted to own businesses and control them."

Among Birfield's portfolio was a trio of investments in continental European automotive transmission manufacturers, all of which made CVJs. It owned 39.5% of a company called Uni-Cardan, based in Lohmar, West Germany. Uni-Cardan in turn controlled Glaenzer Spicer, which was located in Poissy, France and in which Birfield held 33%; and it and Birfield each owned 50% of Birfield Trasmissioni, which they had set up as a green-field joint venture in Brunico, Northern Italy.

These interests came as something of a pleasant surprise to GKN: "Ray Brookes had never heard of Uni-Cardan," said Hughes. Up to this point, GKN's continental European operations were extremely limited: they consisted of the Stenman fasteners business, an Italian welding machine company, and a small minority stake in a Viennese maker of biros and pencils. Now, quite unexpectedly and at a stroke, it found itself with a major bridgehead in the three largest vehicle markets in mainland Europe.

Brookes told shareholders that the Uni-Cardan operations "are complementary to the existing and increasingly international trend in GKN. They should constitute secure and natural bases for future expansion." As we have seen, the GKN chairman was not given to understatement. But those words in April 1967 are the greatest understatement in the history of the group.

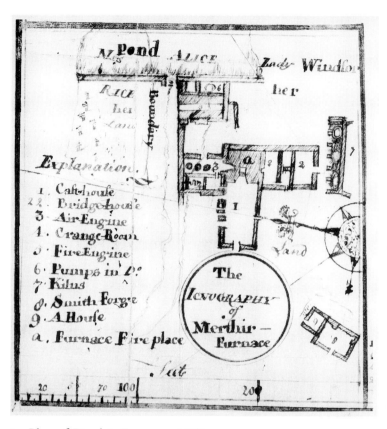

1. Plan of Dowlais Furnance 1763
   *Glamorgan Record Office*

*All images courtesy of GKN unless otherwise stated*

2. General View of Merthyr in 1811 by John George Wood.
   *The British Library*

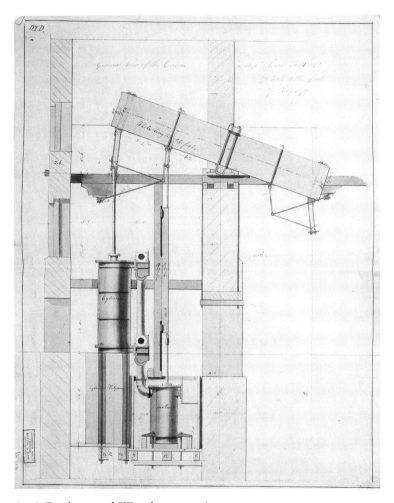

3. A Boulton and Watt beam-engine.
*Birmingham Reference Library*

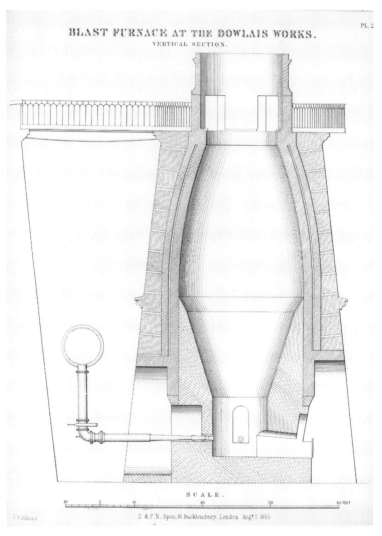

BLAST FURNACE AT THE DOWLAIS WORKS.
VERTICAL SECTION.

SCALE.

4. A section through a Dowlais Furnace taken from William
Truran's *The Iron Manufacture of Great Britain* (1855).
   *The British Library*

5. Sir John Guest from a mezzotint by William Walker of the painting by Richard Buckner.
 *Glamorgan Record Office*

6. An engraving of Dowlais House (c. 1840).
   *John A. Owen (Works Manager for BSC Dowlais Works)*

7. A blast furnace at Dowlais
   *Glamorgan Record Office*

8. John Sutton Nettlefold

9. Joseph Chamberlain (1836–1914)

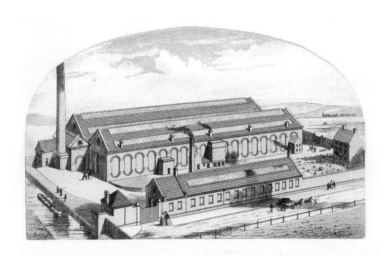

10. The original screw mill of 1854
*European Industrial Services*

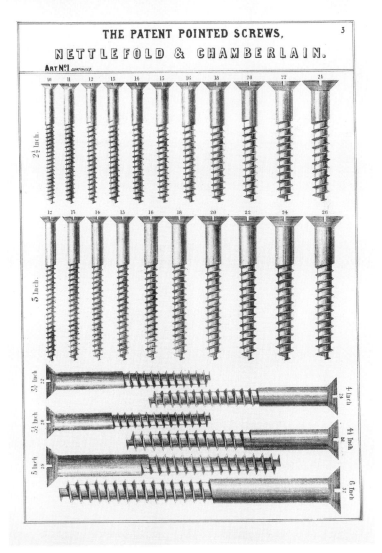

11. A page form Nettlefold & Chamberlain's 1871 screw catalogue

12. Arthur Keen and family.
*Photo courtesy of Mrs M. H. Dent (granddaughter of Arthur Keen).*

13. The London Works in Smethwick

14. Arthur Keen (1835–1915), former Chairman, Patent Nut and Bolt Co., First Chairman, Guest, Keen and Nettlefolds Ltd.
*Photo courtesy of Mrs M. H. Dent (granddaughter of Arthur Keen).*

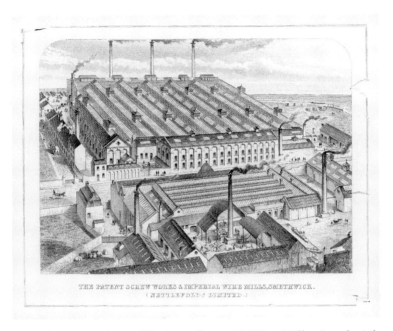

THE PATENT SCREW WORKS & IMPERIAL WIRE MILLS, SMETHWICK.
( NETTLEFOLDS LIMITED.)

15. The patent Screw Works & Imperial Wire Mills, Smethwick in the 1880s. Nettlefolds Ltd.

16. The furnaces at Dowlais c. 1865–70.
*Glamorgan Record Office*

17. The Goat Mill
   *Glamorgan Record Office*

18. G. T. Clark
*Merthyr Central Library*

19. William Menelaus
*Merthyr Central Library*

20. A Bessemer coverter at Dowlais
   *John A. Owen (Works Manager for BSC Dowlais Works)*

21. Dowlais-Cardiff blast furnaces being built
*National Library of Wales*

22. The three blast furnaces at Dowlais-Cardiff
*National Library of Wales*

23. E. P. Martin
*Institution of Mechanical Engineers*

24.  A display of Nettlefolds woodscrews, nuts, bolts, colters, nails and hooks.

*A GKN photo*

# CHAPTER 10

# White Heat and
# Cold Comfort

1967. The Sixties were in full swing, the Beatles were releasing "Sergeant Pepper's Lonely Hearts Club Band", England was King of Football having won the previous year's World Cup. But British industry was in no mood to join the party. The country's long-standing and deep-rooted economic problems, which had beset the Wilson government since it took office, were coalescing into a full-blown crisis.

Brookes surveyed the national scene in early 1967 and, while acknowledging the quality of some Ministers, remarked that: "In vital areas of decision they appear handicapped by the historic prejudice of pressure groups. The obscurity of ultimate intentions toward business, capital, profits and dividends allied to existing repressive tax legislation affecting corporate and personal incentives, are factors destructive to the mainsprings of national endeavour and the root causes of present stagnation. The bleakness of these uncertainties is fundamental to the persisting lack of confidence."

Stop-go was back with a vengeance. Frenzied efforts were made through the Prices and Incomes Board to regulate domestic demand and narrow the balance of payments gap. Between June 1965 and November 1967, hire purchase and credit terms were changed seven times.

None of this alleviated the pressure on the pound – it only increased as Britain endured a troubled summer. In June, the Six-Day War between Israel and Egypt led to an oil embargo on Britain by some Middle East producers on the grounds that the country was supporting Israel. Still more damage was done by a national dock strike, which closed most of the major ports. The first devaluation for 18 years duly followed. On 19 November, the exchange rate was cut to $2.40, a 14.3% reduction. Wilson told the British public, not entirely accurately: "We're on our own now. It means Britain first. It does not mean, of course, that the pound here in Britain, in your pocket or purse or in your bank has been devalued."

Brookes took a somewhat different view when, a few months later, he reported on a year when GKN's pre-tax profits declined slightly: "We failed over a fairly wide front to achieve budgeted financial objectives, which when determined towards the end of 1966 did not and perhaps could not have taken into account the ensuing near-total collapse of UK Government policies and associated economic predictions culminating in devaluation." And, when he looked ahead to 1968, he anticipated "the near-certainty of siege economy conditions".

The GKN that fought its way through the hostile British economic and political landscape of the late Sixties was quite a different animal from the group of even two years earlier. Its automotive operations, already expanded by Birfield, advanced further with the £12.3 m purchase of Vandervell, the engine bearings group. Partly because of the two acquisitions, GKN's automotive-related operations, including the OffHighway agricultural machinery business, now represented almost 40% of its UK sales, and one-third of overall group turnover.

The other reason for the group's increased dependence on automotive markets took effect on 28 July 1967, when the GKN Steel Company was formally transferred into public ownership for the second time in 16 years.

GKN tried to lead a rearguard action against renationalisation. Its problem was that the steel industry was hopelessly divided by internal rivalries – which provided Labour's justification for uniting the industry through public ownership. "They brought it on themselves," Brookes concluded. "I went regularly to what they used to call 'the steel barons' meeting, which took place about once a month, and I pleaded passionately for urgent consultations the following morning. But they had this silly thought that they were going to avoid nationalisation or escape it somehow. Failing that, they couldn't achieve sufficient unity of purpose as to who would merge with whom, so the clock went round."

Brookes worked closely with the then-Chancellor Jim Callaghan to produce a private–public sector alternative in which there would be enforced mergers with the government taking a stake of around 50% to ensure control without full public ownership: a part-nationalisation.

The effort foundered on the reluctance of GKN's fellow steel-makers. Eventually, the industry proposed to concentrate crude steel-making on the five largest and most modern works, including Scunthorpe, backed by further investment and the closure of obsolete capacity. Then it came up with a draft plan for the consolidation that would be required among the companies. But it was too little, too late – particularly with Labour's left wing pushing continuously for the government to stick to its nationalisation commitment.

So the 14 largest companies, including GKN, which accounted for 90% of crude steel production were brought together to form the British Steel Corporation (BSC). "It would have been possible to avoid nationalisation at that time," Brookes said. "The Cabinet was about evenly divided. What made it necessary to nationalise was not in finality the absolute bloody-mindedness of the Labour government. It was the intransigence and lack of unity among the steel barons themselves."

Nationalisation this time round was more limited in scope – it involved only the steel-making businesses at Cardiff, Scunthorpe and Brymbo, not the re-rolling and bright steel products operations. But, much to Brookes's chagrin, it still went further than it should have done.

"It was admitted to me by Richard Marsh [the Industry Minister] that Brymbo was an accident of nationalisation," Brookes said in 1974. Brymbo was caught up in the process by a legal technicality: "We brought it on ourselves because this was one of the few areas in which we turned companies into divisions". GKN Steel was one of the only subgroups (along with Fasteners) where the major constituent companies had been disincorporated and reconstituted as "Works".

"If Brymbo Steel Works had been called Brymbo Steel Works Limited, it would not have been nationalised," Brookes said. "The absence of the word 'Limited' resulted in nationalisation. Within weeks of nationalisation taking place, Dick Marsh said to me: 'Well, obviously you can't frame an Act to except a circumstance like that: it's happened, I'll get it back to you.'"

Marsh then invited Brookes to become chairman of BSC, either along with or instead of his chairmanship of GKN. Brookes declined but did eventually agree to become an advisor in BSC's creation and a non-executive director once the Corporation was established. The position made sense in principle, since GKN now depended on BSC for most of its crude steel supply and had to co-exist with the Corporation. However, Brookes later resigned after a boardroom row over BSC's refusal to admit that it was selling steel plate to Scandinavian shipyards at much lower prices than it would sell to British yards, thereby rendering the UK builders uncompetitive.

Brookes had accepted Marsh's request that he participate in BSC on one condition: that Brymbo would be duly returned to GKN. "I said, 'I'll not serve unless I have your word on that'. He gave me his word and I think, in all fairness to him, he tried to carry out his word. But I think he was then obstructed by forces in the Corporation."

So GKN had to wait for the promise to be kept. It was Mary Tudor who had declared that, when she was "dead and opened, you shall find 'Calais' lying in my heart" – a reference to the devastating loss during her reign of the last English possession on French soil. Brookes recalled the Calais story and told Marsh and Lord Melchett, the first chairman of BSC, that "Brymbo was engraved on my heart and it was going to stay that way".

GKN now had to negotiate a respectable compensation settlement. On 28 January 1969, it announced that it would receive just over £42 m (almost £500 m at current prices) for the nationalised assets. GKN got the money in the form of Treasury stock, which it sold immediately. "The settlement is higher than that which Government had sought to impose, but lower than the realistic worth to GKN," Brookes reported. But the only alternative would have been protracted arbitration, affecting the time value of whatever money GKN would receive.

That value was particularly vulnerable because of the inflation now afflicting the UK economy. Inflation had been 2.5% in 1967; within two years, it increased to 5.4%. Part of the rise was in-built by devaluation, but much of it was now being driven by wage claims demanded by increasingly militant union leaders and frequently conceded by back-pedalling managements.

GKN was affected directly by disputes, but the main impact on the group was indirect through strikes at customers, notably in the motor industry. Brookes estimated that GKN lost £1.6 m in profits in 1969 because of industrial action. As he noted, however, the damage went well beyond the immediately financial: "The indirect adversities are incalculable, including constant switching of production lines, appalling strains on top management, and the diminution of hard-won customer goodwill sometimes resulting in the permanent loss of home and export business."

In 1969, Wilson made one final attempt to re-impose order on increasingly chaotic labour relations by supporting his Employment secretary Barbara Castle's sensible reform plan, *In Place of Strife*, which would have exposed unions to fines if they broke proposed new rules on strike ballots and cooling-off periods. But the plan was torpedoed by union barons backed by Jim Callaghan, who had been appointed Home Secretary after resigning as Chancellor over devaluation.

Brookes made no secret of GKN's views on the defeat of *In Place of Strife*. "In contrast with the proliferation of other interventionism, the dismal retreat by Government from intended legislation is seen to be a retreat from the responsibility to govern. The burden of this expediency, which has encouraged unbridled arrogance from some Trades Union leaders, will prove heavy."

His was an all-too-accurate prediction. In 1970, officially-recorded strikes totalled 250, costing more than 1.5 m lost working days. Because of the continued upsurge in unofficial action, the actual number of disputes and days lost was far higher. While the public sector was hit by what seemed a continuous wave of disruption, particularly after the surprise election of Edward Heath and the Conservatives in 1970, the motor industry was the arena where the most destructive private sector battles were fought.

By 1970, the rot was setting into the British car industry. Output that year was 1.64 m vehicles, well below the levels of the mid-1960s. Production for the UK market was at its lowest point since 1962. Moreover, France and Germany were increasing their exports to other European countries far faster and further than Britain. While UK exports to Europe, helped by devaluation, had risen from 142,000 in 1960 to 346,000 a decade later, France increased exports from 243,000 cars to 834,000 and Germany from 434,000 in 1960 to almost 1.1 m in 1970.

One factor in this relative decline was Britain's exclusion from the EEC – something Heath remedied in 1971 when he at last won French agreement to admit Britain. But the industrial problems now plaguing the UK industry clearly played an important part. Brookes told shareholders: "The destructive militancy of minorities is alien to the decencies and preferences of the majority of people." But, for the ruinous moment, the militant minority held sway over the silent majority.

GKN suffered serious disputes in 1970 at Sankey and Scottish Stampings. The Sankey pressings and fabrications strike dragged on for weeks, through August and September, and cost the group £1.8 m in lost profits. GKN began the efforts to end the strike by negotiating with the local officials, and ended it at a crunch arbitration meeting with the top union officials under the auspices of the Engineering Employers' Federation.

Jim Parsons recalled: "The case for Sankey was put by its managing director Tom Honess and the case for the unions was put by Moss Evans [a future general secretary of the TGWU]. The other top union official present was George Wright of the Engineering Workers' Union, the AUEW."

George Wright was a leading Communist, but after both sides had said their piece, there was a long silence broken when Wright declared: "Well, it's clear that the unions are wrong and the management are right." That was the end of the Sankey strike – the worst dispute in GKN at any time in the 1970s. Unfortunately, it was not the last dispute from which GKN suffered – not by a long chalk.

The following March, when he looked back back on 1970 and forward into 1971, Brookes gloomily surveyed the state of the nation's economy: "The chronic and persisting lack of effective growth in UK productivity has at its roots years of unrewarding obsession with outdated political prejudices and discredited economic theories, enforced adherence to restrictive practices, confusion of liberty with licence, excessive tax disincentives, diminishing cash flows and depleted investor confidence," he said.

At the same time, Brookes highlighted one of the most insidious and, in the long term, damaging effects of the inflation that was now becoming ingrained in the UK system: its deterrent effect on investment. "In conditions prevailing in 1970, it was virtually impossible for industry in the UK to finance the maintenance – let alone the expansion – of operations from its own cash flow," he said. "The deficiency has had to be met by capital markets, the demands on which, coupled with an insistence by investors that long-term interest rates must also have some regard to continuance of inflation, have forced long-term interest rates up to a level which would have astounded our predecessors." To help meet its own needs, GKN issued £20 m in debenture stock in mid-1970 – the first of a succession of cash-calls to which the group resorted during the decade in order to help fund its UK operations.

Despite the exacting industrial environment, the group was still growing. In 1971, sales exceeded £500 m for the first time and pre-tax profits edged up to £45 m. GKN was the 12th largest company in Britain and 43rd in the

American magazine *Fortune's* list of the world's biggest industrial businesses.

Apart from the main automotive and steel businesses, GKN's sprawling portfolio encompassed locks and hinges, power station cooling towers, grandstands and scaffolding (it equipped the stadiums for the 1970 Edinburgh Commonwealth Games and The Open golf championship at St Andrews), beer barrels, vending machines, air filters, central heating and desks and shelves. It refurbished a railway in the Congo and supplied equipment for a Brazilian steelworks. It installed double-glazing and converted swathes of England to natural gas. It was a vast and ubiquitous component of British industrial life.

Geographically, however, the group was making a historic change of direction. In a shift which paralleled that of the country, GKN was moving away from its focus on the Commonwealth markets and towards continental Europe. Two significant corporate developments exemplified this fundamental reorientation.

In mid-1970, GKN and Broken Hill Proprietary (BHP), the giant Australian steel and mining group, signed a deal under which BHP took a 50% stake in John Lysaght Australia. The agreement to some extent represented a recognition of the inevitable by Brookes and the Board: over the preceding years, Lysaght had become increasingly dependent on BHP for its raw steel and, as a result, the Australian group had begun to exert a stranglehold on Lysaght's operations.

GKN could have gone it alone, but as Brookes recognised: "Our position in Australia was untenable – not necessarily in terms of the past, but in terms of the future." Because Lysaght had never invested in raw steel-making capacity, the company had long depended on BHP for supplies. And as the market, and Lysaght, had grown, so that dependence had increased. Lysaght had evolved very successfully: from the original galvanised sheet trading business which had been supplied by exports from the UK, it had moved to an in-country finishing operation, installed a coil plant, then hot-rolling and finally cold-rolling. But having extended its footprint and expanded with the market, it now faced the challenge of investing big money to maintain its market leadership.

"GKN were at a point when some involvement of BHP in Lysaghts had to be sought," Brookes said. Identifying the objective was one thing; achieving an agreement with BHP was another. It took Brookes and his team three years' hard talking to reach an acceptable deal. "They did not want a partnership at any time, but were persuaded and connived at," he said. "They did not want it because, in fact, Lysaghts was a sitting duck."

Brookes took a GKN team including James Insch, the group's deputy chairman, and Geoffrey Hughes, to BHP's home city of Melbourne to try and clinch a deal. "We used to have breakfast at the Melbourne Club, which was very stiff even by British standards in those days," Hughes recalled. Brookes and Ian McLennan, BHP's hard-as-nails managing director, did most of the negotiating on McLennan's nearby farm.

Eventually, a deal was struck. It included a condition that the next hot strip mill for the operation would be put down by Lysaght, not BHP, and an agreement in principle that a steel-making plant would be built at Lysaght's Westernport site in Victoria to support the hot- and cold-rolling facilities there. The agreement also provided an obvious exit route should GKN ever decide to sell out of Lysaght.

In mainland European auto components, by contrast, the group was on the threshold of a new world. And the key to the door was Uni-Cardan.

CHAPTER 11

# Crossroads

The company that became the cornerstone of GKN's global driveline business was – rather like Guest, Keen & Nettlefolds itself – the product of a three-way merger inspired by one man. Uni-Cardan (U-C), based in Lohmar, North Rhine-Westphalia, was created in 1964 largely by the inspiration of Bernard Walterscheid-Muller.

Walterscheid-Muller was the adopted son of Jean Walterscheid, whose eponymous family business was primarily a producer of driveshafts for agricultural use – including power take-off (PTO) shafts for connecting the tractor to the agricultural implement. The other two members of the group also had their own areas of specialisation: Lohr & Bromkamp focused on joints and shafts for passenger cars, and had an embryonic interest in CVJs. It supplied Volkswagen and BMW. The third company, Gelenkwellenbau (meaning "drive-shaft build"), was controlled by the Stratmann family and was mainly involved in the truck market with heavier universal joints and propshafts.

The companies' product ranges overlapped slightly, but together they comprised a well-balanced and very extensive producer of shafts and joints. Birfield's entrée into the business was through Gelenkwellenbau, in which Herbert Hill had acquired a minority stake.

After the Uni-Cardan group was formed, Fiat and other Italian vehicle producers pressed it to set up an Italian operation rather than to sell into the country from Germany. So Walterscheid-Muller allied with Hill to set up Birfield Trasmissioni as a green-field venture in Italy. He also expanded into France by buying a majority stake in Glaenzer Spicer, the leading French driveshaft producer. Having established manufacturing operations in the three main production centres of mainland Western Europe, Walterscheid-Muller then began to extend Uni-Cardan's network through service companies elsewhere in Europe, including the Netherlands and Austria.

Birfield's 38.8% stake in Uni-Cardan was a large holding, but very much a minority. The British company had minimal influence over Uni-Cardan and GKN inherited that state of affairs when it acquired Birfield. However, having discovered Uni-Cardan, GKN behaved in character. It wanted to take control.

The Uni-Cardan minority stake, as Brookes later noted, created a dilemma: "A holding of that dimension, when the people are engaged in selling to the same markets and, by and large, the same or similar products as your own wholly-owned subsidiary, is enough to make it self-destructive to invade their market. But it is not enough to stop you wanting to invade it. The immediate problem was: 'Could we or could we not get a majority?' "

Brookes did not join the Uni-Cardan board: he had a philosophy – no doubt influenced by what he had seen happen to Kenneth Peacock – of not going on the boards of subsidiaries. For more than two years after the acquisition, the Uni-Cardan directors whom GKN had nominated told Brookes repeatedly that he could not gain a majority. Brookes decided that he needed to find out for himself whether this was indeed the case. So he asked Walterscheid-Muller and some of his Uni-Cardan colleagues if he could accompany them on a tour of the plants. "I didn't particularly want to see the factories, but I did want to spend three days in close proximity to this highly-individualistic chap," Brookes recalled. "I had decided that on the third day, I would broach this question of majority control."

To promote intimacy, Brookes chartered a private jet "where you are huddled like rabbits in a hutch and it is not conducive to dignity". This certainly produced a result, although not quite according to Brookes' premeditated timetable. Within three hours of meeting Walterscheid-Muller, when they were airborne on the first leg of their tour, Brookes decided to confront the issue head on.

"I don't know what made me do it," Brookes recalled. He fired a verbal broadside at the unsuspecting Walterscheid-Muller. "I've had enough of this nonsense," Brookes thundered. "I understand that you are opposed to us having control but I am not going to stay out of the European market. I am going to enter it and compete with our own minority interest. I believe that because we are more efficient and, in my view, infinitely better than Uni-Cardan, we will take you to the cleaners even though we will be taking our own 38% to the cleaners in the process."

This would not be an unfriendly act, Brookes claimed with what, at the very least, was a degree of cheek. "GKN started in the propshaft and joint business at BRD out of desperation for not having any alternative, but with a very fine labour force and very good management, and having conquered Hardy Spicer and Birfield we are not going to let this momentum be halted by a continental minority interest. Uni-Cardan must be the next tree to fall." Finally, Brookes informed his German counterpart: "You are the real architect of Uni-Cardan and you need the support of a big and powerful brother. It is in your best interests and that of your family holdings for us to have a majority."

As an exposition of why it was GKN's manifest destiny to control Uni-Cardan, Brookes's oration could not have been surpassed. In truth, GKN was by no means superior to the German company in engineering terms – "Uni-Cardan was wonderful from a technical viewpoint but terrible in terms of financial management," Hughes said. But GKN was certainly the larger company and used to getting its way.

Some seconds passed as the jet flew on and Walterscheid-Muller digested Brookes' onslaught. The Uni-Cardan chief habitually used an interpreter, even though his English was excellent. Brookes suspected it was a device to give him additional time to consider his responses. He certainly deployed the tactic on this occasion. "You have raised momentous issues," he said finally. "I would like to think about this for a long time." Brookes, determined to press home his first mover advantage, retorted: "Well, you can't have a long time to think about it because I am going to move quickly."

Walterscheid-Muller took less than 48 hours to respond. The party stayed the following night in Paris, but next morning, when they were due to fly on, the airport was fog-bound and their jet could not take off. While they were waiting for the fog to clear, Brookes and Walterscheid-Muller took a walk down a disused runway. This time, the German did not bring his interpreter.

The scene was somewhat reminiscent of the final moments in the film "Casablanca", even if Walterscheid-Muller didn't look much like Claude Rains and Brookes was certainly no Humphrey Bogart.

"I haven't been to sleep all night because I want to do the right thing," said Walterscheid-Muller.

"Yes, I believe you do, Bernard. And I think you know what the right thing is."

"Well, what holding do you want?"

"51% would be adequate."

"I give you my word that I will do my best to bring that about."

"I want more than that; I want your word that you *will* bring it about."

"Well, the situation is not entirely in my control."

"It is if you are sufficiently hard with the people who are just riding on your backs and ours and creating an impossible situation."

"Right, I will do it."

Brookes did not reply, although he might have said: "Bernard, this could be the beginning of a beautiful friendship."

It might have been better had Walterscheid-Muller used his interpreter. Despite his pledge to Brookes, more than a year went by and nothing happened. Brookes recalled: "The polite, but scarcely-concealed, attitude inside GKN was: 'Ray Brookes has, as usual, trusted somebody and it hasn't happened'."

So Brookes called his counterpart. "I am a little disappointed," he rebuked Walterscheid-Muller. "I know this was a difficult exercise – what's the problem?"

The answer illuminated how English idiom could get lost in translation to German literalism. "My difficulty with all the family interests which are involved is to get you exactly 51%," said Walterscheid-Muller. "I can get you more." Brookes laughed: "How silly we – or I – have been. I don't mind if it is more. I don't mind if it is the lot." Walterscheid-Muller duly delivered on his promise to Brookes. In 1971, GKN increased its holding from 39.5% to 58.7% and Uni-Cardan became a subsidiary of the group.

Even as Brookes was cementing GKN's hold on Uni-Cardan, however, he was being lured back to the future. The result was an intense, behind-the-scenes boardroom debate about the strategic direction that GKN should take, a debate in which the other main protagonist was Trevor Holdsworth.

Having served his GKN "apprenticeship" as group chief accountant, Holdsworth had been despatched by Brookes to gain operational management experience by running Fasteners. In 1970, he was brought back to headquarters with the title of Group Controller, clearly earmarked for higher office. As GKN's newest, youngest director, Holdsworth now had a baptism of fire: in no time at all, he found himself leading the opposition to the direction in which his chairman wished to take the company.

Brookes wanted GKN to buy back all its nationalised steel businesses. "The chairman wanted steel back because it was a 'big man's business'," Holdsworth recalled. "I decided that I had to oppose him because I knew it was the wrong thing to do. It was too commodity and political. There was always the risk of renationalisation. We had a big argument." Moreover, Brookes – possibly frustrated at the time by the delay in gaining control of Uni-Cardan – wanted to sell out of the business.

Holdsworth had no doubt that both moves would be massive mistakes. Reacquiring the steel business in its entirety and pulling out of Uni-Cardan would have meant turning back the clock. "When I arrived at GKN, we were basically just an iron and steel maker, producing steel and steel products for a huge range of industries," he said. "What we needed was technology, proprietary products and internationalisation. By going into automotive in a big way, we got all that. The move into automotive changed the culture of the group, because the steel culture was 'produce the most you can' whereas our automotive business was increasingly about quality rather than just quantity."

At this critical juncture – a true watershed for the group – Brookes demonstrated his ability to bow to a superior argument and change his mind. "I persuaded him," Holdsworth said. "He did listen, and he accepted my arguments. Basically, I wanted to concentrate on the automotive industry."

Brookes and Holdsworth agreed that, instead of buying back all the nationalised steel operations, GKN would only reacquire Brymbo. "It was small and specialised," Holdsworth said. And, far from selling the Uni-Cardan stake, GKN would look to increase it. "Thank goodness he gave in, or the constant velocity technology – which became central to our strategy – would have been lost," Holdsworth later remarked.

GKN completed the reacquisition of Brymbo on 29 September 1973, paying a net £20 m for the business. As part of the transaction, British Steel acquired the foundries in Merthyr and Cardiff which had continued after nationalisation under the ownership of GKN Dowlais Ltd.

"I would have taken Brymbo back if it had been making a loss," Brookes said later. "Because I would have known I could have made it make a profit again. But that wasn't the situation: it was making nice profits. In fact, we had to buy our own profits and I didn't like doing that at all."

For Brookes, Brymbo eliminated a crucial weakness in GKN's armoury: its lack of an in-house source of special steels for its forgings and castings operations. Now the objective was secured. Brookes was sure that Brymbo itself would be delighted to be back in the GKN fold. His confidence was quickly justified. About 10 days after completion of the deal, Brookes wrote to the managing director, welcoming Brymbo back. "I got a letter back with complete GKN heading and everything. They had the paper all ready."

CHAPTER 12

# In Face of Strife

Holdsworth's disagreement with Brookes certainly strained relations between the two men: "He was rather annoyed with me," Holdsworth recalled with characteristic understatement.

But Holdsworth had no doubt that the argument was worth it. The commitment to Uni-Cardan not only underpinned GKN's future in driveline products, it also transformed the territorial balance of the group. "Geographically, we were all Commonwealth," said Holdsworth. "Australia, India, Canada, South Africa. We had nothing in Europe and the US. That also changed with the constant velocity joint business. It gave us a whole new range of customers in different geographies."

The difference Uni-Cardan made to GKN's mainland European operations was marked. In 1970, the group had profits of only £1 m on sales of £15 m on the continent; the following year, with Uni-Cardan consolidated, it reported profits of £7.4 m on sales of £81 m.

Mainland Europe – which effectively meant the Uni-Cardan businesses – leapfrogged every other overseas territory to become GKN's largest region of activity outside the UK. And that was only the start of its growth. "Generally speaking, going into automotive was the best thing we did," said Holdsworth. "But the best single move we ever made was Uni-Cardan. That changed everything."

GKN immediately took steps to remove the mismatch between Uni-Cardan's outstanding technology and its somewhat rudimentary financial systems. In June 1971, it dispatched two young accountants from head office to Lohmar. It was, as one of the duo later recalled, a straight-forward mission: "Our role was to put in GKN reporting systems, monthly accounts – typical post-acquisition-type activities. Their budgeting was pretty embryonic in those days," said Trevor Bonner. He didn't know it, but he was to stay for 27 years.

Bonner was well out of what was happening back home. There, the industrial earthquake that had been building for decades was finally convulsing the country.

Like most seismic economic events, the British catas-trophe of the 1970s was triggered by the combination of long-standing, deep-rooted faults with stresses of much more recent origin. In this case, the fragility of the pound, the sustained relative decline in UK productivity and the increasing anarchy in labour relations undermined the country's economic foundations. On that unstable plat-form, the Heath government piled what became known as the "Barber boom" after the irascible Chancellor of the Exchequer, Anthony Barber.

Between the first quarter of 1972 and the third quarter of 1973, British gross domestic product (GDP) increased by 10.5%. That growth was fuelled by another event with totally unforeseen consequences: the Bank of England's 1971 decision to remove restrictions on lending by the major banks and finance houses.

Credit growth erupted. New bank lending to the private sector more than trebled from £1.86 bn in 1971 to £6.43 bn in 1973. Inflation surged. So did pay claims. A vicious wage-price spiral ensued. Britain was beset by strikes. The National Union of Mineworkers (NUM) demanded a rise of 45% in 1972 and forced Heath into a humiliating settlement at 20%.

For a while, the government tried to ride two horses at once: maintaining low interest rates and disregard for the falling level of sterling while seeking to contain inflation through pay and price controls. In November 1972, the formerly free market Conservatives introduced a statutory prices and wages freeze, known as Phase I.

Phases II and III followed in 1973, restricting annual pay rises to £250 and £350 respectively, and consequently compressing differentials to an unprecedented extent. Controlling prices was the easy part; wages were another matter entirely. The policy's main effect was to squeeze UK industry, which found itself unable to raise prices while being subjected to ever-increasing wage-fuelled inflation.

Brookes was quick to highlight the damage being done. "In their severity and bureaucratic complexity, the counter-inflationary measures constitute a major milestone in State control and intervention in industry," he told shareholders. "British industry does not earn a high enough rate of profit in real terms to sustain future growth and new investment ... Whilst counter-inflationary measures of some sort may have been inevitable, there is clearly the danger that the overall effect, particularly if the measures are prolonged, may be to strangle rather than to apply a tourniquet."

Against this worrying backdrop, GKN drove on with organic and inorganic expansion. Its largest acquisition at this time came in 1972 with the purchase of Firth Cleveland, a conglomerate whose main industrial businesses – wire, steel strip and fastener manufacture – complemented those of GKN. The acquisition also brought Ian Donald, Firth Cleveland's chairman, into the group. As a main board director, Donald played an important role in helping to shape the group's strategy in the ensuing years.

Brookes' view of one of Firth Cleveland's other businesses – a chain of 450 television, radio and electrical appliance shops called Civic Stores – was revealing of the group's corporate psychology. Since GKN had no retail expertise whatsoever, Civic seemed to be an obvious case for immediate disposal. Brookes, however, was not so sure.

"We must go further downstream," he said a few months after the acquisition. "We have got to go much more heavily into the distributive trades. It is not very important what they are, but if they happen to link in with the things we make, that is an added bonus. We must do that because there is more profit the nearer you get to the public and less capital secured – and we are too capital-intensive.

"I think we have got to create a whole new generation of downstream terminal products, preferably of the kind that people will require into the age to which we are going, not the age that we are at now. Finally, we have got to get into this motor component after-market, chiefly because more and more people want to do things for themselves, because they cannot afford to pay a garage mechanic."

To an extent, the GKN chairman was clearly shooting the breeze. In the same interview, he hinted that GKN might attempt to expand into gas turbine engines – clearly implying that it might be interested in buying Rolls-Royce, which had been nationalised after collapsing the previous year. And, far from venturing into retailing, GKN sold Civic Stores less than two years later.

However, between the lines of blue-sky thinking could be discerned some clear signposts to the group's future, informed by the strategy being developed by Holdsworth and Basil Woods, who had joined the group in a business development role. GKN did indeed embark on a substantial diversification into distribution – or, as it came to be known, industrial services. That included, as Brookes foretold with uncanny accuracy, a major investment in the auto after-market.

For the present, the group's drive into services was focused on the industry with which Brookes felt most comfortable – steel. In 1973, GKN launched a takeover bid for Miles Druce, a large UK steel stockholder whose acquisition would enlarge GKN's existing steel stock business, extend its range into stainless products, and expand its geographical coverage.

The bid was fiercely resisted by the Miles Druce management. It was a protracted fight, prolonged by being subject to approval from a competition authority with which British companies had previously not been forced to contend – the European Commission in Brussels.

The case might have been a long one, but it was also open and shut. "I learned in the first month that we were going to win," Geoffrey Hughes said. "Miles Druce tried every device, but to no avail. Ray Brookes used to fume about it. John Howard [then GKN's company secretary] was instrumental in calming him down. But we were bound to win. There was no serious competition issue."

Brookes did indeed become exasperated by the struggle, describing it as an "unedifying and avoidable fracas". But by the time GKN prevailed in 1974, his focus had switched to other, bigger issues. In particular, he was increasingly concerned about the condition and prospects of the British economy.

Brookes' 1973 report to shareholders highlighted the UK's growing problems. The GKN chairman showed that, while inflation had increased 54% since 1966, UK gross domestic product had risen only 19% while the earnings of GKN's UK workers had more than doubled – massively outpacing GDP growth and far ahead of inflation.

To the group's credit, it had kept earnings per share (eps) moving ahead. Eps were 14.5 p in 1966 and 27.2 p in 1973 – an advance of 88%, more than matching overall inflation. But inflation restricted GKN's ability to pass those eps gains through to shareholders: "The shareholder comes off worst because dividends have not kept pace with inflation," Brookes reported. Indeed, dividends were only up 34% over the seven years.

As Brookes noted, the eps improvement masked a fundamental and growing weakness in the body economic:

"Neither GKN nor British industry in general earns a high enough rate of surplus in real terms to sustain future growth and new investment. The excesses of taxation and ill-considered prejudices against profits exacerbate this problem."

A powerful group such as GKN could continue to grow nominal profits in this environment – the consumer boom helped group pre-tax profits exceed £50 m for the first time in 1972, while sales reached £623 m.

But at the same time, the real long-term competitiveness of GKN's UK operations was being impacted. Brookes said that the UK automotive businesses suffered from "inadequacy of profit margins on domestic sales" and that "our manufacturing operations and investments in Europe yield better results than the present price structure in the UK permits".

The beleaguered Heath government resorted to interest rate rises in an attempt to curb rampant inflation. In the space of five months from June 1973 the bank rate was raised from 7.5% to 13%. But the attempt to slow growth and bring down inflation was rendered futile by the October Yom Kippur War between Israel and the Arab states. As in the Six-Day War, the Arabs used their oil as a weapon in a bid to pressure Israel's Western allies to support concessions by the Jewish state. This time, though, they went much further in imposing embargoes and driving up the price.

On the eve of the war, oil had been $2.59 a barrel. By January 1974, the Arab-dominated Organisation of Petroleum Exporting Countries (OPEC) had raised the price to $11.65 a barrel – more than quadruple the pre-war price. In Britain, the price of petrol doubled within weeks, from around 30 p to 60 p a gallon. Inflation surged from more than 9% in 1973 to 16.1% in 1974.

Apart from a few nuclear power stations, Britain was dependent for its energy needs on oil and coal. Confronted with the OPEC embargo, the government prepared for petrol rationing and imposed a series of speed limits on Britain's roads – 70 mph on motorways, which had never been subject to a limit, and 60 mph on other main roads. Rationing never materialised but the speed limits stayed. Learner-drivers who drove their first miles in a golden age of cheap petrol passed their tests to find that, instead of the freedom to hit 100 mph on the open road, they had entered a harsh new world where they had to keep a close eye on the speedometer.

For GKN, the first oil price shock had profound consequences. In anything other than the immediate short term, it was hugely beneficial for its expanding Driveline business because it triggered a massive shift to front-wheel drive (FWD) throughout the Western car industry. Petrol prices were being driven to their highest levels since the invention of the motor car. That made the fuel-saving economics of front wheel drive irresistible.

Appropriately, considering its formative role in the history of the car industry, Western Europe got the message first. A rush to develop new FWD models ensued. But while this transformation encompassed all the major vehicle manufacturing nations, the British industry's ability to benefit was hobbled by its crisis in labour relations and competitiveness. The consequences for GKN were far-reaching.

# CHAPTER 13

# Farewell to a Hot Forger

Raymond Brookes was now entering the twilight of his chairmanship. He had earmarked Barrie Heath, then head of the glass company Triplex, as his successor. Holdsworth was seen as too young for the top job and was to become deputy chairman.

Brookes still had some unfinished business to resolve, notably with GKN's Australian partner BHP. Despite the hard-won agreement for BHP to become GKN's partner in Lysaghts, there had continued to be intense jockeying for position between the two groups. The battle centred on whether, under the agreement, Lysaghts or BHP had the right to build and own the next hot strip mill that the partners would have to construct. Brookes was determined that Lysaghts should do it because he knew that, if it went to BHP, Lysaghts' subservience to the Australian giant would be well and truly cemented.

A summit meeting was arranged at a half-way house – San Francisco. Brookes told McLennan: "We've been frigging around now for about two years trying to resolve this problem, so you had better know where you stand. The hot strip mill is going down. Lysaghts are going to own it. They have that right. You are committed to that under the original partnership agreement and that is the end of the matter."

The GKN boss then said that if BHP would not support Lysaghts' construction of the mill, GKN would fund the whole project. "You realise you are talking about not less than $120 m ... (about £64 m ...)?" McLennan asked him. "Yes, I do, and it doesn't alter my view at all," replied Brookes. "As far as I am concerned, that decision is taken. Your decision is, do you want to stay as a partner or don't you? If you stay as a partner, you are part of it. If you don't want to be part of it, you are in breach of your partnership."

Sabre-rattling it might have been, but it did the trick. BHP agreed that the strip mill should be built through Lysaghts, and Westernport in Victoria was selected as the location. Brookes' relationship with McLennan held firm. In fact, the two families became fast friends.

Brookes' last year in charge of GKN, 1974, was eventful, to say the least. The domestic economic environment could not have been much grimmer. The year began with the Heath government imposing a three-day working week on British industry in an attempt to preserve coal supplies against a threatened mineworkers' strike and save on fuel imports because of the sky-high oil price. Power cuts affected the whole country. Television was closed down at 10.30 pm each night to save electricity. The government really did advise people to brush their teeth in the dark.

For once-Great Britain, it seemed to be the nadir of the long post-war decline. In the face of the widespread union unrest, Heath called a general election and lost to Wilson's Labour, which had the highest number of seats in a minority government. Eight months later, Wilson won an overall majority of just three seats.

Inside GKN – as in many companies – a spirit akin to that of World War Two took hold. Energy Emergency Committees were established in most GKN factories to combat the electricity crisis. It was all hands to the pump or the private generator. As Brookes noted in his last chairman's report, "manual workers, supervisors, staff, union officials and management maximised the use of available resources, minimised difficulties and significantly reduced the financial and economic adversities". To GKN's chairman, it must have seemed as if the group had become a giant Garringtons – the 1941 vintage.

Helped by the contributions from its recent acquisitions, GKN powered through the short-time working and the political upheavals. For the first time in its history, turnover exceeded £1 billion. Trading profits were also a record, passing the £100 m mark for the first time. Both sales and profits had trebled in the 12 years of Brookes' chairmanship. While the UK still accounted for more than 60% of profits, GKN's orientation in overseas markets was shifting away from the traditional Commonwealth markets and towards continental Europe. "One thing I did do," Brookes remarked. "I made GKN international in spirit."

By the force of his personality and his intellect, he changed the character of the company for good – in both senses of the word. Not that he was a revolutionary. To at least one leading member of the new generation of management, he cut a rather old-fashioned figure. But by the portfolio changes he oversaw – notably the move into proprietary automotive products – and by the people he brought on – Holdsworth in particular – he opened the way to the future.

In one element alone – the choice of Heath as his successor – Brookes harked back to the "gentleman industrialist" spirit of the old GKN. In every other respect, his objective and clinical approach to industrial management established a new, professional approach. Other changes, such as his reduction of the executive retirement age from 65 to 60, substantiated this culture. His organisational changes – the subgroups, later consolidated into bigger groups that were essentially divisions – provided the new corporate culture with a structural spine. "He modernised GKN and he organised it," said one contemporary.

Brookes both epitomised and to some extent institutionalised the unusual combination of pragmatism and vision that distinguishes GKN. "I think there are two great dangers in business," he told one interviewer. "There is the danger of not knowing where you are going or where you wish to go; and there is the danger of being too rigid in knowing where you are going and therefore getting into a situation where an opportunity presents itself, or a bright idea comes up, and someone says, 'That doesn't fit the Plan, so it will not be done'."

Before Brookes, GKN had been a centripetal organisation, a sum of semi-independent parts run by the barons who controlled those independent businesses. Brookes did not remove all those baronies – Sankey remained a semi-autonomous bastion for years after him – but he did change the group's balance. He turned GKN into more of a centrifugal entity in which strategic leadership by the board could make the group something greater than the sum of its parts.

"The centre at GKN has not been doing enough. The role of the GKN board has been to check, to examine history and to approve capital expenditure. It has never really, as a board, talked in depth as to where we want to take this business. Evolutionary offensive and defensive thinking happens in the operating companies. But the gap, to my mind, has been to get the board into a situation where it says, finally, 'The overall policy is our responsibility, not merely to approve but to influence and, if need be, regenerate'."

As a student of GKN's strengths and weaknesses, and despite his occasional flights of fancy, Brookes was also a great believer in sticking to the knitting. "We are exceptionally good at mass production and really understand it – making vast quantities of things that have fairly similar characteristics and which are sometimes loosely described as being low-technology, although they are nothing like as low in technology as they might appear to be," he reflected late in his career.

Brookes also recognised the importance of working with the corporate grain in a cultural sense. Jim Parsons recalled a discussion one December evening at the group's Kingsway offices in London, which Brookes had established as GKN's base in the capital. After 6 o'clock, the chairman would invite people up to his office "for a scotch and a talk, while he puffed on his pipe".

On this particular night, less than a fortnight from his retirement, Brookes was musing to Woods and Parsons about the character of GKN. "I really feel we are different from a lot of big companies," he ruminated. "I wonder why that is. What can I tell Barrie Heath about why GKN is different?" He asked Woods for his thoughts on the subject. Parsons decided that he would produce some too.

"Over many years," Parsons wrote, "the group has developed a tradition of respect for the individual, of the fair and decent treatment of individuals, of sensitivity, sympathy, understanding and true humanity. Closely allied to this, a good quality of management – with appropriate standards of behaviour and professional competence – has been established."

Parsons continued, remarking on the group's combination of decentralised management and robust financial controls and its low-profile, firm but informative approach to industrial relations – which had kept GKN freer for longer from the contemporary wave of shop-floor disruption. His last point was one of the most fundamental: "Amongst 'top' management, there is no complacency. On the contrary, there is a readiness to question and review the validity of established methods and policies."

Brookes left a copy of the memorandum to Heath, who told Parsons he would "keep it in my top drawer and refer to it from time to time when I have to be reminded how GKN really should be doing things". The memo proved to be a remarkably durable document. Heath was the first new GKN leader to read it, but not the last.

The final piece of Brookes' legacy was the longest-lasting of all: the establishment, first at Garringtons and then throughout the group, of a support network for former GKN employees. The Evergreen Association, whose work continues today, employs voluntary social workers throughout the UK to help retired GKN workers and their spouses who need some form of advice and assistance.

Evergreen is a true descendant of the social conscience manifested by John Guest at Dowlais. Brookes said: "I have tried to ensure that in the crucial and potentially lonely post-retirement years, people should not have a sense or reality of severance; that we should be in touch with their necessities of mind and body; that they should be in touch with each other and with the point of their past employment."

On his retirement, Brookes became life president of GKN. Shortly after that, he was ennobled for services to British industry. Inside the company, there was a joke that he got his knighthood for selling Brymbo and his peerage for buying it back. The truth is that few British industrialists have more deserved elevation to the peerage. Not a bad outcome for someone who liked to describe himself simply as "a Staffordshire lad and a hot forger".

His abiding influence is reflected in the memories of those who came into GKN during his chairmanship. "Talk about a tough character," said Jim McFarlane, who held senior management and, latterly, board positions through the 1970s. "He wasn't always right, nor would claim to be, but I remember at my first annual general meeting being tremendously impressed by the authority that this man had."

Howard Wheeldon, a City analyst who hailed from the West Midlands, met Brookes at the outset of his career. "He was the last of the great Sixties engineering giants," Wheeldon said. John Jessop, who joined GKN in 1971 as a young manager with engineering and business degrees, attended Brookes' last post-annual meeting conference. "He used to gather all the senior management from every subgroup. About 200 would be there at Heath Street. He was an inspirational speaker. He just commanded attention. He had charisma."

It was fitting, then, that Jessop should play the key role in making one of Brookes' last objectives – the establishment of a meaningful business in industrial services and distribution – a reality.

# CHAPTER 14

# A Pallet Pool Is Born

It started with a visit to Australia by Geoffrey Blake, managing director of the Building Supplies and Services (BSS) subgroup. BSS was one of the spearheads of GKN's drive into services. It was an odd collection of disparate businesses: constantly on the lookout for opportunities, either through acquisition or start-up.

Jessop, who had joined the subgroup as planning manager, said: "BSS consisted of companies that were by-products of the mainstream GKN business. So we had a Foundations business which was based on steel pile [and which led to the creation of Keller, today a highly-successful public company in its own right]; a scaffolding business based on a steel product made by Exors of James Mills [a rolled and bright steel business], a reinforcement business, again based on steel."

"Then we had a very weird business called Servotomic, which did small bore radiators. It must have been some offshoot of a steel derivative type of product." Servotomic subsequently entered the market for converting Britain to North Sea gas. Jessop analysed the portfolio. "I thought, there isn't a lot of 'Service' about these companies, except for Servotomic." He recommended to Blake that they look for more pure Services operations.

Blake went to Australia primarily to look at GKN's scaffolding business, which was a smaller mirror-image of the UK scaffolding side. But while he was there, he met Oliver Richter, head of the diversified Australian services group Brambles. One of the main Brambles subsidiaries was a company called CHEP, which maintained a pallet "pool" – hiring out wooden pallets to industrial and commercial users in Australia. Richter thought the future lay in plastic pallets, and he knew about Sankey's expertise in plastic extrusions. He reckoned that Sankey might be able to make a new, plastic pallet for Brambles.

"I can certainly introduce you to the Sankey people," Blake said. "But what is your business exactly?" So Richter explained exactly how CHEP started and what it was.

At the end of World War Two, the American forces had left a huge amount of mechanical handling equipment in the countries around the Pacific Rim. The Australian government bought up this equipment, turned to its domestic industry – which was still quite unautomated – and invited companies to hire some of the plant. When a company was satisfied that mechanical handling saved money, it could buy its own equipment and return the rented gear.

When the scheme was well-established, the government withdrew from running it. Seeing a private sector opportunity, Brambles bought the government-owned equipment, along with a fleet of forklift trucks – and a host of pallets. Richter, whose brainchild this was, saw a chance to build a business hiring out those pallets to companies, such as big retailers, who used large quantities of pallets but had no need to own them and carry them on their own balance sheet. He called it the Commonwealth Handling Equipment Pool – CHEP.

On his return to England, Blake went to see Jessop. "I know we are looking for new business ideas," he said. "What about this?" The pair invited Richter to England and Jessop took him to see Sankey. But the plastic pallet was a sideshow. Jessop was much more interested in the main event – CHEP itself. Could it work in the UK? That, Jessop soon discovered, was exactly what Richter was wondering too.

"Oliver had an ulterior motive for approaching us," Jessop recalled. "He was very interested in whether pallet pools could work in other countries, particularly the UK. I think he tried New Zealand and didn't get far. Possibly he looked at Canada. He thought the US was too big."

Blake and Jessop agreed with Richter that it was worth a try. So GKN and Brambles formed a fully-fledged research organisation to examine the potential for developing CHEP in Britain. "To me, having studied the situation, it seemed such an obvious solution to a problem," Jessop said.

The natural market was in distributing fast moving consumer goods (FMCG) products to British retailers. The UK food retail sector of the early 1970s was modernising and consolidating. But the distribution system which obtained at this time was archaic – costly and cumbersome.

An FMCG producer would take a product from the production line and put it on a pallet. The pallet – which could be carrying one ton of product – went into a very big warehouse owned by one of the retailers. Alongside it would be a thousand other products, all on pallets. The warehouse had relatively small storage yards.

As the product was used up in the supermarket, the pallet became empty and went back into the yard – alongside a thousand other emptied pallets. Some of the pallets belonged to the same FMCG company, but most were from different manufacturers. The retailer's warehousemen could not possibly sort the pallets into orderly racks. So they would pile them up on a stack and if a driver from the supplier came into the yard and asked for the firm's pallets back, the warehouse would tell him to go and get them.

"He could never get his exact pallets back – they were probably broken anyway," said Jessop. "The stack of pallets looked like a bonfire ready to be lit – they were all piled up, higgledy-piggledy, many of them broken and with no indication who they belonged to."

As a result of this wastage, some producers started using lighter and less-expensive pallets in order to save money. But these caused the warehouses huge problems because they were not robust; they were easily dented or broken, often damaging the goods on them or on other pallets, and even threatening Health and Safety on site. On top of that, those drivers who came to collect empty pallets would find themselves with pallets of different weights, some of which were not strong enough to carry the supplier's product.

"It was anarchy," said Jessop. "The retailers wanted this problem gone. The manufacturers were buying more new pallets than their total stock in a year, in order to keep the production lines going – so it was costing them an absolute fortune."

It was now obvious to Jessop and Blake that CHEP had great potential in Britain. GKN was a decentralised business with strong central cost controls, so they did not need approval to establish a joint venture which required no up-front investment. GKN wanted Brambles to carry an equal share of the risk involved, and therefore pressed for the Australians to take a 50% stake in the joint venture. But Richter, who was very happy to do that, was overruled by his chairman who wanted to minimise what he saw as Brambles' risk. As a result, GKN started with 80% of the UK enterprise.

"We opened an office opposite the GKN head office in Kingsway," Jessop said. "A couple of people came from Brambles in Australia; I got a couple of other people from GKN and we just did it as an exercise within the subgroup, until we were ready to take it further. That's when it got interesting."

Jessop and Blake faced two high hurdles. They had to get GKN board approval for the joint venture to proceed. And they had to find some customers. Jessop wrote a full proposal for the board. "The problem was that they had no real means of judging it. They had a capital expenditure panel and a technical panel, but they had nothing that could assess a pure service activity like this."

To prepare the ground, Jessop marketed the venture to individual directors. Basil Woods, whose strategy called for extensive expansion in services, supported it. Sir Douglas Bruce-Gardner, one of the most senior executive directors, was also in favour. Crucially, so was the new chairman, Barrie Heath – "although he told me he wanted to call it Prang, not CHEP," Jessop recalled. "I think that was a joke."

Roy Roberts, a newly-elected director who had responsibility for GKN's distribution businesses, also supported CHEP. "Eventually, it got through by the narrowest of margins," Jessop said. "We were able to show the board that the concept worked somewhere else – ie, Australia. The board agreed that we should give it a go."

If winning board approval had been tough, it was nothing compared with the struggle Jessop and his fledgling team now had to get CHEP off the ground. They had designed the product: "A distinctive, heavy-duty, very high-quality pallet. It was blue – I'm not sure where the choice of colour came from. It had different dimensions from the Australian one – the Aussie one was square; we designed a more rectangular pallet."

They had the logo: "We got a man in who came up with a logo and I sat up and played around with it. We got the 'C' of CHEP partly looking like a 'C' but with a touch of 'G' – the G of GKN." In order to work properly, the CHEP network had to be national from the start. So Jessop and his team carefully researched and identified eight sites for depots, staffed by a total of 100 people, to provide nationwide coverage.

But despite all the planning, CHEP could not take off: "We sat for the best part of a year and did almost no business at all," said Jessop. The problem was not the retailers

– "every retailer said they wanted it". It was getting the FMCG companies to adopt it. "We couldn't persuade anyone to be the first company to use the system – no-one wanted to be first when they were putting at risk their product line if they couldn't get the pallets they needed. No-one was sure that it was going to work. As they saw it, the fact that Brambles did it in Australia was neither here nor there."

Jessop intensified his marketing offensive. But he recognised that he needed reinforcements if he was going to persuade enough companies to give CHEP a chance. "What helped was that GKN was then one of the top 20 UK companies. So what we were selling them was based on the strength of GKN and the fact that GKN would never let them down. Our immense resources and reliability. I would roll up at the manufacturer with at least one GKN main board director, and give them this speech."

He also enlisted the help of the supermarkets. "We knew that they were on board. So whenever we could, we would ask the most senior director from a supermarket that we could to come along to one of these lunches with suppliers. They did a lot of our selling for us."

Geoffrey Blake never lost faith in the venture, Jessop said. "He stuck with CHEP. We had board meetings telling him what we were doing, but despite the lack of business there was no review. He used to say, 'You are still doing the right thing.' Nobody from above him tried to intervene. To give the business a whole year to get going was quite something."

Finally, Jessop and his colleagues broke through. Three major FMCG suppliers – Spillers, Tate & Lyle and Nestlé

– agreed to adopt the system. "With our eight depots, we promised to supply pallets from whichever site was closest to the manufacturer. The company would then tell us where the pallets were going. As part of the retailers' side of the deal, we said: 'We will sort your pallets separately and we'll encourage the people who come in with your pallets to take an equal number of pallets away'," Jessop said.

If any pallets were damaged, the retailer simply brought them back to CHEP, who repaired them. If the retailer told CHEP its pallet stock was too high, CHEP would reduce it to a manageable level and keep the supplier's production lines going by delivering pallets there. "The system works like a bank: at the end of the month, a particular supplier would have so many pallets on hire."

The economics were overwhelmingly positive. "We could cut the supplier's costs by 50% and still make a very healthy living for ourselves," Jessop said. "The great advantage of the business is that it thrives on itself, because the bigger the pallet pool, the more the economies of scale. One pallet is more efficient than two, two is more efficient than three. So it was in everybody's interests to make one pallet work as hard as possible."

When other suppliers saw the advantages of the system, they soon joined the pool. And as the business scaled up, CHEP increased its density of coverage by expanding the number of depots. At the same time, CHEP extended its range of activities: "Baked beans, for instance, come in tins and the tins come in cartons," said Jessop. "The cartons can come into the factories on pallets. Tomato sauce bottles can come in on pallets to be filled. So you can follow the whole supply chain back through."

CHEP never made a pallet. That meant it employed relatively little capital and its returns, once it was up and running, were handsome. Jessop recalled: "By the time I finished in the UK, we had 80% of the UK retail market and people were starting to talk about monopoly. Lots of other people wanted to start up, but they never could because of the scale they needed and which we already had." To this day, no authentic rival to CHEP has emerged in Britain.

Jessop knew CHEP UK had made it when he heard from Heath. "When we finally did some business, the chairman phoned me up. 'Why didn't you tell me?' he asked. 'You promised to let me know when you really got it going.' What he was really saying was, I've been keeping an eye on you."

CHAPTER 15

# Shot Down

Barrie Heath was also keeping his eye on a larger target – the markets of Continental Europe. In fact, the keynote of his five-year chairmanship was the group's attempt to expand its operations – and, in particular, its automotive component business – in mainland Western Europe.

For GKN's new chairman, this endeavour carried a certain personal irony. Heath had been a Spitfire fighter pilot in the Battle of Britain, and a very good one. Indeed, he had been awarded the Distinguished Flying Cross for his courage and achievements in action. He wore the decoration with pride – his annual reports to shareholders were headed "Statement by the Chairman Barrie Heath DFC".

He was, in many respects, a larger-than-life character. There are more stories about Barrie Heath per year of chairmanship than about any of his predecessors or successors. According to Jim Parsons, "Barrie's fighter pilot mentality and personality remained unchanged throughout his life. He enjoyed singing officers' mess songs, sometimes bawdy, and was prone to break into song after dinner." His after-dinner speeches could also be an event. On one occasion, at a formal dinner in Italy, he made his speech and sat down while his host responded. Whereupon, the GKN chairman jumped to his feet and made a second full-length speech.

In 1978, at the opening of Uni-Cardan's new office at Siegburg, near Bonn, Heath met the local mayor. When the mayor learned about Heath's Second World War career, he told the GKN chairman: "I was a pilot too. We might have been in the same dogfight in the Battle of Britain." "Maybe," responded Heath. "What did you fly?" "A Junkers-88," replied the mayor. The Ju-88 was a bomber. Barrie Heath had little time for bombers: "No," he told the mayor categorically. "We couldn't have been in the same dogfight." "Why not?" asked the puzzled dignitary. "Because if we had been, I would have shot you down," Heath said.

Heath was not renowned for his patience. During a stay at the famous Taj Mahal Palace hotel in Bombay, he ordered a soft boiled egg for breakfast. When the egg came, it was hard. He called the waiter, who brought another egg. This one was also hard. So Heath sent it back again – only to get a third hard-boiled egg. The exasperated GKN chairman picked up the egg and hurled it against the restaurant wall as the waiters scattered and other diners ducked.

Heath did not expand GKN's rather sparse presence in aerospace, but he certainly built up its corporate aircraft fleet. "Profitability was high, and Barrie created his own mini-airforce," said Parsons. There was a Hawker Siddeley

125 business jet, a twin-engined Messerschmidt helicopter, an Islander monoplane for short take-off and landing, and Kingair and Queenair turbo-props. The Queenair was based in Germany for Uni-Cardan's use.

Sir David Lees remembered the helicopter. One day in the late 1970s, when Lees was general manager, Finance – deputy Finance Director – he was asked by Heath to accompany him to a lunch in Norwich with the chairman of Norwich Union, then one of the largest and most august investors in British companies. It was to be a high-powered lunch: Norwich Union had assembled an array of fund managers to whom the GKN team would talk about the group and its strategy.

"Paddy Custis, GKN's finance director, was to accompany Barrie," Lees recalled. "I suspect that Paddy would have done the talking because Barrie wasn't a detail man at all. But on the day in question, Paddy couldn't go, so I was called to the colours. I didn't know who was the most apprehensive, Barrie or I."

They went down by helicopter and arrived late. "Lunch was in this big hall with seas of expectant faces. We duly had the meal. Came the moment and the chairman of Norwich Union was about to say a few words of introduction. Then I saw Barrie suddenly say to the chairman, 'I'm frightfully sorry, but I've got a very pressing engagement in London and we've got to go.' He rose to his feet. I followed him out to the helicopter. He turned to me – it was a wonderful summer's day – and said: 'Why don't we go the long way back, up the Thames – it's a wonderful view.' I don't think the Norwich Union ever did buy a share in GKN."

As a big picture man, Heath did not need a helicopter to see that GKN had an urgent strategic problem. The UK, where two-thirds of GKN's business originated, was in trouble. Inflation exceeded 24% in 1975. "Looking at our business as a whole, the most destructive outside influence is inflation, which affects all countries where we operate, but is especially severe in the United Kingdom," Heath wrote in his first report to shareholders.

Within the UK economy, manufacturing – despite the moves into services, still by far the greatest area of activity for GKN – was in desperate straits. In 1975, UK steel output fell to the lowest level since 1954. "The United Kingdom has a diminishing manufacturing base," Heath remarked. And within UK manufacturing, the motor industry – GKN's largest single business sector – was in just about the worst trouble of all.

British Leyland, the UK's main car and truck maker, was the most high-profile symbol of the country's manufacturing decline. Its output slumped from 789,000 cars in 1970, when it held 38% of the domestic market, to 605,000 units five years later as imports ate into its home market share.

In the new registration month of August 1973, total imports for the first time exceeded BL's UK sales, taking a record 32% of the market. The number one foreign seller was Datsun, with a share of almost 5%. Datsun was the name adopted by Nissan for its export sales. The Japanese were coming. UK passenger car production in 1975 fell to 1.27 m vehicles, down from 1.64 m in 1970. French output was now double the British figure, Germany's higher still.

The dramatic decoupling of continental from UK production rates had a major impact inside GKN. Most of its British automotive operations increasingly found growth hard to come by. Some – notably Hardy Spicer – did enjoy an absolute increase in demand thanks to the rise of front wheel drive. But they were progressively overshadowed by the expansion, both absolute and relative, of Uni-Cardan with its bases in the flourishing continental markets of Germany, France and Italy.

For Heath, the message was clear. GKN must expand in mainland Europe, both by exporting more from the UK and through enlarging its continental manufacturing presence. His first annual report, which gave financial details in German, French and Dutch as well as English, set the tone. GKN also listed its shares in Amsterdam, Antwerp, Brussels, Frankfurt and Dusseldorf. The listings were essentially symbolic – trading through these exchanges was minimal – but again emphasised the Europeanisation theme.

There was nothing symbolic about Heath's biggest move to enlarge GKN's European presence. In 1975, the group approached Sachs AG, one of the largest private companies in Germany, with a takeover proposal. Eventually, the two companies agreed that GKN would pay DM330 m for just under 75% of Sachs. The main subsidiary, Fichtel & Sachs, employed more than 16,000 people making clutches, shock absorbers and cycle hubs. In every respect, the proposed purchase was one of the largest and most ambitious in GKN's history.

It had personality interest, too. Sachs was headed by the colourful and romantic multi-millionaire Gunter Sachs.

Sachs told Jim Parsons how, during his courtship of Bardot, he had checked the time of day when she would be on the beach near her home in St.Tropez. He hired a plane and parachuted on to the beach nearby. Bardot was impressed. They were married for nine years.

Sachs and his management team struck up good relations with Heath and the GKN executives. Heath said the acquisition would "broaden our product base and provide new market opportunities and additional export channels in continental Europe and elsewhere. From a more substantial presence in Europe, we will be able to develop even closer relationships with our international customers."

However, the deal had to be approved by both the European Commission and West Germany's Kartelamt – its equivalent of the Monopolies Commission which administered Germany's Cartel Law. GKN did not anticipate any problems with the competition authorities. The Sachs management was fully on board. Sachs' product range did not overlap with Uni-Cardan's. The deal would not therefore increase GKN's German market share in any product segment.

A GKN team including Heath and Geoffrey Hughes flew over to the Kartelamt office in Berlin for the first meeting about the proposed deal. They anticipated a formality. "All of us and the Sachs side were convinced that we would be cleared," said Hughes. "Sachs had hired an ex-director of the Kartelamt as an adviser. He knew the Cartel Act inside out."

Much to GKN's shock and surprise, however, the initial feedback was negative. Far from waving the acquisition through, the Kartelamt planned to go over it with a fine toothcomb and was very concerned about the issues it raised. GKN concluded that there was a political dimension to the Office's inquiries which it had not anticipated.

"We arranged a private meeting with the Kartelamt man in charge of the case," said Hughes. "He was very bright but very left-wing. We didn't get anywhere." Then came the final meeting in the process. Despite the bad signals, GKN was still hopeful. "The crucial meeting started at 11 am and we went in thinking, 'This won't take long'." Instead, the meeting lasted three hours and the Kartelamt said it was going to block the deal.

"The most we thought would happen was that they might impose conditions and we had various provisional undertakings ready in case we had to dispose of this or that business," said Hughes. The meeting ended at 2 pm. "We had to have lunch at the Kartelamt canteen and all they had left by that time was fish fingers." No crumbs of comfort there.

Heath and his team now realised, as Hughes recalled, "that we were in for a long haul". One element that GKN had failed to consider was the influence on the Kartelamt of US competition law. "The US had developed something called the 'Deep Pocket Theory'," said Hughes. The theory maintained that, even if a transaction was not going to create too large a market share in a particular product, if the buyer was financially very strong then the deal could distort the market. "The Germans applied that theory to our case, even though it was not enshrined in the Cartel Law."

However, Hughes and his colleagues had no doubt that there was more to the Kartelamt's opposition than any American-inspired competition theory. "I think it was more about keeping Sachs German than keeping GKN out. Plus, they weren't used to big bids. I think they were at a stage when they weren't at all sure that Anglo-Saxon partnership was a good thing."

Heath was nothing if not determined, and he was determined not to take the Kartelamt judgment lying down. The EC cleared the deal, but at that time, it could not overrule the Kartelamt. Thus began a three-year battle in the German courts to have the Kartelamt ruling over-turned. In the process, GKN acquired just under 25% of Sachs, the maximum minority shareholding allowed without requiring German competition authority approval, for DM110 m. The group won its appeal to the Berlin Appeal Court but the Kartelamt then appealed in turn to the West German Supreme Court.

In February 1978, the Supreme Court found against GKN and upheld the Kartelamt veto on the group's planned acquisition of the outstanding 50.01% of Sachs shares. GKN filed an appeal with the West German Ministry of Economics, which had authority over public interest aspects of takeovers. But that was a long shot, and in the end, the group decided not to proceed. GKN folded its tents. In early 1979, it sold the near-25% stake for DM130 m, at least booking a DM20 m profit on the disposal.

That was scant consolation for a frustrated and disap-pointed Heath. Positive as ever, he put a brave face on the defeat. Lees recalled: "By coincidence, he and I were over in Nuremberg visiting our people in West Germany the day the final ruling against the bid came through. Barrie said, 'OK, we've lost this but let's have a party in any case'. He was a big man in every sense; he had the common touch."

One GKN man was not surprised by the failure to win Sachs. Trevor Bonner had been based in Uni-Cardan for four years when GKN made the bid, and was by now Finance Director of Uni-Cardan. Bonner was an objective observer of GKN's legal battle against the Kartelamt because Uni-Cardan was not involved in the bid, despite its local knowledge.

Below chairman level, the Sachs project was led throughout by the GKN team from London, headed by Gordon Griffiths, the main board director in charge of the group's automotive businesses. The decision not to involve Uni-Cardan reflected a degree of internal politics. Uni-Cardan and the UK Transmissions group reported separately into head office.

Bonner said later: "That deal would have changed the face of the group, but I was not surprised that it did not happen. We in Uni-Cardan were always leery that a combination of things would lead to the bid being abortive." One element "was the politics of a foreign company being allowed to own such a prize German asset. Sachs was perceived as exactly that; it was very high profile, because of Gunter Sachs.

"So it wasn't only discussed in the business papers but also in the BildZeitung [Germany's top-selling tabloid]. In my view, it was always going to be high-profile because of Gunter and that didn't do GKN any good. If you spoke to someone from the Kartelamt, they would tell you that was all irrelevant, but I don't believe it."

Bonner also thought that at least one of Sachs' customers, although neutral in public, might in private have opposed the deal "although I could never prove that". As a result, he said, "We got a ruling that was unexpected and probably questionable from a competition policy standpoint."

The Sachs failure was a turning-point for GKN, and had several important results. Most obviously, it significantly increased the group's reliance in automotive components on driveline products. Within driveline, it emphasised the importance of Uni-Cardan, GKN's only business of scale in mainland Europe, as the UK operations ran into increasing difficulty. That in turn began the process whereby the centre of gravity in GKN automotive shifted towards Siegburg. The reorientation accelerated after September 1978, when GKN bought out more of the minority holders and increased its shareholding from 58.7% to 81.9%.

"You got Uni-Cardan growing and developing quite rapidly," said Bonner. "You had the automotive side of GKN in the UK struggling as a result of what was happening in the customer base. And inevitably, within the automotive group through the Seventies and into the early Eighties, that led to a progressive transfer of political power to Germany."

Uni-Cardan's influence increased as it extended the scope of its European operations. "After General Franco's death in 1975, we were able to begin to build a presence in Spain," said Bonner. "We brought that forward as a project." If the UK had led the Spanish drive, it would have been difficult to realise because of the continuing political antagonism between the two countries over Gibraltar.

At the same time, the Sachs rebuff led GKN under Heath to turn, at long last, towards the United States. Hughes said: "When we launched the offer, we thought

Germany was where our future lay. We planned to extend our involvement in the European auto component industry into other segments. In effect, it was the Sachs outcome that made us decide that we had to go into the US automotive industry."

By any standards, let alone those of an international group the size of GKN, the company's US sales were miniscule. They had trebled between 1970 and 1976, but since they totalled all of £8 m at the start of the decade, that was not saying a great deal. In 1976, GKN made a profit in the US of £400,000.

But in that year, it secured a significant contract to supply CVJs to Chrysler. The order was a rare example, at that time, of teamwork between the UK Transmission business and Uni-Cardan: GKN would supply Chrysler through exports from both Hardy Spicer and Uni-Cardan's plants. The contract could be worth about $20 m sales a year from 1979.

Even as the Chrysler contract was being signed, a second and still more significant American opportunity emerged. To help meet the post-oil shock market for smaller cars – cars with front wheel drive – Ford decided to make a US version of the Escort. One of GKN's biggest customers in the UK and mainland Europe, it turned to the British group for CVJ supply. However, unlike Chrysler, Ford would not accept exports from existing European plants. It insisted on in-country supply. GKN would have to build its first North American factory, or lose the order.

The GKN board duly approved construction of a CVJ factory in the US. However, in a step which made GKN something of a pathfinder, it chose not to site the plant in Motown country – the indigenous industry's historic heartland of Detroit. Instead, GKN selected Sanford, North Carolina as the location, a pioneering strategy to invest in virgin auto industry land which was subsequently adopted by the Japanese and German vehicle makers when they established transplants in the US. Initially, the Sanford plant was dedicated to supplying Ford, although later some of the Chrysler business was also gradually transitioned into the plant. Initial capacity was 400,000 driveshaft sets a year.

The move catalysed GKN's thinking about the need to streamline its fragmented driveline operation, which was currently split three ways – the UK, Continental Europe and the US, each with its own chief executive, each reporting directly to corporate headquarters. "That wasn't deemed to be totally sensible," recalled Bonner dryly.

So a single company was established – GKN Universal Transmissions – combining all the group's CVJ and propshaft manufacturing into a single organisation. The CEOs of the three regional operations sat on the board of the company and Bernard Walterscheid-Muller was its first chairman. At the outset, it was primarily a co-ordinating body, although none the less valuable for that. But to Bonner, it had the potential to become much more.

The strengthening of Uni-Cardan and the move into the US came just in time. At home, the British motor industry was sliding even deeper into crisis.

# CHAPTER 16

# On the Front Line

Jim McFarlane took over as managing director of Garringtons in 1977. He walked straight into the kind of labour relations scene that could be found all over the shop-floors of British industry in the late 1970s.

McFarlane had run the Smith Clayton aerospace forgings business at Lincoln for more than seven years and had known his share of tough situations. On 4 February 1971, he had been at a lunch in London when he learned that Rolls-Royce had collapsed and called in the receiver. Rolls accounted for 40% of Smith Clayton's business. Two weeks earlier, the firm had commissioned a multi-million pound forging plant to make turbine discs for Rolls' RB211 engine – the largest investment in its history. McFarlane had some nail-biting days before the British government stepped in and saved Rolls.

But even for an experienced hand like McFarlane, the Garringtons situation proved exacting. "I asked GKN why they wanted me to move to Garringtons. They said, 'We want a firmer hand over the workforce." Garringtons had been a little bit inclined to make concessions rather than face up to having a strike. "They had a very tough shop steward there, an AEU [the engineering workers' union] man in charge of the majority of fitters. The EEPTU [the electricians' union, ETU for short] was in charge of the electricians and they thought they were superior to the fitters and should be paid more. It was thoroughly unjusti-fied. The AEU man stopped me on the floor and said, 'If you give them an extra shilling [5 p] an hour, you'll have to pay us an extra five shillings [25 p] an hour.' So if I bought off the electricians, I would have to buy off the fitters. I did my best to avoid that."

McFarlane went to talk to the ETU. As was usual in those days when the plethora of different unions was one of the main problems besetting UK industry, each union had its own room at the plant. McFarlane walked in and urged the stewards not to push their claim. "I said, Please don't do this. It will be a long strike, that I can guarantee, and I don't know what the solution would be because if I make a concession to you, I'll have to make an even bigger one to the AEU. So please don't push it. They ignored me."

It was a classic Seventies dispute. It involved pay dif-ferentials, demarcation, union rivalry – most of the ingre-dients that undermined British manufacturers' ability to produce and deliver reliable products on time and to budget. Other elements which played an important part in the labour relations landscape also soon reared their heads: the attitude of the parent company and the response of customers.

GKN was certainly worried about the cost of the dispute. Garringtons employed 5000 people at Bromsgrove, Darlaston and Witton. By any measure, it was a large business, accounting for about half the whole Forgings group. Its management and workforce knew that – they called themselves "Big G". "Garringtons was a big company and it was losing profit," McFarlane recalled. "Not only that, but its customers were not going to wait around for supplies to be restored."

After the strike had lasted three weeks, McFarlane got a call from Gordon Griffiths, the main board director responsible for Garringtons. "Gordon said, 'This has been going on a long time, Don't you think you should find an answer to it?' I said, 'Well Gordon, there isn't a solution except to weather it. If you want to get rid of me and put someone else in charge who'll make a concession, it's your privilege to do that. I am not going to make a concession because it will only make the problem worse.' GKN gave its managing directors a good deal of latitude. Neither Gordon nor anyone else overruled me."

The strike went on for another three weeks. Then McFarlane got a call from the ETU local organiser – a full-time paid union official, unlike the stewards. "He said, 'This can't go on. I think we should meet.'" The meeting took place at one of the Russell Square hotels that were the favoured London stopovers for union representatives. "He started off by saying, 'You'll have to give way, you know.' I said, 'I don't think so.' He said, 'GKN will sack you if you don't.' I told him that I had been through this with GKN and they hadn't sacked me. He said, 'You and I better find a solution. Can you come up to our annual conference in Scarborough? We'll get the members there and talk about it.'"

"We hatched a little plot – You say this, I'll say that. I told him, 'If you depart from this text, there will be hell to pay.' He replied, 'Likewise.'" So the pair, manager and union official, played out the two-hander in front of the Garringtons stewards. A peace formula was agreed: the electricians would go back to work while the company employed a consultant to evaluate the job and whether the electricians warranted more pay than the fitters. The AEU also signed up to this.

"Then the unions said, 'We've been out of work for six weeks – are you going to recompense us?' And I said, 'Come off it – not bloody likely. Are you going to recompense us for all the money we've lost?'" McFarlane told them that the company was willing to pay for the consultant, but that they were also party to the arrangement and so, as a reflection of their commitment to it, they should pay something, however nominal, towards the consultant's cost. "Then we can say with complete honesty that the unions are paying towards this as well as the management. They were taken aback, and asked how much I was talking about. I said, 'You could give us £50 each.' The ETU agreed; the AEU said they would have to refer it to their executive committee, but they agreed in the end."

When the job evaluation began, the unions started being uncooperative again. The evaluation was never completed. "But that didn't matter," McFarlane recounted. "They were all back at work and they never went on strike again. Maybe if British management had been a bit firmer from the outset, we as a country wouldn't have destroyed the motor industry in the way we did."

Certainly, many plant managing directors were not as determined as McFarlane. And many boards were less resolutely behind their managers than GKN. Nor were customers always as supportive as they might have been. McFarlane himself acknowledged the sharp contrast between working predominantly with the aerospace industry and finding himself immersed in car making. "It came as quite a shock – the customers weren't as understanding as Rolls-Royce, Hawker Siddeley or the British Aircraft Corporation. My God, they were tough."

He had had some forewarning: "At Smith Clayton, we made the shaft for the rear axle of the Ford Transit – a very big seller. We were the only forge that could make it in the UK but we were making a loss on the business. I thought that this was ridiculous. So I went to Ford's chief buyer in the UK and told him that we weren't going to go on making it at that price – we would have to have an increase."

About a year later, McFarlane had to requote for a crankshaft Smith Clayton supplied to Ford, and the chief buyer asked for his price for the next year. "I told him, The price of steel and labour has gone up, so our price has to rise too. He said, 'I'm afraid you won't get the business then. There are plenty of people who can make this component and I still owe you for the Transit axle shaft last year.'"

This adversarial, supplier–customer relationship was par for the course in the 1970s. It only began to end after the arrival in the West of the Japanese vehicle makers with their collaborative approach to the supply chain. The win–lose attitude was a lever that union representatives could use to pressurise component-makers into conceding pay and conditions demands.

Other factors were critical in destroying the competitiveness of the British-owned motor industry – management failure to develop reliable products that enough customers wanted and to sell them at commercial prices, for one thing. But union militancy was decisive. McFarlane, who left GKN in 1982 to become director-general of the Engineering Employers' Federation, recalled an interview in the late 1970s with a national newspaper labour correspondent.

He had come to see Oscar Hahn, also a GKN director, and McFarlane: "He asked us, 'How much time do you spend with customers?' I said 'Customers? I'm forever talking to works committees and shop stewards – I haven't got time to talk to customers. But our German, French, Italian and Swedish counterparts do. That's why we are losing business to them.'"

Disruption to deliveries was widespread. "We had what a colleague called 'Decibel Scheduling'," McFarlane recalled. "The customers who shouted loudest and most often were the ones who got served. You didn't do it in an orderly way. You were merely responding to the latest panic or crisis."

The UK's fatal flaw was the increasing productivity gap with its rivals. That was why the impact of British union power was so devastating. Both in itself and in the inflation that it generated through unjustified wage increases, militancy undermined the economy's competitive infrastructure.

Successive GKN chairmen had warned for years about the inadequacy of real rates of return on investment. Now there was a massive additional disincentive to invest: "So much of our energy as managers was taken up with industrial relations," said McFarlane. "We knew things were wrong and we didn't really know how to put them right, and we knew that we were to a degree destroying ourselves. But we seemed almost powerless to prevent it. Whatever we tried to do, the unions wouldn't cooperate. It got to the stage where I would go to buy some new equipment and think, 'Oh, God, all this bloody argument we are going to have with the unions about what will the piece-work rate be for operating this. Either they will refuse to operate it at all, or it will cost us so much to get their agreement that the financial case for having this equipment will be undermined. It's just not worth investing.' What a defeatist mindset! But I'm not a defeatist, and if I was thinking that, then others would be thinking it in spades."

Legions of British managements did indeed reach the same conclusion. Those who invested found their rates of return crippled by the price exacted by unions for operating the new plant. Those who didn't were condemned to fall further behind the overseas competition. According to the National Economic Development Office statistics on British Industrial Performance, UK manufacturing's cost-competitiveness declined by about 40% during the mid-Seventies.

What was needed to transform the picture? McFarlane had no doubt: "The root of the problem was that the unions had legal immunity. You couldn't prosecute them or sue them for the damage that they did. It's not surprising that they got a bit above themselves. The law was on their side. It was ridiculous. Managements could have done better than they did, but they were very seriously handicapped by this legal immunity. Some managements were a bit feeble and gave in when they shouldn't have done so. But behind it all was the feeling that you couldn't win, or that you could only win by expending an enormous amount of time and money and effort. And that tended to be a Pyrrhic victory. We pointed this out to the Labour government, but they didn't do anything about it."

Far from intervening to restore the lost balance of power in industry, the government – pushed by ministers including Tony Benn, the energy secretary – launched a drive to promote greater "industrial democracy". By this, they meant to give employee representatives a much bigger say in company affairs, including the possibility of legislation to impose worker directors. However, even if the verdict was pre-ordained, due process had to be observed. In 1976, the government therefore established a committee of inquiry on industrial democracy under Sir Alan Bullock, master of St Catherine's College, Oxford University.

From the outset, this committee was loaded in favour of the union cause. It contained Jack Jones, general secretary of the Transport and General Workers, and Clive Jenkins, his counterpart at the white-collar ASTMS, along with David Lea of the Trades Union Congress and the employment rights lawyer Lord Wedderburn from the

London School of Economics. But three industrialists were also invited as members: Sir Jack Callard, chairman of British Home Stores, Sir Norman Biggs, head of the bank Williams and Glyn's – and Barrie Heath.

The committee's terms of reference were even more loaded than the membership: "Accepting the need for a radical extension of industrial democracy in the control of companies ..." they began. But Heath and his fellow industrialists accepted no such thing. As Jim Parsons noted: "The last thing they wanted was Trade Union representation on their boards and they would fight to the death to resist it."

Heath had inveighed long and hard against the demands of the industrial democracy lobby. "There is too much uninformed enthusiasm to enact legislation as though this could provide a panacea for all our ills," he told shareholders. "I strongly doubt whether the mandatory appointment of employee representatives to the Boards of our companies, both great and small, would provide any answer to industrial strife, and it would certainly be no guarantee of commercial success."

Unlike some contemporary company chairmen, who did not believe in consultation of any kind, Heath spoke from a position of authority. Thanks to the work done by Parsons and his Personnel Department over 25 years, GKN had been a pioneer in developing information channels for its employees, through workplace councils and a range of other tools.

Parsons had never forgotten what he had seen on a visit to the US in 1952, when he visited a Westinghouse plant just after the management had defused an exorbitant pay claim. The management had hired a local cinema on a Saturday morning, invited all the union officials involved, together with key employees and their wives, and given a presentation explaining the situation in the industry, the economics of the company, the implications of the claim and why it could not be accepted. The union reduced its demand.

The lesson was drummed home when he stayed in a hotel in Cleveland. A noisy sales conference was in progress when he arrived, but the reps left that afternoon. In the evening, Parsons remarked to the young lift attendant how nice and quiet the hotel now was. "Sir," said the boy with a withering look of contempt, "don't you know that if this hotel isn't running at one-third capacity, we're in the red?"

Parsons worked for years to encourage in the GKN workforce a similar level of economic understanding. He produced a discussion course, Work and Wealth, explaining the basic facts of economic life. Subsidiaries ran workplace briefings to explain their results to employees and promote participation. The group developed information packs – the forerunners of later generations' Employee Reports – summarising the figures and key business developments. This data provided plenty of substance for the joint consultative committees that GKN was among the first UK companies to set up.

The wave of militancy in 1970s Britain tested these systems to the limit and beyond. In places, as at Sankey and Garringtons, the culture of mutual understanding cracked for a time. Generally, though, the foundations Parsons had established did insulate GKN from the worst effects of the prevailing shop-floor anarchy. By the time Parsons retired from GKN, on 31 December 1978, all 110,000 employees worldwide were receiving the briefings.

Bullock provided Parsons with his last hurrah at GKN. Weeks from retirement, he was called by Heath into a rearguard action against the dominant voices of the Left on the committee. The committee, predictably, had split. While the majority was drafting its recommendations for a vast extension of worker involvement in corporate decision-making, the trio of industrialists had decided that they would have to produce a dissenting, minority report.

The report had to be written by industrial relations experts, and it had to be written fast. Parsons' GKN team sprang into action, burning the midnight oil to write, edit and complete the dissident report. Heath thanked Parsons by waiving the rule that executive directors had to retire at 60 – the GKN veteran was allowed to stay to the end of 1978.

The majority report, calling for worker directors on all UK company boards, was met with widespread criticism. Heath added his voice to it, telling GKN investors: "Any such legislation would definitely not add to the efficiency of our company and would cause further uncertainty amongst the country's labour force, as well as having undesirable repercussions on overseas investment in this country."

In the end, the recommendations withered away, consigned to history by the progressive weakening and ultimate fall of the Labour government. Bullock stands today as a relic of that past, and as a reflection and a reminder of the industrial relations extremes to which Britain fell prey in the Seventies.

The wave of strikes reached its peak at the end of 1978 and in the early months of 1979, the so-called "Winter of Discontent", when a host of public and private sector strikes against the government's vain attempt to restrict pay rises to 5% paralysed swathes of the economy. Hospitals had to turn away patients; dustbins overflowed with rubbish; food and petrol supplies were disrupted; hundreds of thousands of workers were laid off. There were even isolated instances of gravediggers refusing to dig graves.

Such images implanted themselves in the national consciousness. They were still fresh in voters' minds when the Callaghan government lost a "no confidence" vote on 28 March. At the ensuing General Election on 4 May, Margaret Thatcher led the Tories to victory with a majority of 43, thereby becoming Britain's first woman Prime Minister.

Compared with the disruption to essential services, the continuing strikes in Britain's motor industry seemed of lesser importance. Here, too, the long decline of the UK-owned manufacturers was entering a conclusive phase. Total UK car sales in 1979 increased to 1.7 m as imports, notably by the Japanese, continued to march onward and upward. But BL's output and market share slumped to record lows. Its production fell by more than 16% to just over 500,000 vehicles; its exports dropped to barely 200,000; BL's UK market share dived below 20% for the first time.

For GKN, the decline of its once-predominant domestic customer, a symptom of the loss of competitiveness by UK manufacturing as a whole, presented a colossal challenge. Facing that challenge was a new management team, led by Trevor Holdsworth. For company as well as country, this was a pivotal moment. But even Holdsworth could not know just how critical the moment would be.

CHAPTER 17

# Baptism of Fire

On 1 January 1980, Trevor Holdsworth became chairman of GKN. Holdsworth, who was knighted two years later, led a generational change at the top of the group. His new team had been in the making for several years as the Raymond Brookes "old guard", who had stayed on under Heath, retired or moved into non-executive roles. Holdsworth himself had become managing director in 1977 in addition to the role as deputy chairman that he had assumed in 1972. He was Heath's natural successor.

Around Holdsworth, a new core team emerged. Roy Roberts, a tough, hands-on, operations man became managing director, Basil Woods was the strategy head, Ian Donald joined the board with responsibility for the driveline business (then called Universal Transmissions) and other activities. David Lees was in place to succeed Paddy Custis, who retired the following year as finance director.

Despite its relative youth, the team had a deep-seated knowledge and understanding of the group. Roberts had joined as a management trainee in 1951; Lees had joined Sankey as chief accountant in 1970 and Donald came in with the 1972 Firth Cleveland acquisition.

Holdsworth himself was now in his 17th year at GKN, and had played a highly influential role in developing its strategy and structure. Brookes, a great talent-spotter, had seen his potential early and had ensured that he received a rounded education in industrial management. "He trained me," Holdsworth recounted. "After my initial spell at head office, he sent me to run Screws and Fasteners because he said it was about time I got some experience managing a business." Holdsworth's main contribution at Fasteners was to oversee development of the Pozidriv, an innovative crosshead screw whose superior design enabled the business to hold back the rising tide of lower-cost imports, at least for a time.

Holdsworth returned to head office in 1970, and effectively became head of strategy and business development. As Deputy Chairman during Heath's tenure, his cerebral approach contrasted sharply with the Chairman's extroversion. Heath liked to burst into rousing song. Holdsworth was an accomplished pianist. Most recently, he had masterminded the replacement of the UK subgroups by a series of larger divisions. GKN's continued size and sprawl were reflected in the fact that there were 20 divisions in total, from Autoparts distribution to Welding.

The Autoparts business was one of two that belonged to larger, international groupings – the other being the Transmissions operations, which were being further expanded in the US by the construction of a second and larger factory in Alamance County, North Carolina.

Autoparts was the product of a breakneck charge into parts distribution which had begun in 1978 with the acquisition of Parts Industries Corporation. Parts Industries, which was based in Elvis Presley country – Memphis, Tennessee – did exactly what its name suggested: it was the fourth-largest distributor of replacement vehicle parts in the US with annual sales of $100 m.

Parts Industries was the most dramatic manifestation to date of Holdsworth's desire, supported by Woods, to establish GKN as a large player in services to counterweight the manufacturing operations. It was a portfolio approach – Transmissions was clearly becoming a very strong business, but it was almost entirely focused on original equipment and had a relatively small aftermarket content.

By contrast, other long-standing components of GKN's manufacturing range were either low-tech metal bashing or in terminal decline, or both – particularly Fasteners, whose home market share was being devoured by cheaper foreign imports. Holdsworth said later: "We all felt that we should have in GKN a counter-balancing offset business so that we would not be dependent solely on the automotive industry. What should it be? We decided that we would go for non-manufacturing, service activity – distribution both wholesale and even retail."

GKN was also encouraged by the success of CHEP UK, which had developed rapidly to the point where, by the end of 1978, the pool totalled 1.5 m pallets. That year, CHEP moved into mainland Europe – although it almost left GKN behind in the process. Brambles had told GKN that it was considering establishing a CHEP operation on the continent, and asked if its British partner wanted to join the venture. But Roy Roberts, on behalf of the board, declined, saying that GKN was happy to concentrate on the UK.

The Brambles team therefore decamped across the Channel and joined forces with the Belgian bank Compagnie Bruxelles Lambert. They also lined up a third party to join the enterprise. But these talks ran into difficulties. Jessop, who had been horrified to learn of the original rebuff to Brambles, saw an opportunity to recover GKN's position. "I called them and said, 'Why don't I come in?' I almost took it back to GKN as a fait accompli," he said. GKN acquired one-third of CHEP Europe, and together with Brambles subsequently bought out Bruxelles Lambert to increase their holdings to 50% each.

Brambles was happy, but GKN had to pay a price for readmission: Brambles demanded 10% more of CHEP UK, reducing GKN's stake to 70%. Brambles' demand and GKN's reluctance to meet it both reflected the transformation of CHEP UK. Within four years it had changed from being an experimental business in which both parties were trying to minimise their exposure to a jewel in both groups' crowns.

GKN's services push continued apace. No sooner had Parts Industries been acquired than the group bought Stern Osmat in the UK. This was a big step into the DIY and leisure market, since Stern was a distributor of gardening equipment, ironmongery and hand tools, supplying 2500 UK retailers.

The main focus, however, remained autoparts, with further expansion in the US, UK and France. In early

1980, GKN added a touch of Country & Western to its Elvis catalogue when it acquired Worldparts Corporation, based in Nashville. Worldparts specialised in imported car parts, at the time a fast-growing market as foreign manufacturers increased their share of the US market. By that time, GKN had assembled an autoparts distribution and service business with annual sales of more than £200 m, most of it acquired in the space of two years.

Superficially, there appeared to be a certain logic in an original equipment components manufacturer developing an accessories and replacement parts business. In reality, the market dynamics and the disciplines involved were completely different, as GKN was to discover. "Some people tried to make a case for a connection between distribution and OE, but there wasn't one," Bonner remarked.

For the time being, however, the diversification appeared to be working. It certainly highlighted how the group was changing direction, because the corollary of the acquisition drive was the start of a disposals programme involving some long-standing GKN subsidiaries.

Initially, the disposals were small – a liquid filtration business and GKN's half-share in a South African auto components business. But in June 1979, the group announced it was selling its 50% stake in Lysaght Australia to BHP for £44.2 m. The deal, which was completed in December, marked a historic break with the past. Apart from Guest Keen Williams, Lysaght had for more than half a century been the most prominent of all GKN's overseas operations. The fact that it was one of the group's few surviving steel activities added to the significance of the disposal. The deal reflected GKN's reorientation away from the Commonwealth and towards Europe and the United States.

If Lysaght's sale was a landmark, so was the near-simultaneous disposal of most of the UK bolt and nut business – the major remaining vestige of Arthur Keen's Patent Nut & Bolt Company. There was much, much more to come.

On the eve of the 1980s GKN was still a vast conglomerate. It employed just over 104,000 people. Almost 70% of them – 69,115 to be precise – were in Britain, where GKN had more than 70 operating subsidiaries.

The group had sales of £1.96 billion, of which £1.1 billion were in the UK. West Germany was the largest overseas market; with sales of £168 m, of which £138 m were originated there and the rest was exports. The USA was the only other country where GKN had sales of more than £100 m.

UK operating margins lagged those of the overseas companies, as they had done for years. At 4.9%, the UK return on sales contrasted with 8.2% for the overseas businesses as a whole. The UK profits and returns would have been slightly higher but for the impact of a national strike by engineering workers, the first big dispute faced by the Thatcher government, which was estimated to have cost GKN £15 m. Nevertheless, the group made record pre-tax profits of £125.8 m in 1979 and delivered earnings of 47.6 p a share. It paid dividends totalling 27.7 p. Return on net assets was 11.3%, up from 9.8% the previous year.

Holdsworth was not complacent. He told shareholders that recessionary signs were apparent from the final months of 1979 and that the new-found strength of the pound was beginning to impact exports from the UK, particularly to the US. He described the economic background as "increasingly unsettled" and pledged that GKN would continue "our major programme of strategic realignment, aimed at simplifying and concentrating the group's businesses". But even he could not foresee the scale of the economic deluge that was about to descend on British industry, or the extent of the transformation that was to be required by GKN.

Like the recession of 1973–76, the 1980–82 slump was triggered by a Middle East crisis which caused an upsurge in the oil price. In January 1979, the Ayatollah Khomeini and his supporters forced the Shah of Iran into exile and unleashed a fundamentalist Islamic revolution.

On the eve of the revolution, oil was about $12 a barrel. In its wake, the price soared as the militant Khomeini regime and its supporters sought to drive up prices to pressurise the West over Israel. Iranian oil went to $40 in December 1979 as OPEC failed to reconcile the views of the moderates with those of the hawks among its members. The price shock did not really bite until 1980, triggering a rapid decline in Western GDP growth and an upsurge in unemployment.

In the United States, the "Big Three" vehicle-makers – General Motors, Ford and Chrysler – made combined losses for the year of more than £2 billion as sales slumped, and Chrysler had to be bailed out by the American government. It was one of the overseas vehicle makers to which Holdsworth was referring when he said: "Two major international groups, both important customers for GKN, have had to be sustained by concerted action by bankers, and in other cases governments have given direct support."

All developed economies suffered. But the hardest-hit of all was Britain.

In three years, UK unemployment more than doubled, from just over 1.2 m when the Thatcher government took office to 3 m in the autumn of 1982. Manufacturing industry was particularly impacted. By the time Thatcher was re-elected for the second time in June 1987, 2 m manufacturing jobs had been lost since 1979: employment in the sector was down from 7.1 m to 5.1 m.

The decline in manufacturing output was equally enormous. Output had increased by an average 1.2% a year in the three years before 1980. In 1980, output plummeted by 8.7%; the following year, it slumped a further 6%. Not until July 1987 did manufacturing output regain its 1979 level.

Britain was hit so much harder than its peers for two reasons. First, far from falling as it had done during every post-war recession, the pound rose in value. The reason was Britain's discovery and successful development of its North Sea oil reserves: crude North Sea oil production increased by almost 50% to 77 m tonnes in 1979, its largest annual jump en route to its mid-1980s peak.

North Sea oil turned the pound into a petro-currency: every cent rise in the oil price was another reason for currency dealers to buy sterling. The pound peaked against the US dollar in late 1980 at almost $2.40 – the 1967 devaluation level. As a result, manufacturing industry suddenly found its exports being priced out of overseas markets while imports became increasingly price-competitive.

This would have been a severe challenge in itself. Industry looked to government policy to provide relief.

But, instead, it found Thatcher and her Chancellor, Sir Geoffrey Howe, unyielding. The Prime Minister had come to power dedicated to eradicating inflation from the British body economic. Now that problem had been exacerbated by the rise in the price of oil.

Thatcher and her fellow monetarists saw inflation as the fundamental reason for Britain's post-war economic decline. Inflation had offered an easy way out. It was an alibi for companies reluctant to take the hard road to improve their real competitiveness. The cost of living went up, so pay claims and awards went up, and prices were raised to finance the wage increases. As one manager told the *Financial Times* in 1983: "For many years, we lived on the fairy gold of stock inflation. We made stock profits and borrowed from the banks to provide cash for working capital. How wrong we were."

Thatcher and her allies were determined to break the habit, and the mould. By controlling the money supply, they aimed to squeeze an addiction to inflation out of Britain's economic bloodstream.

So, far from relieving the impact of the high pound by cutting interest rates and pumping money into the system through increased borrowing, they tightened the screw. They hiked interest rates to 17% – rates did not fall below 12% until August 1982. In Howe's first Budget in 1979, basic and higher income tax rates had been cut but VAT was almost doubled to 15% – inadvertently giving another twist to price inflation at the very moment recession was taking hold. In 1980, inflation jumped to 18%. That made the subsequent counter-inflationary drive even more severe.

It was all too much for many British industrialists. Sir Michael Edwardes, executive chairman of BL, told the Confederation of British Industry's annual conference in Brighton in November 1980 that: "If the Cabinet does not have the wit and imagination to reconcile our industrial needs with the fact of North Sea oil, they would do better to leave the bloody stuff in the ground."

Holdsworth chose his words with greater care. Characteristically, he saw both sides of the issue. On the one hand, he rebuked the government for economic policies which "have turned the world recession into an unprecedented national depression". However, Holdsworth told shareholders, "We must not forget that the central economic problem of the United Kingdom has, for a long time, been our disastrously low national productiveness.

"A depreciating currency, borrowing to finance national revenue deficits and reduced profitability of industry have enabled the nation to pay itself more than it has earned and to avoid facing this central issue. High inflation has resulted. No previous policies – and many have been tried – have succeeded in reversing this long-term deterioration. If our national standard of living is not to decline steadily and permanently, then we have to make substantial changes.

"The continual deferment of these necessary changes has meant that they are now happening with extreme and painful speed during a period of general recession. Alternative policies proposed by alternative political parties and others are either, at best, unconvincing or, at the worst, unthinkable."

GKN was certainly feeling the pain. It made a pre-tax loss in 1980 of £1.2 m – a downturn of £127 m from the previous year's record profit. It was the group's worst performance since the start of the Depression in 1930. The dividend was slashed by more than two-thirds to 8 p. The news made the front page of the *Financial Times*. It symbolised the crisis enveloping British manufacturing.

GKN also had to cope with the first major public sector strike of the Thatcher era. On 20 January 1980, almost all the 166,400 employees of the British Steel Corporation walked out in the first national steel strike for 70 years. The strike, against management plans for plant closures, lasted 13 weeks. Less than half-way through, the Iron and Steel Trades Confederation (ISTC), the steel union, spread the strike to the private steel-making sector, including GKN. Although the Court of Appeal ruled that this extension was illegal under employment law, the judgment was overruled by the House of Lords.

When the strike was over, the rate of job loss at BSC was unprecedented: almost 46,000 jobs were cut in a year, most of them within six months of the strike's end.

Holdsworth commented: "The reasons for that strike and any gains achieved must now surely seem irrelevant to those who created the situation. The cost to GKN was great, not only in our specific steel-making areas but also in the general disruption caused throughout the steel-using and steel distribution activities."

Despite the steel strike, the group and its predominant UK operations stayed in profit for the first six months of the year. The damage was done in the second half, when the UK business racked up operating losses of £40 m as the recession struck. "No major part of the UK activities has escaped the effects," Holdsworth reported.

General Steels suffered a fall in overall demand of such severity that, in the second half, its output plummetted by more than 50%. Both it and Special Steels and Forgings dropped into the red. By far the biggest impact, however, was felt by the UK automotive operations, the largest single business in the group, as output slumped.

Worldwide, car production fell by 8% and commercial vehicle production by 10.5% – although Japanese production actually increased by 14% in cars and 15.8% in commercial vehicles. But in almost every territory where GKN operated or exported, demand for the group's transmission components held up. In the US, despite the problems of the Big Three, the increase in market share of front wheel drive cars more than offset the overall production cutbacks. In mainland Europe, output held up relatively well until late in the year.

The sole exception was the UK. The combination of the long decline in competitiveness with the onslaught of recession pushed the indigenous car makers over a cliff. British car production dropped to 924,000 vehicles, the lowest level since 1955, when output was on the up as the post-war consumer boom gathered pace.

No manufacturer suffered more than BL, for which the 1980 recession was a truly defining moment – a moment of absolute truth. BL's output fell more than 20% to 396,000 vehicles and its share of the UK market hit an all-time low of 18.2%. There was no way back to the volumes that it had previously achieved. It and its successor entities – Austin Rover, Rover Group – never made more than 500,000 cars in a year again.

The long-term ramifications of the crisis could not be evident to Holdsworth and his team. It was hard enough to achieve some measure of short-term visibility. But one thing was clear to the chairman and his board: drastic measures were needed to preserve the financial and operational integrity of the company. The unthinkable became the inevitable.

CHAPTER 18

# Transformation

The 1980–82 recession changed the face and shape of GKN for good.

Most obviously, it dramatically altered the group in terms of employment: in 1980 alone, GKN made or announced 16,000 redundancies – almost one-quarter of its pre-recession UK workforce – at a cost of £75 m. About a third of that total represented the cost of streamlining continuing operations; the majority reflected closures and disposals.

In 1981, a further 6000 workers went and £37 m was spent on redundancies and cutbacks, £25 m of that on closing or selling businesses. The figures in 1982 approached 1980 levels – £65.4 m in costs, of which £53 m related to closed or disposed subsidiaries. A further 5000 jobs were cut. The following year, a further £21 m restructuring costs were incurred; in 1984, £19 m.

By the end of 1983, therefore, GKN had more than halved its UK workforce to 33,600 from immediate pre-recession levels. The worldwide workforce had been almost halved, to 54,000 people. The group had spent just short of £220 m on rationalising, closing or selling businesses.

As a result, the group's portfolio had been transformed. Hitherto sacred cows were slaughtered on a vast scale. One of the largest was also one of the first: in June 1981, GKN and the British Steel Corporation completed the establishment of a new company, Allied Steel and Wire Holdings (ASW) which combined GKN's General Steels division – the wire and rod-making operations – with that of BSC. The venture was dubbed Phoenix I, and the two parties owned 50% of the company apiece. But it was clear which way each was moving. Following in the footsteps of Lysaght, GKN was on its way out of General Steels.

Bright Steel followed. GKN rolled it into a three-way joint venture company, British Bright Bar, with BSC and the private sector firm Brymill. GKN retained a minority 40% stake for the moment. After these deals, the only steel-making business that GKN still wholly owned was Brymbo.

A host of other businesses went. The Plastics Machinery and Welding Divisions were sold. GKN Contractors was run down as the contracts were worked out. This was more easily planned than executed, because of the problematic nature of some of its projects. Grey Denham, who joined GKN in 1980 as Legal Counsel and had previously specialised in company divestments, found himself part of a small legal team dealing with the extensive divestment programme.

GKN Contractors posed particular issues, because of the unusual nature of its outstanding contracts. One was for refurbishment of tin mines in Zaire. "The Zaire tin mine refurbishment had been fraught with difficulties, including disputes with the local partner, local land right disputes, security issues and political instability in the country – all of which caused work stoppages," Denham recalled. "After one stoppage, a work compound was found to be overrun by snakes. The GKN medical staff also considered the site unsanitary. In order to meet basic requirements, septic tanks had to be imported, disguised as iron ore containers in order to get around import restrictions. In the end, the contract became untenable as the anticipated recovery of tin never materialised."

There was also a contract to build three chicken slaughterhouses in Iraq. "GKN Contractors had successfully completed contracts for chicken farming facilities in Iraq but the slaughterhouse contract coincided with the Iran–Iraq war," recounted Denham. One of the sites was attacked by an Iranian plane. In these very difficult circumstances, performance issues mounted. GKN Contractors invoked a force majeure clause [exempting GKN from any liability due to forces beyond its control], but nevertheless the Saddam Hussein Government attempted to call the performance bonds under the contracts."

GKN avoided money being paid up front by alleging that the call under the bonds had been fraudulent. "The law suit with the Iraqi Rafidain Bank took years to grind through the Courts," Denham said. "All but one of the calls were ruled to be unfounded and the remaining one at issue was still unresolved when Iraq invaded Kuwait. That led to sanctions and the freezing of all Iraq's overseas assets, so we ended up with no liability as the Rafidain Bank was unable to continue the action."

The Zaire and Iraq contracts were effectively the last straw for GKN: they led to the inevitable conclusion that Contracting was not sustainable, and should be closed.

Within many of the businesses that GKN retained, there was extensive rationalisation. Fasteners closed plants and consolidated production on to one site. Forgings and castings were also streamlined. Axles, wheels and pressings were all cut back as demand fell.

Jim McFarlane recalled the atmosphere in the GKN boardroom: "We had certainly felt it was coming. But all the same, it was hard going. We couldn't see much light at the end of the tunnel and we wondered where we would end up. We knew we weren't the only ones making a loss. We felt that we must do something to get out of this mess. Quite a lot of what happened was inevitable and cathartic rather than destructive. But a certain number of babies went out with the bathwater."

In terms of its balance sheet, GKN remained well within borrowing limits: the articles of association set a limit of £707 m on total borrowings, and at the end of 1982 debt had peaked at £392 m.

The situation was far less comfortable in cash flow and P&L terms. From 1980 to 1982, interest cover excluding redundancy costs was less than two times trading profit. In two of those three years, the group suffered a net cash outflow: 1980 being the worst year, with more than £78 m draining out of the company.

One business above all saved GKN from what could have been severe financial trouble: Uni-Cardan came into its own. In 1980, while the UK operations were slumping into loss, mainland Europe – almost entirely Uni-Cardan – made a trading profit of £39 m, after accounting for currency changes. Profits from the other overseas businesses totalled £16 m. At constant rates, Uni-Cardan's performance was even more impressive because of the average 8% rise in the pound that year.

In 1981, as the UK traded back into a marginal profit of £13 m, Europe made £36 m. The following year, it made £26 m, almost half the group's total £54 m. The resilience of the German, French and Italian vehicle markets, and the strength of Uni-Cardan within those markets, saw GKN through. "In 1980 and 1981, Uni-Cardan kept us afloat," said Denham. "It was probably the difference between GKN and oblivion."

Bonner, who succeeded Walterscheid-Muller as chairman and chief executive of Uni-Cardan in 1981, commented: "It's no exaggeration to say that Uni-Cardan went a long way towards saving GKN as a group during this period, because of the profits and cash it generated. It was highly profitable. We were exercising strong working capital control, which meant that we were able to continue to invest ahead of depreciation and still generate cash for the benefit of the group as a whole."

In the darkest days of the UK recession, Uni-Cardan's cash did more than merely provide GKN with the headroom to re-engineer its UK manufacturing base. It also gave the group a sufficient platform to continue the development of its designated growth businesses.

Holdsworth made clear in early 1981 the group's commitment not to be deflected from its three-pronged strategy. "The general thrust of our programme for strategic change and development remains," he told shareholders. GKN would continue "to concentrate upon the manufacture of technologically-orientated products of high added-value; to direct our thrust to world rather than national markets both by direct exports and by overseas investment; to increase substantially the Group's involvement in the services sector".

Money might have been short, but GKN continued to put resources where its mouth was. The group spent £18 m on acquisitions in 1981. Some of the outlay went on Autoparts. But the largest element involved the creation of the waste business Cleanaway, which alongside CHEP became the cornerstone of GKN's industrial services arm for the ensuing two decades.

Once more, the impulse came from Brambles, which had grown a waste business in Australia into a major activity. Brambles wanted to start up in the UK, and its board decided that this should again be done in partnership with GKN.

At first, the GKN board – clearly preoccupied with the UK crisis – turned the proposal down. As with CHEP's European venture, Jessop then intervened and persuaded the board to reconsider. The partners agreed that, unlike CHEP which had been created from scratch, they needed to build on an established business. They identified Redland Purle, the waste arm of the building materials company Redland, as a suitable springboard. It was acquired in

January 1981 and the two companies each took 50% of the business, which they rebranded.

Jessop was relieved: "I could see that Cleanaway was never going to lose us money. But also, I didn't want Brambles to find another partner who might then join them when CHEP went into the US, which was the big outstanding market and had the potential to transform CHEP. So essentially, Cleanaway was a defensive move from my standpoint."

At almost the same time as Jessop was reinforcing GKN's alliance with Brambles, Alec Daly, another of GKN's new generation of managing directors, was helping to establish a new business line. Both in itself and in the road down which it was to lead GKN, this activity was to prove as significant as the Brambles relationship.

Daly had joined GKN in 1978 to head Sankey. He had worked for Ford for 16 years, and been steeped in the company's culture of rigorous analysis, tight cost control and effective execution. If there was a problem, went the Blue Oval axiom, then Ford would fix it. Daly knew Sankey as a reputable supplier – it made the underbodies for the Transit [for which it was still supplying components in 2009]. However, as Daly quickly discovered, Sankey had issues which needed fixing.

"I was struck by the fiefdoms in GKN," Daly said. As baronies went, Sankey was one of the biggest and, because of its long and proud history both during and preceding its ownership by GKN, one of the deepest-rooted. McFarlane observed when he left the GKN board to join the EEF: "I said that I had visited every part of

GKN except Sankey – because they had never invited me to visit."

On the eve of the recession, Daly said: "Sankey had 13,000 employees and it comprised many activities on many sites. I didn't realise how ancient the facilities were or how difficult the unions were. The unions were quite capable of walking all over management at that time. Above all, I hadn't known how lacking in real productivity the company was. They were grossly overmanned, but because they made money – they were never stellar, but they were a consistently good earner for GKN – I don't think anyone was going for the last inch. By contrast, at Ford, no matter what you did, you had 5% annual productivity improvement factored into your targets."

Confronted with the UK motor industry slump, Daly stayed calm: "In the auto industry, people recognised that these were cycles. Car companies are always on the cusp. If they aren't working at 70% capacity or above, the ink flows red. You make money in the good times and try not to lose too much in the bad times. And you take all the costs you can out of the business."

In a way, the recession helped Daly to make a break with Sankey's past. "We had some redundancies, almost all of them voluntary, and we sold operations such as electrical laminations [whose origins dated back to the 1880s]. The guys in Sankey were all Sankey people from long ago and so it was quite difficult to change the culture. I was once told it took five years to change a corporate culture, and it certainly did there. At the first annual budget meeting, I said to them, 'Where's your efficiency plan?' After that, they always came in with a plan."

Once the business was moving in the right direction, Sankey's scale – which had reinforced its complacency and resistance to change – became an asset. "They had an extensive core product range – pressings, clutch plates, underbodies, wheels for trucks, tractors and OffHighway vehicles. Because they were so big, although they did have competitors, it was an orderly market. Usually there were about three people trying to get the business and we were always one or two, so we never suffered badly from people eating our lunch. I was determined that, if we went for new projects – and we were very dependent on the automotive and agri-tech business – we would put in a lot of new facilities. We gradually got Sankey to be a very competitive, well-facilitised business."

One new project stood out. In 1980, the Ministry of Defence (MoD) awarded Sankey a contract for the main development phase of a proposed new family of tracked armoured personnel carriers (APCs) called the MCV 80. MCV stood for Mechanised Combat Vehicle. It became known to the world as the Warrior. It was the brainchild of the Sankey designer Ken Lofts. "Ken was the genius behind Warrior," Daly said simply.

Winning the design contract clearly placed GKN in an outstanding position to win the big prize – the Warrior production contract, scheduled to be for more than 1000 vehicles. However, there were no guarantees. Daly realised that if Sankey did not deliver the prototype on time, to budget and on specification, its design contract victory could go for nothing.

Sankey had a good record in armoured vehicles. It was now producing the Saxon wheeled APC at its Hadley

Castle plant at Telford, and Saxon was being ordered in the hundreds by the British Army and overseas customers including the Netherlands, Malaysia, Brunei, Oman and Nigeria. But Warrior was a much bigger vehicle, several rungs up the technology ladder from Saxon.

"Ken and I worked on it together," Daly said. "It was a vehicle, and I was used to vehicles. I went over there to check on how it was progressing. There was no discipline on costs or timing and very little networking. Everything was done on boards. So I brought in vehicle project management and asked Ken, 'What targets are you setting yourselves for reliability – so many miles before breakdowns, and so on?' He picked that up. We took everything I knew about how Ford did these sort of things and applied them to developing Warrior."

The Warrior team then borrowed another technique from the motor industry – they consulted the end-customer: "We went to the soldiers and asked what they wanted most from the vehicle. They picked out two things: one, they didn't want a mine to be able to blow it up when the vehicle went over one; and two, they wanted it to start every time you pressed the button." Sankey set out to achieve those two priorities.

But GKN was still not assured of winning the production contract. The MoD intended to place an initial order, followed at a later date by the main production contract. Whoever won the initial batch was virtually guaranteed the main order. "I was determined that we weren't going to give it away after doing all the design and development work, but we had to fight for it," Daly said.

216

1. Seymour Berry entertaining GKN directors
   *Photograph: J Clark*

*All images courtesy of GKN unless otherwise stated*

2. Destruction of the blast furnaces at  Dowlais c. 1937.
  *Welsh Industrial & Maritime Museum*

3. A nineteenth century display of Nettlefolds fasteners
*Photograph reproduced by Allen Baker Photography Ltd*

4. Joseph Sankey, founder of the business

5. A pre-war saloon fitted with Sankey wheels (1)

6. T.S. Peacock, joint managing director of GKN 1920–46
*Photograph reproduced by Allen Baker Photography Ltd*

7. J. H. Jolly, joint managing director of GKN from 1934, deputy
chairman 1943 and chairman 4 years later.

8. Sir Kenneth Peacock, chairman of GKN 1953–65
*Photograph reproduced by Allen Baker Photography Ltd*

9. A specialized tank assembled by Lysaghts
   *Source: Rheem Co*

10. Royal Visit 1912

11. Dowlais-Cardiff Steelworks, East Moors, 1949
   *Aerofilms Library*

12. Sir David Lees

13. Trevor Bonner 1996

14. New Technology

15.  Laser machine at Lohmar

16. EH101 19

17. Sir CK Chow

18. A380

19. Raymond Brookes

20. Warrior tank

21. Chep

22. Kevin Smith

23. Roy Brown

24. Trevor Holdsworth
   *Trevor Livingstone Studios, Birmingham*

Michael Heseltine had taken over as Secretary of State for Defence, and he was implementing a radical new approach to procurement. The contract was the first that the MoD had put out to competition – previously, it had simply allotted a contract to a particular company, or companies. The orders tended to be shared around the industry. Heseltine was also determined to end the MoD's traditional "cost-plus" system, whereby if the costs of a contract increased once it was let, the company concerned could simply recoup those overruns from the government.

GKN's main competition came from Alvis, the armoured vehicle maker owned by United Scientific Holdings (USH). Sir Peter Levene, who ran USH, was later recruited by Heseltine to be head of Defence Procurement. "The competition went on and on," said Daly. "We were being encouraged to take big slices off the cost per vehicle. But we decided to take a brave approach and put the emphasis on the quality of our product. We were bigger than Alvis/USH and we had done a great job on the design contract." GKN won. In 1983, it was awarded the initial production contract for 280 Warriors. For the first time in peacetime, GKN had an authentic Defence business.

The Warrior win epitomised how the tide was turning for GKN. In spring 1983, Holdsworth reflected that since he had become chairman, his reports to shareholders "have been largely commentaries on contraction, recitals of retrenchment, reorganisation and restructuring, accompanied by recessionary conditions ... Each year I could only express the hope and belief that the considerable changes made within our on-going businesses, and the costly restructuring which had relieved the group of many severe problems, would give us the opportunity and ability to secure improved profitability quickly when market conditions improved. Some of that hope is now beginning to be fulfilled."

In May, as stock markets gathered steam, discounting the forthcoming economic recovery, the group launched a £77 m rights issue to reinforce its balance sheet and fuel fresh growth. Then it made a takeover bid for its smaller West Midlands motor components rival AE.

AE specialised in engine parts – pistons, piston rings, bearings and cylinder liners. The bid was a second attempt by GKN, following the Sachs failure, to emulate in the engine what it had achieved in the driveline – the creation of a major UK-owned international player. The difference from the Sachs experience was that AE's management, which originally recommended the bid, then changed its mind and opposed the offer. Ultimately, however, history repeated itself: the bid foundered on the attitude of the British competition authorities. In the process, like Sachs, the episode revealed fundamental flaws in the approach by the competition authorities.

There was little doubt that the GKN/AE case raised prima facie competition concerns: the companies' combined share of the UK bearings market was 94% (Vandervell plus the AE business) and in cylinder liners it was 86% (Sheepbridge plus AE). The Monopolies and Mergers Commission judged that such large domestic market shares would be both anti-competitive and cause an increase in imports to the detriment of the UK's indigenous industry.

It was a purist, ivory tower approach which highlighted the failure of the UK Competition law framework to take account of market realities or anticipate industry trends. GKN contended forcefully that the rationale for the AE deal was to establish one strong British engine component company to compete in European and world markets. It told the Commission that component sourcing was becoming increasingly multinational and that the original equipment manufacturers (OEMs) – the vehicle makers – were moving away from fragmented national suppliers to source from companies able to supply them across many different territories.

GKN knew that was true, because of what it was seeing in driveline. Moreover, it was supported by the three major foreign-owned vehicle companies active in Britain at the time – Ford, Vauxhall and Peugeot [then called Talbot]. All of them told the Commission that the merger was in the best interests of British industry. Only BL, which was now increasingly pinned in the UK market, did not back GKN's case.

The Commission rejected these arguments and, in March 1984, blocked the bid. What happened subsequently to AE highlighted the parochialism and short-sightedness of the decision. Three years later, AE was taken over by Turner & Newall, which was diversifying out of building materials into motor components.

The competition authorities waved this bid through, because T&N had no existing interests in engine components. But no competition issue also meant there was no economy of scale in the deal, no creation of a strategic UK engine parts supplier. The epilogue was all too predictable: T&N was subsequently acquired by Federal Mogul, the American auto parts maker.

Holdsworth took the AE rebuff philosophically and GKN moved on. It did not become a major engine components supplier and, as a result, the Vandervell business was left exposed to eventual disposal. However, the group remained active in cylinder liners into the 21st century.

The main effect of the AE setback was to accentuate the importance of the driveline business, both to GKN's motor components activities and to the group as a whole. While Hardy Spicer and BRD were grappling with the impact of the UK industry's tribulations, Uni-Cardan's sales in mainland Western Europe were still strong. And with the increasingly significant US operation now recovering from a tough 1982, when North American car production hit its lowest level for 20 years, driveline was changing and raising its game.

Despite falling victim to the regulators, the group continued to wield influence in the corridors of power. GKN was one of the foremost supporters of the legislation that Thatcher brought forward to remove union immunity and curb the wildcat and secondary action that had cost British industry so dear in the Seventies.

In March 1980, the group – along with other leading companies – was consulted over the planned first Employment Bill. GKN told the government that the problems of defining secondary strikes and picketing were so great that it was better completely to remove union immunities from legal action over secondary disputes.

However, the company recognised that this might not be politically possible at this stage.

In the event, there were three Employment Acts, each going further than its predecessor in restricting union power by outlawing secondary action, introducing mandatory secret ballots for strike calls or union elections, and restricting strikes to issues concerned solely or mainly with wages and conditions. The main result was to remove legal immunity from unions or union members, thereby rendering them liable to actions for damages, fines or sequestration of their funds.

The laws were highly effective and paved the way for a sea-change in labour relations in Britain. Many of those who benefited were surprised by Thatcher's determination to push through the reforms. Jim McFarlane, however, was not. He had met her when he was running Smith Clayton in the early 1970s, well before she defeated Heath in the Tory leadership election of 1975.

"The EEF had asked her to come and talk to them at a dinner," he recalled. "A group of us were chatting to her before dinner, and in her forthright way, she told us what she planned to do in industry, reform the union laws and so on. I said, 'That sounds very attractive, Mrs Thatcher, but we have learned over the years that we can't always believe what politicians tell us they are going to do.' She turned on me – I shall never forget those eyes – and said: 'You Can Believe Me.'"

As Holdsworth's balanced judgment on the Thatcher government's economic policies made clear, GKN was not one of those British companies that paid uncritical homage to the Prime Minister. Writing at the peak of the recession,

Holdsworth said: "The private sector of manufacturing industry has taken action and achieved substantial change. However, the same degree of adjustment has not yet taken place in much of the public sector.

"We are still faced with absorbing without choice many increased charges for goods and services – and the UK has nearly half its economy in the public sector – from providers complacently continuing to deal with their employees as if maintaining their standard of living or their jobs was an unquestionable right. To effect change in these cases is the clear responsibility of Government, and so far they have not succeeded."

Holdsworth recalled: "I got along all right with Mrs Thatcher, although she did once say to me, 'I'm not sure that you are one of us' [the classic Thatcherite phrase for its diehard supporters]." Holdsworth got on very well with Denis Thatcher, whose knowledge of industry played an important role in informing Mrs Thatcher's approach. "Denis had run a chemical company and I was also chairman of [the chemicals firm] Allied Colloids, so we had that in common and we had some great times." As he tended to do with industrialists he liked, Denis would invite Holdsworth back to Number 10 for an evening drink. On occasion, the Prime Minister would be there too. The relationship continued when Sir David Lees succeeded Holdsworth.

As a prominent British manufacturer – one of an ever-decreasing number – GKN's relationship with the Thatcher and succeeding governments remained important. But one of the consequences of the early 1980s transformation was fundamentally to change the axis of the group.

In 1983, motor components – of which driveline was by far the biggest element – generated no less than 68% of GKN's £119 m trading profits. Despite the modest UK upturn, nearly half the trading profit – £55 m – was made in mainland Europe, almost entirely from Uni-Cardan.

From his base in Siegburg, Trevor Bonner now began to implement an expansion and integration strategy which would make driveline not only GKN's most international business, but one of the first genuinely global operations in the manufacturing world.

# CHAPTER 19

# The Japanese Connection

Even while Uni-Cardan's earnings were sustaining GKN during the Anglo-Saxon recession, Trevor Bonner and his team were looking ahead. "We were beginning to see that growth in continental European vehicle production, which had sustained and driven Uni-Cardan through the Seventies, wouldn't go on for ever," Bonner recalled.

"North America was still a growth engine, but there was a need to balance an already-plateauing UK situation and a progressively-plateauing one in continental Europe through a presence in emerging markets."

The first market they addressed was not exactly an emerging one. By the early 1980s, the Japanese motor industry had emerged as the most potent growth force in the world vehicle market. Its leading manufacturers – Nissan, Toyota, Honda, Mitsubishi and Mazda – were already making big inroads into most Western markets. Only the likes of France and Italy, which operated draconian import restrictions, kept the Japanese out.

Their first target was the US, where collective Japanese market share increased from 4% to 23% during the 1970s. But the Japanese sales were all exports from home, and they triggered a rising tide of anti-Japanese sentiment and protectionist lobbying in the US. What ensued was one of the largest and most sustained waves of inward investment any industry has ever seen. From the early 1980s, the Japanese vehicle makers began to lay down factories – "transplants" – first in North America, next in the UK, then across the world.

By the turn of the decade, Nissan was making plans to build a plant in America. It was followed by the others, with Toyota announcing in 1985 that it would build two factories, one in the US and the other in Canada. Like GKN with its North Carolina sites, most of the Japanese avoided the indigenous motown around Detroit. Instead, they went south, into areas new to the car industry like Tennessee (Nissan) and Kentucky (Toyota). GKN was waiting for them.

The Japanese knew GKN was there because the group had played the game the Japanese way: the long way. Eiji Toyoda, cousin of Toyota's founder and the chairman who led Toyota to post-war leadership in its home market and expansion overseas, was once asked: "Will you have fulfilled your ambitions in 10 years' time?" and replied: "I don't know; 10 years is a short time in the car industry." Most of his Western peers thought a year was a long time and a decade was a lifetime.

Uni-Cardan's contacts with the Japanese began in the early 1970s. It faced one domestic rival, NTN Toyo Bearing. NTN was originally a bearings manufacturer, but it had been granted licences to make CVJs by Birfield before the British company was acquired by GKN. It saw the opportunity presented by the move to front wheel drive, and decided to major in CVJs.

"Japanese vehicle production at the time Birfield licensed NTN was still very limited," said Bonner. "Either the British didn't foresee the explosion in Japanese vehicle production and therefore were willing to grant licences, or they felt Japan was a stretch too far (which you could fully understand in the Sixties) and therefore were willing to grant exclusive licences.

"Given the particular demographics of Japan, and also the infrastructure or lack of it at the time, most of the vehicles produced were small cars with front-wheel drive," Bonner said. "But sole supply of automotive parts in those days was almost unheard-of." The Japanese car makers wanted a second indigenous supplier. They approached Uni-Cardan, which they recognised as a world leader in the technology. Uni-Cardan saw its chance to plant a Trojan Horse in NTN's backyard, and grabbed it.

"Uni-Cardan was quite shrewd," Bonner said. "It told the OEMs, 'We are not prepared to put another competitor into the business, but we will grant a licence to you, Mr Customer, to produce our products under licence.' That enabled Uni-Cardan to obtain long-term supply agreements in exchange for licences." In the late 1970s, Uni-Cardan did that with Toyota and Nissan; in the early 1980s, it made a similar agreement with Honda.

Uni-Cardan granted all of them full production rights in Japan – but it added a rider: if any of the OEM licensees subsequently started production outside Japan, they committed to buy from Uni-Cardan. "You could see by then that some transplant production was going to happen," said Bonner.

At the same time, GKN as a group had been building a footprint in Japan. It had been present there since the Sixties, with two offices in Osaka and Tokyo established as a trading post for fasteners. But in the late 1970s, GKN upgraded these into fully-fledged representation and customer interface operations for its automotive business.

"For a Western manufacturer, we realised quite early on the importance of the Japanese," said Bonner. "The licensing deals and our local presence – deliberately not a manufacturing presence – created the platform for us to develop a relationship with the Japanese OEMs. That in turn opened the door for us to become the supplier of choice to the transplants as they began to appear on the scene both in North America and Europe in the Eighties."

As head of first Uni-Cardan and then GKN's whole driveline business, Bonner was a regular visitor. "Between about 1981 and 1986, I personally would have gone to Japan at least twice a year, even when there was no pressing need," he recalled. "It was just to put our face in front of Toyota, Nissan and Honda, to keep a dialogue going and to make them aware of our development, both technical and geographical."

Crucially, GKN's Japanese drive was supported by two of the most senior directors: Holdsworth travelled there frequently and, after his retirement, served on the British government's UK-Japan 2000 group of industrialists. Ian Donald, then deputy managing director, saw the growing

importance of Japan very early and was extremely supportive of Bonner's business-building efforts.

Outside Japan, GKN benefited most from its patient
relationship-building through the Japanese expansion in
North America. "The Japanese marques had developed a
stronger position in the US earlier," said Bonner. "The
transplants were more important to GKN in the US."

This was partly because of the scale of the volumes,
compared with the European transplants, and partly
because – despite its early link with Chrysler and its close
relationship with Ford – GKN never established the kind
of presence with the Big Three as a whole that it enjoyed
in Europe. GM, the largest US car maker, actually owned
an in-house CVJ producer, which was GKN's main competitor in the American market.

Nevertheless, GKN's success with the Japanese in
Britain had a symbolic and historical significance which
the US inevitably lacked. In January 1984, after a campaign lasting at least two years, the British government
secured Nissan's agreement to build a transplant in the
UK. Although no-one in the Thatcher government dared
mention the phrase, this was in fact a triumph for industrial strategy and interventionism.

Without the government's commitment, including
that of the Prime Minister herself, and without its money
– £125 m in aid out of a total project cost of £350 m –
Nissan would almost certainly not have picked Britain as
the location for its first car plant in Western Europe.

Following the strategy it had pursued in the US, Nissan
chose a site in Washington, near Sunderland Airport –
far from the UK's own West Midlands motown. And,

honouring the commitment it had made to Uni-Cardan, it selected GKN as sole supplier of CVJs for the models it built there. Nissan was followed by Honda, which converted an engine factory at Swindon into a full-scale car transplant, and then by Toyota. GKN was contracted as sole supplier to both of them.

The impact of the Japanese transplants was everything that the Thatcher government had hoped for. While the British car industry faded out – its home-owned brands and plants were sold in the late 1980s and 1990s to Ford, BMW, Peugeot and Volkswagen – the car industry in Britain was reborn.

By 1997, the Japanese trio accounted for almost 40% of total car exports from the UK. In that year, UK passenger car output reached almost 1.7 m vehicles – the highest level for a quarter of a century. Like other British-based suppliers, GKN's UK driveline operations gained a new lease of life thanks to the Japanese transplants.

Under Bonner, the increasingly integrated driveline operation also developed a cultural affinity with the Japanese. Toyota, Nissan and their peers brought to their Lean manufacturing philosophy the concept of kaizen – continuous improvement in products and processes. Kaizen had originally been inspired by an American, W. Edwards Deming, whose teaching on manufacturing quality and productivity had been religiously adopted by Japanese industry after World War Two. It became a pillar of the famous Toyota Production System, probably the most efficient production system since Henry Ford invented the assembly line.

Ironically, given Deming's nationality, the vehicle makers of his native country largely ignored what he advocated – until the Japanese began to eat their lunch. The Anglo-Saxon preference was for the far more dramatic quantum leap, the idea that a new technology or product innovation would lift a company to the next level. Kaizen was a far less ostentatious form of progress, but much more dependable if executed properly.

The constant velocity joint owed its success in the 1960s to a Western-style "event" – the front wheel drive breakthrough by Issigonis on the Mini. But by the early 1980s, GKN's CVJ operations had ingrained into their *modus operandi* a culture of continuous improvement. In their different areas of specialism, the Uni-Cardan companies Lohr & Bromkamp, Glaenzer Spicer and Birfield Trasmissioni invested consistently in incremental improvement to both the joints themselves and their methods of manufacture.

In 1985, for instance, Uni-Cardan introduced a new fixed ball-joint, known as the "undercut-free joint" which was capable of operating at maximum angles up to 50 degrees – thereby improving turning-circles – and a new plunging tripod-joint which reduced NVH (noise, vibration and harshness).

The same philosophy was inculcated into Hardy Spicer, which consistently refined its CVJ designs and manufacturing processes. The size and weight of the joints were repeatedly refined, saving materials and cutting fuel consumption in the vehicle. At about the same time, at the Birmingham factory, a purpose-designed flow line was introduced, including robots and employees whose job demarcations had been scrapped.

The expansion of driveline into the US and Japan meant that in 1984 almost three-quarters of GKN's motor component sales were to non-UK customers. The figure reflected the internationalisation of GKN – that year, for the first time, non-UK sales exceeded 60% of the group total of £2.16 billion. After five years' hard labour, trading profits at last passed the pre-recession peak, reaching £143 m.

"In any business with as long a history as GKN, there will almost certainly have been a number of periods of reformation and renaissance preceding a new surge forward," Holdsworth declaimed. "I believe that 1980–84 will prove to have been such a period. GKN has been transformed from a business with the crude designation of a "Midlands metal-basher" into a world leader in innovation and development of sophisticated new engineering products and in the use of the most advanced technology in design and production."

The group was also pushing ahead with expansion in industrial services and distribution, which accounted for just over half group sales by 1985. It had trebled the original size of Parts Industries, including the 1984 acquisition of Beck/Arnley which enlarged the imported parts side. It was also branching out into other areas of the US aftermarket, buying Meineke Discount Muffler Shops, America's second-largest exhaust repair and refit chain which had 400 franchised outlets.

In Industrial Services and Supplies, it created a major UK building services and scaffolding operation by merging

GKN Mills with the Kwikform subsidiary of the building group Costain to form GKN Kwikform. GKN took 60% of the venture, Costain the balance. It subsequently concluded a parallel deal to establish the new venture in Australia.

Defence was still developing rapidly: in 1985, Sankey clinched the full contract for 1048 Warriors, valued at about £500 m – one of the largest single contracts in the group's history.

The drive to expand in automotive components also continued, with two significant moves. One was a rare example of a product which GKN effectively invented: the Composite Leaf Spring. The leaf spring was a glass fibre-reinforced composite road spring which offered significant advantages to vehicle-makers in terms of weight (and therefore fuel) savings and durability. It took seven years to bring to pilot production and GKN now built a manufacturing facility at the Sankey site at Telford. Hopes for the CLS were high. GKN went on to form a joint venture called Translite KK in Japan, where there had been considerable early interest in the product; it held 60% and Mitsubishi Steel held the rest.

Contemporaneously, Uni-Cardan formed a 50–50 joint venture called Viscodrive with the German transmission components maker ZF, to develop and sell another innovative product, the viscous coupling. Within three years, Viscodrive became wholly owned by GKN. This coupling was designed for four-wheel drive vehicles, or as limited slip differentials on front or rear wheel drive cars. GKN and ZF very quickly took Viscodrive into Japan through a joint venture with a Japanese partner, Tochigi

Fuji Sangyo (TFS), in which GKN held 51%. It was the first Japanese manufacturing venture in which GKN had been involved.

Other initiatives were somewhat less ground-breaking. One – in which GKN took such pride that it launched a UK national advertising campaign around it – was a decision to tender to the recently-privatised British Telecommunications for a contract to build a new generation of pay telephone boxes to replace the venerable red boxes. GKN won the contract, which was undertaken by Sankey. The point of the ad campaign was to highlight how the group was changing and diversifying. In fact, the contract was redolent of the old, steel-led, vertically-integrated metal-basher. Eventually, the ad campaign was quietly dropped.

In 1985, a few months after the payphone contract win, a much more meaningful symbol of the new group emerged. As Holdsworth told shareholders: "To crystallise the transformation which has taken place in the composition of the group's businesses over the last two decades, we think it appropriate and timely to propose a change in the company name to GKN plc.

"The names 'Guest', 'Keen' and 'Nettlefolds' are historically linked with businesses in steel, bolts and nuts and fasteners which have all now ceased to be part of our mainstream strategy," Holdsworth said. "We are now known universally as GKN and the change of name will not only recognise this, but also underline the new direction which the Group has taken."

After 83 years, the decision was a landmark moment. At the time, there was a growing trend in the UK for companies to adopt initials instead of names, but GKN's switch went well beyond mere fashion. As Holdsworth said, it reflected the fundamental change in the nature of the business away from its historic constituents.

Control of the last two of those historic businesses – Steel and Fasteners – now passed to other companies. What remained of Fasteners in the UK and mainland Europe was the subject of a clean, albeit somewhat costly break, part of the dissolution of the General Industries division. The Fasteners and Hardware Distribution Division, as it was now called, was sold to management buyouts along with two other small subsidiaries from General Industries. The total proceeds were £38.9 m, but Fasteners was sold at a loss of more than £12 m.

For GKN, this was a small price to pay for the disposal of what was now officially a "strategically peripheral" business. After decades of struggling to hold back the advance of low-cost – and increasingly higher quality – imports from emerging markets, Fasteners had at last been overwhelmed.

Like other British industries, Fasteners had lived long, profitably and complacently on the basis that it dominated a captive, cartelised market. When that market was consigned to history by the competition authorities, Fasteners found itself plunged into a new world with which it was not equipped to cope. It had become an anachronism, its exit from GKN the subject of a few lines in the annual report. They were not much of an epitaph.

Other symbolic changes were taking place. Holdsworth had already moved the annual meeting from its historic home in Smethwick to a hotel in London's West End. He also relocated the London "headquarters" from Kingsway to Cleveland Row, near Queen Elizabeth the Queen Mother's home, Clarence House. Then, in mid-1984, the group's administrative headquarters was moved from Smethwick where it had resided since the creation of Guest Keen, to Ipsley House in Redditch. GKN now operated a dual headquarters, with its strategic base in London.

Kingsway was a classic Sixties corporate office, but it was also a manifestation of long-standing custom and practice. This, in the boardroom and in the City, was still the age of the long lunch. Fortnum & Mason did the catering at Kingsway: "There were no sandwiches in those days – it was five courses or nothing," recalled one Kingsway denizen.

The building became an anachronism because of the recession and GKN's radical reshaping. "With Kingsway, the concept was that we would gather under one roof all these offices of the various different businesses in London," said Tony George, who joined GKN in 1970 as deputy company secretary to Mike Chester, and succeeded him in 1987. "But they all hated this idea. We acquired the office and fitted it out at great expense – mahogany panelling, expensive flooring etc."

The offices at 7 Cleveland Row had been owned by Firth Cleveland. But its discreet, elegant and slightly old-fashioned ambience evoked the heritage of GKN. The wood-panelled rooms were appropriate hosts to oil paintings from the age of John Guest. The Victorian lift was a genuine working antique. All in all, the office exuded a calm, low-profile, businesslike approach which personified the character of the remodelled GKN. It remained GKN's

London base until 2008, when the group moved to smaller offices in Pall Mall while reinforcing Redditch's position as its headquarters.

The pictures of 19th century steel-making on the Cleveland Row office walls outlasted the group's involvement with the actual business. In 1985, GKN concluded an agreement with British Steel to form a joint venture in engineering and special steels and forgings to be called United Engineering Steels (UES), in which GKN would initially hold a 39.1% minority stake. It had taken the best part of two years to finalise the venture, codenamed Phoenix II, which was completed in March 1986. GKN's contribution to UES was Brymbo and its forgings operations, including Garringtons and Smith Clayton.

Holdsworth, no doubt mindful of his argument with Brookes about whether the group should return to steel-making, saw the deal as epitomising his long-held and painstakingly-pursued strategy of exiting commodity manufacturing. Lees recalled: "The Phoenixes were quite an inspired way of divestment because the companies that GKN owned at the time were rather like house-builders in the 2008 recession – they were just unsaleable. Yet they were going nowhere – indeed some of them were in serious danger of running into losses.

"The cost of closing them would have been horrendous – hundreds of millions, I guess. Privatisation was the political order of the day, and these Joint Ventures with British Steel represented privatisation, even though British Steel was still a stakeholder [it was eventually privatised on 5 December 1988]. And they proved to be great successes because the operations became efficient; there was a better balance of demand and capacity." In other words, they lived up to the Phoenix tag.

"The ventures were not transformational, because the strategy was clear – we had to be out of them," Lees said. "But the methodology was innovative. People think of joint ventures typically as a way into businesses, but they can also be a way out of businesses. The Phoenixes were good examples of an exit strategy and it worked."

Lees himself was emerging as the leader of a new generation top management team. Bonner joined the board in January 1985 and was followed a year later by four new directors: Daly, Jessop, Michael Borlenghi – head of strategic and business development – and Brian Insch, son of James, who was already a GKN veteran having joined the group in 1963. He had oversight of all the group's continuing interests in steel. This group was clearly being positioned to lead GKN into the 1990s.

For the moment, Holdsworth, Roberts and Donald continued to drive the international reshaping strategy. In 1986, GKN disengaged from steel services, selling the steel stockholding subsidiary for just over £50 m, taking a loss on the disposal of £10 m. In Germany, Uni-Cardan formed a joint venture called Emitec with Interatom, part of the German electrical and electronics giant Siemens, to make metal substrates for catalytic converters, now a fast-growing market.

GKN also established itself as a leader in the UK vending services market by buying British Vending Industries, a move which doubled the size of its vending services business. And, in a further sign of its commitment to growing industrial services, it formed a joint venture with the British drain-cleaning company Dyno-Rod to start a similar business in the US, with GKN holding 60%.

But at the same time, GKN encountered a setback in one of its core future growth businesses – autoparts distribution. It was a harbinger of problems to come with the diversification into services.

# CHAPTER 20

# An Era Ends

The problems became apparent in early August 1986 when Holdsworth unveiled the group's interim results. As usual in such instances, it was not the numbers for the period just ended that worried the market – it was the outlook for the second half. To the City's dismay, the GKN chairman revealed that the group now expected full-year profits would be at a standstill compared with those of 1985. In other words, GKN would suffer a profits downturn in the second half.

Inevitably, the shares plunged – and stayed down. Early in 1987, the group was evicted – temporarily – from the FTSE 100 Index of Britain's largest companies, the first time it had suffered such an indignity.

Several factors were at play: the American driveline business had won new, long-term contracts from established customers, but at the cost of lowering its prices. As a result, initial profitability was lower than under the previous contracts. OffHighway was hit by a significant fall in demand from European agricultural markets. A sharp fall in UK commercial vehicle output impacted Sankey.

These problems were either temporary or due to external and cyclical factors. The Autoparts problems were more worrying, because they seemed more structural. Annual profits in the distribution division halved to £11 m because of problems in the US and UK autoparts business.

For the first time since its acquisition seven years earlier, Parts Industries delivered no real sales growth. Meanwhile, the imported parts operation, bringing in replacement parts for the growing Japanese vehicle parc, was pummelled by a slump in the value of the dollar against the yen, an exchange rate change which was clearly not going to reverse overnight. In Britain, GKN reported that the market "remained very difficult". Autoparts France had to be restructured, at substantial cost.

It took GKN's shares the best part of a year to recover their level immediately before the profit warning. When they did pick up, in mid-1987, the recovery was partly due to speculation about a possible takeover bid for the group. As is sometimes the way in the City, the market had got hold of the right story at the wrong time.

Months earlier, Holdsworth and his board had indeed considered a megadeal. They had approached Lucas Industries, Britain's other major motor components manufacturer, about a merger. In theory, Lucas was ahead of GKN on the value curve, since its products, such as braking systems, were beginning to move into the higher-growth area of electronics.

GKN executives were beginning to think that they would have to take the automotive components portfolio into the ostensibly high-growth area of electronic systems. Analysts thought so too, because there was a general expectation that CVJs would run out of growth at some point in the not-too-distant future.

A GKN–Lucas merger would have created a group with annual sales of more than £3.5 billion. Moreover, it would almost certainly have passed scrutiny by the Office of Fair Trading because there was no product overlap between the two groups. But after studying the GKN proposal, Lucas decided against pursuing it. The idea was dropped and the two companies went their own ways. A decade later, Lucas merged with the American company Varity and the enlarged LucasVarity was subsequently taken over by TRW, the American engineering group.

With the Lucas plan abandoned, GKN now set about expanding entirely under its own steam. Its first significant attempt, however, ended in disappointment. The Ministry of Defence, impressed with GKN's performance on Warrior and Saxon, asked whether the group wanted to bid for Royal Ordnance (RO), its own vehicles and munitions company which was up for privatisation.

RO was not deemed suitable for a stock market float, so the hunt was on for a trade buyer. GKN was indeed interested. It assembled a bid of £160 m for the business. This was a hefty amount considering that the group's stock market value at the time was less than £900 m. The rationale was that, while the UK market was very low-growth, in the right hands RO could be built into a serious export contract winner. In the event, this hope proved somewhat illusory. "We were quite a force in fighting vehicles at the time," said Lees. "That was really our claim to market knowledge, if that's the right word in the defence industry."

However, there was a catch. Or rather, two catches. First, the MoD wanted the quickest sale it could get. GKN's bid was going to take some time, because the price of RO meant it would be a "Class 1" transaction, requiring a special meeting of shareholders to approve the deal. The other catch was that GKN had a rival – the former state-owned British Aerospace. BAe was much bigger than GKN, so it could afford to outbid the group and buy RO on the spot without needing shareholder approval.

An auction ensued, run by the MoD's John Bourne, who later became the highly-respected Comptroller-General of the National Audit Office. "Came the hour, and he ran a parallel contract procedure," said Lees. "We both had contracts, both were marked up and we both made bids. People worked all day and night getting these contracts sorted. The day came – and we lost: we were outbid."

BAe paid £190 m for RO. For the best part of two decades, the business struggled to make a good return, but – when BAe finally managed to consolidate the entire UK armoured vehicles market under its control – the deal at last paid off. GKN played a part in that end game too. "I don't think it was a great loss for us," said Lees. "I doubt we would have won any more exports than BAe did." The experience, however, was not lost on GKN. Planning an acquisition in the defence arena and learning how to handle contacts with the MoD in those circumstances proved to be useful additions to the corporate skill set.

Despite the RO defeat and continuing underperformance by Autoparts, Holdsworth's eight years as chairman and his quarter-century in the company ended on a high note. Pre-tax profits in 1987, the last full year of his chairmanship, were an all-time record of £146.5 m; RoNA reached 16.6%, earnings per share climbed to 34.7 p and the dividend was raised to 14.5 p, further banishing memories of the 1980 cut.

Fittingly, Holdsworth's last 12 months contained a number of signature moments – projections of the strategy that he had put in place and pursued with such consistency, not just as chairman but in the years leading up to his assumption of that role.

The group sold its stake in Allied Steel & Wire for £84 m, leaving only the minority holdings in Bright Bar and UES as the last vestiges of its interest in steel.

CHEP UK achieved its highest annual growth rate ever, increasing the pool by more than one million additional pallets. CHEP Europe approached the five million pallet mark and opened for business in Spain. GKN bought out the minority shareholdings in Kwikform Industries in Australia and took full control. In the UK, the vending business expanded further by acquiring a coffee service firm.

At Sankey, Daly concluded a joint venture, called Venture Pressings (VP), with Sir John Egan's privatised and revitalised Jaguar company to produce all body pressings for Jaguar and Daimler models from 1991. Following the takeover of Jaguar by Ford, the company was sold by the joint venture partners. On the other side of the slate,

GKN sold Vandervell for just under £13 m, concluding the attempt to develop an international engine components business that had climaxed with the AE bid.

Above all, the driveline business under Bonner continued its global advance with a welter of incremental steps on numerous fronts. The US operation not only won orders from Toyota and Honda's transplants, but secured a breakthrough order to export driveshafts from Alamance to Toyota in Japan – the first time a US-based GKN subsidiary had won an export order there.

In mainland Europe, the motor components business was extended in December 1987 when Uni-Cardan bought ZF out of Viscodrive and took full control of the business. In the UK, Hardy Spicer began deliveries to the Nissan Sunderland factory. A Taiwanese associate, in which GKN held 20%, started CVJ production. In Australia, GKN bought 30% of the joint maker Unidrive. It doubled its holding in its Spanish driveshaft business to 40%. And it increased its holding in Uni-Cardan itself by acquiring another 10.2% for almost £38 m, bringing its shareholding to 96.7%.

Then, in March 1988, Uni-Cardan made its first move into China by forming a joint venture, Shanghai GKN Driveshaft Company, with Shanghai Automotive Industries Corporation (SAIC). This prescient step was the result of Bonner's "Follow the Customer" principle: Volkswagen, one of Uni-Cardan's biggest customers, had decided to build a factory in the People's Republic and wanted its key suppliers to support it. GKN was the first global automotive component supplier to establish a manufacturing presence in China.

GKN agreed to inject its CVJ technology into the partnership with SAIC, and to improve and expand the universal joint and propshaft activities that SAIC contributed. It was the start of a long and increasingly important relationship. Five months later, GKN established a CVJ joint venture in India, Invel Transmissions, in which it took a 40% share.

Uni-Cardan had held a minority stake in a Brazilian CVJ operation since 1973, so – almost two decades ahead of its time – driveline now had bridgeheads in three of the four great emerging markets later acroynmed BRIC: Brazil, Russia, India and China. Russia was closed for the moment, but even when it opened up after the fall of the Berlin Wall, Bonner remained wary of going there. "It was about weighing risk and opportunities," he said. Most of the stakes were minority ones because that was what the relevant governments demanded.

"We set up joint ventures partly because we had to, given the laws and regulations in most of these countries at the time," said Bonner. In Mexico, where in 1981 Uni-Cardan had started Velcon, a 25%-owned CVJ joint venture, foreign companies were not allowed to have more than 25% of the equity; in China and India the limit was 50%. "So we needed partners for that reason, and also because we had little local knowledge. We had the product and production technology and the customer interface, but we didn't really know how to operate in those countries."

As with Uni-Cardan itself, Bonner had every intention of increasing those stakes when the opportunity arose as government limits were relaxed. The global network, like the CVJs themselves, was being developed on the kaizen principle – step by step, by continuous improvement. "I think we would claim to be the most international automotive supplier in the world," Holdsworth said on the eve of his retirement.

Managing the succession – the hardest of all tasks for successful, long-standing chairmen – was the final challenge. Holdsworth interviewed the six next-generation directors – Lees, Bonner, Daly, Jessop, Insch and Borlenghi – and asked each of them one question: excluding himself, who did the interviewee think should be Chairman? Lees was the overwhelming – in fact, the unanimous – choice.

But the succession involved more than simply identifying a new chairman. Roy Roberts and Ian Donald were retiring at the same time. There was no single obvious successor for Roberts, who had proved an outstanding hands-on managing director, complementing Holdsworth's more intellectual approach.

So Holdsworth, with impeccable intellectual logic, replaced the structure that he had created. In its stead, there would be a chairman and three managing directors, Bonner, Daly and Jessop, each with responsibility for his particular part of the business. Borlenghi and Insch, who now became Human Resources director, together with Brian Walsh, who was recruited to succeed Lees as finance director, completed the new team. All told, it was a fundamental passing of the baton – one of the most extensive management transitions, outside of the early 20th century mergers, that GKN had implemented.

The curtain fell on a momentous and tempestuous era – momentous because of the transformation the group had undergone under Holdsworth's leadership, tempestuous because of the extreme macro-economic environment in which that transformation was executed: "Driven both by unfavourable economic forces and our own strategic necessity, these eight years have been a period of quite exceptional change," Holdsworth reflected. "I think we've completed, as much as anyone ever completed anything, the total break by GKN from its 200-year history."

CHAPTER 21

# A Stake in Westland

Sir David Lees (he was knighted in 1991) was chairman of GKN for 16 years and is a towering figure in the history of the group. Longevity alone would give him a certain distinction – he was the longest-serving active chairman since Sir John Guest, albeit in a non-executive capacity for just under half his tenure.

However, it is what Lees achieved and the degree of change he oversaw that distinguishes him. If Holdsworth engineered the strategic break from GKN's past and began the process of sweeping change, it was Lees who carried that incipient transformation through to fulfilment.

Lees was systematic, logical, objective, pragmatic, consistent, unsentimental and, perhaps above all, totally determined – hallmarks both personal and in keeping with the corporate grain. "The group might have exited the steel business, but David Lees made up for that: he had the steel to drive the further change we needed," said one former executive.

As Finance Director, Lees had already demonstrated his readiness to set new standards of effectiveness by jettisoning customs and practices which had outlived their usefulness. The stockbroker's lunch was, at that time, a City institution. Such lunches were organised by a securities house and attended by company management on one side and "buy-side" fund managers from different institutions on the other. The standard and seniority of the institutional representatives varied wildly, to the frequent frustration of the company and some of the other institutional guests. Moreover, the company had no say in targeting particular fund managers with whom it wanted to talk.

In December 1986, after one wasted lunch too many, Lees decided to ditch these events. Instead, GKN would go direct to the buy-side – in the first instance, to its own shareholders, later to non-holders. The move was immediately and widely misinterpreted as a decision by the group to stop talking to the City. In fact, it blazed a trail which was subsequently followed by many other companies until it became the new norm.

Each year, Lees would see GKN's top 10 institutional shareholders individually and the next rank of significant holders in groups of five or six. As a result, by the time he succeeded Holdsworth, he had put in place a system which meant that, every year, the company was meeting holders of more than half its shares face-to-face. Widespread adoption of this practice went a long way to bridging the communications gap between management and owner which had bedevilled British industry for decades. The science of investor relations was born.

Lees brought a similar clear-headedness to running the group. "We had a very logical management structure," he said. "I relied heavily on the three business heads [Bonner, Jessop and Daly]. Basically, I saw my expertise as strategy and numbers. I would have meetings every month with the three individually, with the Finance Director [initially Brian Walsh, later David Turner] at my side. We'd go through a lot of the detail. I think it worked because the governance pressures then weren't as great as they are today. You spent a certain amount of time with shareholders and the media, but still had enough to run the business that way."

Lees took over with some firm objectives. "I certainly believed that the group needed to focus much better and as quickly as made sense," he recalled. "The internationalisation was clearly very important. Our US involvement was still pretty small and our Japanese involvement was only just beginning. I was profit and cash driven. The strategic track was to do a lot of acquisitions in our core businesses and a lot of divestments in the non-core ones."

Holdsworth had been pitched into the deep end within months of becoming chairman because of the UK recession. Lees faced a different kind of early challenge – to explain to a surprised market why the group was making a dramatic move into a new sector.

The first inkling the outside world had about this momentous step was in October, barely five months after Lees had become chairman. GKN announced that it had paid £47.8 m for a stake of 22.02% in the military and civil helicopter manufacturer Westland Group.

This was national news, thanks to the famous, or infamous, Westland Crisis three years earlier – a political furore which almost brought about the downfall of Mrs Thatcher.

The origins of that crisis lay in a collapse of the helicopter market in the early 1980s. Westland, a relatively small player in the global business, was exposed to the point that its order book from 1986 through the rest of the decade was left completely empty. From the early 1990s, it stood to gain substantial orders for the new EH101 helicopter that it was developing for both the Royal Navy and the RAF. But the chances were increasing that Westland would not survive to build the EH101.

By July 1985, the future of the company was clearly at stake and the government backed the replacement of Westland's then chairman, Sir Basil Blackwell, by Sir John Cuckney. Cuckney was a former MI5 stalwart and an outstanding business troubleshooter.

Having helped to install Cuckney, the government – in its classic non-interventionist, hands-off style – left him to find a self-help solution to fill Westland's looming orders black hole. Cuckney later recalled: "One was told at the time that the MoD didn't mind if Westland went bust. And the Department of Trade and Industry [DTI] weren't prepared to fund Westland in any way." He went to Mrs Thatcher, and was bluntly informed that Westland "was a private sector problem and it was on its own".

This, Cuckney said, "concentrated the mind wonderfully. Emotionally, one felt an inevitable degree of patriotism about Westland, because it was a defence company and this was of course after the Falklands War [in which its aircraft had served with distinction]. One felt jingoistic about it in a number of respects, and it was very sobering to be told these things."

So Cuckney went to the market and found his own answer in the nick of time – Westland was by now on the brink of financial collapse. His chosen partner was Sikorsky, the helicopter arm of United Technologies Corporation (UTC) which was one of the industry leaders. "Once you've been told it's totally a private sector problem, your concern is the shareholders, the banks, the employees, the customers," he said.

"It didn't matter to me whether the [rescue] participants were Guatemalan, Korean or what. If you have 11,000 employees and you know that the moment you make your next preliminary results announcement, you are bust, then you want to get the best agreement, fully underwritten and legally binding, that you can in the time available. In those days, you announced your financial results at 9.30 am. The final meeting with the support banks was concluded at 4.30 am."

UTC/Sikorsky agreed to take a significant minority stake in Westland in return for injecting fresh capital into the group, guaranteeing a sufficient level of production to keep the workforce going, and licensing the company to build and sell its own Black Hawk helicopter in Europe and certain other markets. The deal would be mutually beneficial – Westland would be saved and Sikorsky would gain a platform into the European market. Late in 1985, Italy's Fiat joined UTC in what thus became a consortium to save Westland.

Rival European helicopter firms, who had previously shown no interest in preventing Westland going to the wall, now jumped into action. Germany's MBB and Aerospatiale of France enlisted the support of Britain's BAe and GEC and cobbled together a rival rescue package. This would almost certainly have fallen rapidly and quietly by the wayside – Cuckney viewed it as clearly inferior to the well-defined UTC/Fiat offer – had it not been taken up and championed by Michael Heseltine, the pro-European Defence Secretary who regarded Westland as an acid test for European defence collaboration.

Heseltine's support for the European consortium put him directly at odds with Thatcher and with Leon Brittan, the DTI Secretary, both of whom backed Cuckney's UTC/ Fiat deal. Westland was transformed at a stroke from an industrial issue into a Cabinet battle of nuclear proportions which made front-page news and broadcast headlines for days on end. Early in 1986, the ferocious conflict culminated in the resignations of both Heseltine and Brittan while Thatcher only just survived a House of Commons debate which could have brought her down.

When the smoke cleared and the casualties had departed the political battlefield, UTC and Fiat emerged with about 7.5% apiece of Westland's ordinary voting shares. The two also owned some of Westland's class of preferred voting shares.

This meant that, if the preference shares were converted into ordinary, UTC and Fiat together would each own just under 15% – making a combined total of 29.9% of Westland. This was the maximum allowed under Britain's Takeover Code before the companies would be required to launch a full takeover bid. The rest of the share register was a strange amalgam of conventional fund managers such as M&G and Schroders and others, notably the giant industrial conglomerate Hanson, whose chairman Lord Hanson was an arch-Thatcherite and had bought a 14.6% stake to support the UTC/Fiat offer.

The deal worked – Westland was saved and obtained enough work to keep it going until the EH101 was due to come on stream. A footnote to the battle went completely unremarked at the time, except at GKN: "One day, at the height of the row, Michael Heseltine came into lunch in our boardroom," recalled Daly. "He got up about six times during the meal to speak to his German counterpart about Westland."

Now, as Westland settled down under its new ownership structure, GKN was doing some thinking. Lees believed that, while the group should focus on its core businesses, that core should include another major activity. That meant either buying a business which would be completely new to the group – a risky proposition – or building one of the existing smaller operations into something much more substantial.

"The main motivation for buying into Westland was that I was always quite keen on the third leg strategy," he recounted. "I've always felt that three legs to a business was about the limit you could achieve without conglomeration." GKN had automotive and industrial services. Daly recalled: "We were always looking for something else. One day, David Lees said to me that the notion that we should get bigger in Defence was a good one."

GKN's defence business had annual sales at the time of about £100 m – about 5% of the group total. Certainly there was scope for growth. There was also, Daly maintained, the opportunity to make a decent return. This view derived from the group's experience in the Warrior competition. Just as Daly had concluded that bringing motor industry disciplines to Sankey's bid would give GKN an edge over the traditional armoured vehicle makers, so the group believed that it could add significant value through an acquisition at the macro, corporate level.

"Cost-plus had ingrained a certain culture of management and mind-set," said Daly. "The notion that you would do something with 70 men instead of 100 was anathema – you wanted to say you needed 150 because you then got your cost-plus on 150. That permeated everything. If you could get hold of a defence company, we reckoned we could tear costs out like there was no tomorrow."

Daly was assigned the task of identifying the right target. Because GKN was new to the industry, it hired the consultancy firm Arthur D. Little, although the group did much of the work itself. "The search was not massively cerebral. It had to be a British defence company and when you went through the UK list, it was pretty short: Vickers, VSEL [the Barrow-based submarine builder], United Scientific Holdings/Alvis, Westland. They were the only games in town," Daly recounted.

The shortlist was rapidly shortened. Neither Lees – son of a Rear-Admiral – nor Daly had the slightest interest in VSEL: "You could forget about submarines – we didn't want to get into that," said Daly. "And we concluded that the tank had basically had its day, in the sense that no-one was going to buy tanks in the future in great numbers – we were also told that by defence experts to whom we spoke." That was Vickers. As for USH/Alvis, it largely duplicated what GKN Defence already had.

"We had a lot of advice on future defence scenarios, and the one thing that kept coming up was the Rapid Reaction Force concept. The view was that future conflict would either be mega – nuclear war – or small-scale, requiring, in equipment terms, Warriors, tanks and helicopters," said Daly. "So Westland came on the scene."

Daly's team researched Westland further. "Initially, there was no logic to it other than that it was another defence company," he said. Then GKN started talking to Westland itself. "I went round it a few times and could see the scope for efficiency improvement. So if we could get it for a price deemed by the GKN number-crunchers as good, then we would be able to take a lot of costs out. But we had to make a complete case for it. Above all, we had to deal with the 'What's a Warrior got to do with a helicopter?' argument."

From their work on the Rapid Reaction Force, Daly and his team developed the concept of "Battlefield Mobility" – the interactivity and complementarity of quickly-deployable armoured fighting vehicles and helicopters. At the time, some analysts were sceptical about this argument, but Lees maintained that "it was market-led" and subsequent conflicts – the 1990 Gulf War and the Balkan war later in the decade – vindicated the group. The Warrior communications systems had to talk to helicopters, so that was another synergy. And Westland had a good relationship with Italy's helicopter maker Agusta, which GKN respected for its engineering capability.

As they looked even closer, Daly's team discovered another aspect of Westland that was interesting: it had a small business on the Isle of Wight with an offshoot at the main Yeovil helicopter plant which specialised in composite structures – new materials which could be used to replace traditional aerospace metals such as titanium in the wings or the engine. GKN was working on composite technologies at its technology centre at Wolverhampton, where it had a significant number of materials engineers. "When we understood a bit more about Westland's composite business, we recognised there was potential there," said Lees.

By now, Daly had more than enough information to make a good business case for an acquisition. "I did a full-scale presentation to the board, but there was a lot of nervousness about it," he said. The board made its decision: instead of taking the plunge and launching a full takeover attempt, it would dip a foot in the Westland water by taking a minority stake and seeking boardroom representation. That way, it could learn much more about the business before deciding whether to go the whole way.

GKN prepared with care. The group did the rounds in Whitehall, talking particularly to the MoD to ensure that it was onside. Ministers and officials were supportive – the credit GKN was earning from Warrior again served it well. Next, executives identified the shareholders who were likely to sell. The two most obvious were Hanson and Fiat.

In June 1988, Fiat formally announced that it wanted to sell its Westland stake, and added that it was in discussions with UTC, which had a right of first refusal under the terms of the original partnership between the two groups. But when GKN emerged, UTC made clear that it was happy to stay where it was.

With Fiat's stake available, Lees lined up a deal with Hanson to acquire its holding. The structure was slightly complex: "We took Hanson's stake by way of an option deal," Lees recalled. "The money lay in the option and the option was exercisable for £1. I went along to Lord Hanson's Knightsbridge offices to sign the contract to exercise the option. I'd heard a lot about Hanson and I thought, for a joke, because it was a £1 consideration, I would give him a pound." The joke fell somewhat flat, because Hanson did not get it. "He didn't know what to do with the coin. Eventually, he called the company secretary, and solemnly gave him the pound."

So GKN had its 22.02%. The price the group paid effectively valued Westland at almost £240 m – more than double its actual market worth. Some observers, surprised by the valuation, reckoned it reflected GKN's determination not to be outbid, as it had been over Royal Ordnance. That loss, however, was very much GKN's gain now. "BAe might have come in," said Daly. "But they had their hands full with RO and anyway, they didn't have the appetite for Westland."

As far as Lees and Daly were concerned, it was a price worth paying. They now had an effective option to take over Westland – UTC clearly did not intend to make a full bid, and was a potential seller at the right time on the right terms. And they had an inside track.

As Westland's largest single shareholder, GKN negotiated the right to appoint two directors to the company's board. One was Daly, who became deputy chairman. Daly deliberately invited Walsh to join him. "Brian was also ex-Ford and he was a really good finance guy. He was also a massive sceptic about Westland. I knew that, if he came along with me, then we would eventually do it."

In the event, it was more than five years before GKN made its end-game moves. They were five epoch-making years – years that changed the world in which GKN did business.

# CHAPTER 22

# Reformation

The acquisition of the Westland stake continued the transformation of GKN's portfolio. But Lees soon demonstrated
that reformation was also on his agenda.

His first focus was the Autoparts empire that GKN had
built so rapidly, but which was now underperforming,
particularly in the US. Initial analysis led to the conclusion
that the US domestic parts distribution was sound, and
should be expanded further. So within months of the
change of chairmanship, GKN expanded its American
network by acquiring Mid-America Industries for £9.2 m.
Meineke also seemed to be meeting expectations, and
continued to grow. By the end of 1988, it had more than
750 outlets.

The imported parts side was a different matter. It continued to suffer from the impact of the weakening dollar
on the price competitiveness of foreign components. In
September 1988, barely four years after it was acquired,
Beck/Arnley was sold along with the rest of the business

for just under £30 m. The following year, the UK autoparts distribution business followed it out of the group in a £30 m sale, including property assets.

Symbolically, the most significant early step of the Lees regime was to list GKN's shares on the Tokyo Stock Exchange. No-one at GKN expected this to open a channel for substantial Japanese investment in the company's stock, but it was viewed as a way to reinforce the increasingly close relationship that the group was developing with the country's leading car makers. Sales to Japanese car makers worldwide, which had been only £1 m in 1986, reached £70 m in 1989 and accelerated thereafter.

Lees continued to trim the industrial services portfolio: GKN disengaged from the Californian joint venture with Dyno-Rod. Daly maintained his efficiency drive at Sankey, consolidating all autostructures production at the Hadley Castle works in Telford with the closure of two smaller plants, including Bilston, the original home of Joseph Sankey.

Such changes were refinements of what seemed to be a smooth-running machine. The group was firing on all cylinders, setting new financial records: pre-tax profits of almost £215 m; earnings of 50p a share; RoNA of 20.2%. At 20p, the total dividend was back in the twenties for the first time since 1979.

On the world stage, one historic event heralded the opening of a new age and a whole new market in Europe. On 10 November, the East German regime opened the 28-year-old Berlin Wall to its citizens. Thousands of Berliners, from both sides of the barrier, promptly scaled the edifice and began to knock lumps out of it.

Two weeks later, Czechoslovakia's Communist government resigned and Vaclav Havel ushered in the "Velvet Revolution". At 11.45 am Greenwich Mean Time on 3 December, the Soviet president Mikhail Gorbachev and his American counterpart George Bush declared that the Cold War was over.

The extraordinary developments in Eastern Europe had two immediate impacts on GKN. They caused the group to pause in its Defence expansion strategy, because no-one could be sure what the future held for the Defence industry. For many months after 3 December, as the Soviet Union crumbled and, eventually, Russia's Communist regime itself fell, the European air crackled with euphoric talk of the "Peace Dividend".

On the stock markets, defence shares took a battering. Inevitably, questions were raised about the future level of Britain's defence budget. The MoD launched a programme, called "Options for Change", which examined the ramifications for defence strategy and spending of the seismic change in the European military landscape. Certainly, GKN looked prescient in having concluded previously that the halcyon days of the tank were over: in the foreseeable future, there would be no Soviet tank brigades pouring over the North German plain. However, a further GKN move on Westland was off the agenda until the dust cloud from tumbling Communist monuments began to clear and the outlines of the new world order could be discerned.

Lees was positive, but cautious: "The changing political scene will have a bearing on our Defence business, although it is too soon to speculate on changes in the pattern of UK defence expenditure," he noted. "Assuming mobility is an important factor in future military strategy, we will continue to have considerable strengths as a supplier."

In Driveline, there was no doubting the benefit of political change. The breaching of the Wall and the subsequent domino-like collapse of the Soviet satellite governments opened the highway to Eastern Europe, hitherto a no-go area. "We were totally excluded from Eastern Europe until the fall of Communism," said Bonner.

First, the group acquired Gelenkwellenwerk Mosel, the main CVJ producer in east Germany, based near Zwickau, Leipzig. "It had been set up under a Citroën licence, initially as a perceived centre of excellence within Comecon [the Soviet economic bloc]," said Bonner. "It didn't work out that way, because the Russians never wanted to buy from East Germany and Romania went its own way. Following a period of restructuring, that became a profitable and successful operation."

The discussions had started as a joint venture negotiation with the East German government, which at the time only allowed 49% foreign ownership. However, as discussions proceeded, the Wall fell, the ownership rule was consequently relaxed, and GKN was able to own 100%. Later, Uni-Cardan bought Fiat's in-house manufacturing operation in Poland, which it relocated and expanded.

"These two moves were partly about establishing a presence in Eastern Europe as that market opened up," Bonner said. "But the opening up was not just about the opportunity to acquire assets: it was linked to our customers who were doing the same thing: Fiat in Poland, Volkswagen in East Germany." The Zwickau CVJ plant was next door to an assembly plant taken over by VW. VW went on to beat off competition from Renault and acquire Skoda, the Czech vehicle maker.

Driveline's expansion into Eastern Europe filled one of the few remaining gaps in its global network. In a broader context, it furthered GKN's continental European reorientation. In 1989, group sales originated in mainland Europe exceeded those from the UK for the first time in GKN's history. Trading profits from mainland European operations – mainly Uni-Cardan and CHEP – reached a new peak of £91 m, close to half the group's total £192 m. That, plus the growth in the US reduced the UK share of group sales to 36.5%. A decade earlier, on the eve of the 1980 recession, the UK share had been 68%.

The wisdom of the internationalisation strategy was about to be tested – and proven. At GKN's 1990 interim results announced in August, Lees reported that demand was weakening in many of the group's markets. That weakness, he said, was unlikely to be reversed "in the short term".

The GKN chairman was right. What he had observed was the start of a widespread cyclical downturn in Western markets. This time, unlike 1980–82, much of continental Europe was also impacted. Only Germany was, for the time being, immune from the recession now gathering pace. It enjoyed a boom in the run-up to, and aftermath of, the reunification of East and West, which was officially completed on 3 October.

The US was hit – car sales declined by 5.8% year-on-year – but to nowhere near the extent of the early 1980s. Furthermore, GKN was protected from the worst effects of the American slowdown by its presence with the Japanese, who were generally able to offset the overall volume decline by increasing their market shares.

In one respect, however, the recession of 1990–92 was all too like its predecessor a decade earlier: by far the worst-hit country was Britain. As in the earlier slump, an international slowdown was hugely exacerbated by domestic economic problems – on this occasion, an economic boom which triggered high inflation. When, in June 1988, the government had to start pouring cold water on the massively overheating economy, an old-fashioned "bust" began to beckon. Interest rates were raised no less than four times that month alone, from 7.5% to 9.5%.

It was too little, too late. Unlike Brookes or Holdsworth, Lees desisted from telling shareholders what he thought of government economic policy. However, he noted in his first annual report, written in March 1989, that "the shadow of inflation is darker now than it was a year ago. Inflation is an evil that must be suppressed and if its suppression results in a temporary slowdown in economic growth, that may be a small price to pay."

High interest rates and the artificially high value of sterling – which was locked into the European Exchange Rate Mechanism, forerunner to the Euro – undermined British companies' price competitiveness. There was also another Middle East crisis – on 2 August 1990, Saddam Hussein's Iraq invaded Kuwait. That pushed up oil prices sharply, but – unlike the early Eighties – this was only a minor contributory factor to a transatlantic slump that was by this time well entrenched.

In Britain, as the late 1980s' housing market boom collapsed under the high interest rates, property owners were plunged into negative equity. New company formation evaporated. Consumer spending slumped. Car sales dived 12.7% in 1990, forcing GKN and other suppliers to cut jobs at their UK plants.

Echoes of 1980 reverberated: Sir Brian Corby, president of the Confederation of British Industry, disregarded government complaints that industry was merely moaning: "I don't find it helpful to suggest that the lookout on the boat who points out that there are rocks ahead is whingeing," Corby said. "Nor do I find it obvious that it is necessary to crash the boat on to the rocks in order to find salvation."

Lees took the long view. "The effect on industry of rapidly-rising inflation followed by tough monetary measures to effect a cure is self-evidently debilitating. The cure, however, will have been worthwhile if, once inflation in the UK has been reduced to the levels experienced by competitors, it is held there," he told shareholders.

As Holdsworth had done in 1980, he vowed that GKN would do what was necessary to combat the immediate pressures while continuing to pursue its long-term objectives. The company "will continue to tighten the control of costs and cash but without prejudicing the strategic actions necessary to secure the considerable medium and long-term potential of the group".

GKN delivered across the board on that commitment, despite a plunge in earnings second only to that experienced between 1980 and 1982. Pre-tax profits dropped by two-thirds over two years to £69 m and earnings per share declined by more than 90% to 4.1p because the slump in lower-taxed UK earnings increased the group's overall tax charge.

This time, however, the dividend was held throughout at 20.5p, despite being uncovered (after redundancy and closure costs) and therefore paid partly out of reserves for two successive years. But the integrity of the balance sheet remained intact with debt gearing actually being reduced from 44.6% on the eve of recession to 23.3% at the end of 1992. That was thanks to tight cash control and prompt action to lower the cost base.

The recession catalysed Lees's reformation of GKN. In 1991, the costs of selling or closing wholly- and partly-owned businesses totalled £59 m. Another £26 m was incurred the following year. Thousands left the group through sale, closure and redundancy. At the start of 1990, GKN employed 35,900 people worldwide, including 15,700 in the UK. Four years later, the total workforce was down to 26,500.

As in 1980–82, the streamlining was rigorous and relentless. One casualty was the composite leaf spring. Despite years of investment, it had never gained industry traction. Now, amid the market slump, it was a luxury that GKN could no longer afford. The purpose-built Telford facility was closed.

Rationalisation of the group business portfolio – sustained through the entire first half of the new decade – now embraced a number of the industrial services businesses that GKN had acquired relatively recently. The first disposals included Foundations, sold for just over £26 m – a premium to net asset value – to a management buy-out. The Australian automotive aftermarket business went, again for a respectable price. ACS Coffee, part of the Vending business, was also sold. But the most evocative action was a plant shutdown. United Engineering Steels – faced with overcapacity caused by a 15% drop in finished steel deliveries in 1990 alone – closed Brymbo. Brookes, watching from his post as GKN's Life President, was deeply saddened by the decision.

At the same time, and as Lees had promised, the group continued to make cornerstone investments for future growth. One investment stood out – the decision, made along with Brambles, to launch CHEP in the giant US market. The two partners deliberated for more than a year before pressing the button, analysing the market to the nth degree.

"The qualms were about how to do it," said Jessop. "You had to have a national network from Day One. Heinz would make tomato sauce in one place, so if you supplied the pallets, you had to be prepared for the pallet to go anywhere. So you had to have the means to cover everywhere it went. That meant you faced a massive expense just setting up the depots."

The answer, GKN and Brambles agreed, was to establish the network through subcontracting: "We made arrangements with other people's premises to run subdepots – satellite depots," said Jessop. He ran the CHEP USA team with Peter Williams, the Briton who had run CHEP in Australia before coming back to the UK for the launch there, and Mike McCarthy who had started the CHEP operation in France.

For GKN, it was quite a call. Group profits were tumbling and the Western business environment was at its worst for a decade. But both GKN and Brambles recognised that the call had to be made. For CHEP, America was the great prize. It had been in the partners' sights for years, ever since the mainland Europe venture emulated the success of CHEP UK. The enterprise could be delayed no longer.

"With hindsight, it looks like a guaranteed, copper-bottomed success," said Lees. "But it wasn't like that at the time. It was a big risk. CHEP in the UK was much less of a gamble because the size of the country made it a manageable, practical proposition. But in the US, you were comparing 300 m people with 60 m. That was high risk. It was a very difficult decision, one where we and Brambles reinforced each other's courage."

CHEP USA launched in September 1990 and got off to a good start. The majority of America's top 90 grocery distributors agreed to support the pool, and major manufacturers – Procter & Gamble and Unilever's US arm Lever Brothers among them – were early adopters.

Despite the launch success, GKN continued to monitor the US development closely. Lees said, "We knew that we were in for losses for two to three years. We were monitoring that the loss profile was in accordance with what we thought it was going to be when we went in. So we always knew what it would cost to pull the plug, if we had to. In the event, it was never necessary; but at the time, we didn't know that."

These were tumultuous times for GKN. In the Persian Gulf, the Allies launched Operation Desert Storm on 17

January 1991 with the objective of driving Saddam Hussein's forces out of Kuwait. The 700,000-strong Allied force included 25,000 British servicemen and women, and many of the 500-plus Warriors that Sankey had so far delivered to the British Army.

The Warriors were deployed with the First Armoured Division in Desert Storm. There were six variants of what was now christened Desert Warrior: Section, Infantry Command, Repair, Recovery, Artillery Observation and Battery Command. The vehicle more than met expectations, achieving great reliability and high performance despite the hostile climate and terrain.

The Army's Quartermaster-General visited the Telford production site to thank the workforce there. "The soldiers like the Warrior: it is the best, it is reliable, it does the job," he told them. It was the highest praise, again vindicating the work Daly and his team had done in consulting the soldiers themselves when they were developing the vehicle. Once more, a GKN company had acquitted itself well in war. It was appropriate that Sankey, with a tradition of problem-solving military involvement dating back to the First World War, should be the company at the centre of GKN's Gulf War effort.

Suitably encouraged, GKN embarked on a series of alliances to extend its armoured vehicle range and reach. The MoD wanted a new generation of smaller vehicles, called the Future Family of Light Armoured Vehicles (FFLAV), and was planning a competition to select the prime contractor. GKN lined up with America's FMC, Krupp of Germany and Switzerland's MOWAG. Of these, MOWAG delivered by far the most concrete results. It licensed its 8 × 8 wheeled armoured vehicle Piranha to GKN for manufacture and marketing. One export contract to the Middle East was quickly won.

The armoured vehicle prospects buttressed GKN's confidence in the Defence business in general. Its interest in Westland was similarly reinforced when the MoD confirmed its long-awaited order for 44 EH101s for the Royal Navy. The contract, to be delivered over five years from 1996, assured Westland of a buoyant long-term order book. The group watched Westland, and waited.

# CHAPTER 23

# Lift-Off

GKN held its Westland stake for five years. With the Cold War over, it debated whether to sell the stake but neither the obvious buyer, British Aerospace, nor any other likely candidate emerged. At the same time, GKN examined other possible acquisitions, including the aerospace group Dowty. But Dowty was bought by GKN's engineering peer TI Group for a knockout price.

By late 1993, GKN had not quite escaped the impact of recession. That year pre-tax profits fell from £121.8 m to £97.5 m, hit both by a hefty share of losses on UES and a slump in mainland European car markets as the post-reunification boom in Germany ended abruptly.

For all the diversification of the years since 1979, GKN had undergone a net streamlining on a vast scale. Its payroll told the story: at the end of 1993, the worldwide workforce numbered 26,500 – 75% down on the 104,000 employed at the end of the Seventies. The UK reduction was even more striking: less than 11,000 people now worked for

GKN in Britain: 58,000 had gone in 13 years through the combination of disposals, closures and redundancies.

After the remarkable years since 1990, when both countries and companies struggled to relocate their bearings in an unfamiliar world, there was a sense within the GKN boardroom that stability was returning – and with it, the confidence to take decisions for the long term. The worst of the recession was behind the group and the "peace dividend" had been replaced by a "keeping the peace dividend". As a result, GKN was now more confident of Westland's prospects and was beginning to consider a full bid.

Enter Bob Daniel, chairman of UTC. In November 1993, he flew into London and told Lees he wanted to pull out of Westland. GKN had inherited Fiat's pre-emption rights over the UTC stake, which was effectively 17%. Did it want to exercise those rights? If it did, that would take GKN well beyond the 30% level at which it would be obliged to make a full bid.

Lees knew that, if GKN did not buy the UTC holding, the shares could go to another company which would make an uneasy bedfellow. The board decided that now was the time to take control. However, despite starting with almost 47% of Westland on a fully-converted basis, a full bid was not straightforward. It might be opposed by the independent directors on the Westland board. Moreover, the purchase of the original interest had not been universally welcomed. Some investors thought GKN was asking for trouble – one fund manager had told Alec Daly: "You are going to get a big left hook for this, Mr Daly."

Even Lees confessed to having had concerns after taking the original stake: "It was quite bold of us to buy in. The EH101 development was under way, but not guaranteed to be successful. There was the order book question. In fact, it was a big risk – we might have had to write the whole investment off."

Nor did everyone buy the battlefield mobility concept, even inside GKN. One senior executive recalled: "I was never convinced of the strategic rationale, of the link between Armoured Fighting Vehicles and helicopters. But I was a strong supporter of the acquisition, because I could see the ability to create value. As a tactical move, it was fantastic for GKN."

The view of Westland's increasingly bright prospects was the key to the deal. Visibility was excellent as a result of Daly and Walsh's position on the Westland board. For a period, Daly even became acting chief executive: "That was a big opportunity for me to find out what made the business tick."

What Daly unearthed was Westland's best-kept secret. Strictly speaking, it was not a secret because its existence was in the public domain. But that existence had been long forgotten, and Daly only stumbled across it by accident. "I always asked people who reported to me to tell my secretary where they were going to be each day, in case someone had to be contacted. I soon saw that the company secretary, John Bayley, was always going to Geneva, so I asked him why."

Bayley told Daly about Westland's 14-year-old claim for compensation from the Arab Organisation for

Industrialisation (AOI). The claim related to an order for Lynx helicopters placed by Saudi Arabia, Qatar and the United Arab Emirates before the 1973 Yom Kippur war. Under the deal, Egypt was going to be the centre of competence and Westland would help the Egyptian government finance and build a factory to make the helicopters.

After the war, with the investment having been put down, the AOI unilaterally pulled out of the deal. After trying for several years to reach a negotiated settlement, Westland launched a claim for the full £385 m value of the contract. The suit disappeared into an international court of arbitration in Geneva and few people thought it would ever emerge.

Westland's value had more than doubled since GKN took its original stake, and now stood at more than £220 m. In March 1994, GKN made its bid, valuing Westland at £366 m. Westland's independent directors resisted, battling to force GKN to raise its terms significantly. But Lees and his team refused, and increased their offer only slightly.

They did, however, add an interesting, lower-priced alternative, offering Westland investors a share in any payments from the AOI claim. It was an innovative move, although few took up GKN's alternative offer. But its increased terms were enough to seal victory and the group launched a £240 m rights issue to part-fund the purchase.

In the final analysis, the Arbitration Panel in the AOI claim found in favour of Westland and the award was settled by agreement between the parties. The net amount received by Westland was £178 m of which £15 m had been received prior to the acquisition by GKN. Given that, allowing for the existing stake, the acquisition cost of Westland had been about £440 m, the AOI settlement reduced that considerably.

GKN was now into aerospace in a big way for the first time. It had, of course, previously supplied the industry from Smith-Clayton and BRD. "Westland was a great acquisition because the helicopters business made us a lot of money and we got a very good price for it when we sold it," Lees said. "But just about the most important thing on Westland was that it gave us the entry into aerospace."

As GKN opened one door, it closed another: it divested its minority stake in United Engineering Steels to British Steel for £93 m, severing its last link with the industry on which it had been founded. Selling out of UES was one facet of the reformation that now reached its peak. Over a period of 18 months, the group cut a swathe through its portfolio, divesting businesses including the Vending man-ufacturing and service operations, Axles, Kwikform scaf-folding and its minority stake in Guest Keen Williams (GKW), the Indian company it had acquired 60 years earlier.

The GKW sale – to a group of investors for almost £12 m – was particularly symbolic: the old GKN and the new, passing each other in opposite directions. For GKN, India now was about making CVJs and propshafts as the country's motor industry, freed from decades of state regulation, began to grow. The interest in GKW, a micro-cosm of old GKN with its fasteners and forgings, was an anachronism.

Lees summed up the three objectives underpinning GKN's strategy. They were, he said, "to reduce the cyclical imbalance of the group by concentrating on three core businesses which are influenced by different economic cycles but which all have the potential for growth in international markets; to balance those businesses that are normally cash-generative such as automotive driveline with those that tend to be cash consumers such as CHEP; to improve the geographic balance of the group's activities with the aim of progressively reducing the proportion of profit paid in tax".

Once again, the group was at the forefront of a new trend. This one came with an unwieldy, multi-syllabic tag – deconglomeratisation. With markets globalising, an increasing number of Western companies were finding that they could no longer muster the resources to support a wide spread of businesses and needed to focus on no more than a handful of key activities.

There was no place in this new world for underperforming industrial services operations, even if the group had invested heavily in their expansion. The rationalisation of the industrial services portfolio was driven by Marcus Beresford, recruited in 1992 from Smiths Industries to succeed Jessop as head of the services division. After studying the portfolio he had inherited, Beresford quickly concluded that it should be focused on CHEP and Cleanaway which stood head and shoulders above the other businesses.

"When I arrived, there was still a hope that there was mileage left in the industrial services portfolio that had been laboriously built up," Beresford recalled. "But the more you got into it, the more you realised that there was no future in the likes of scaffolding, autoparts, vending and so on."

The dismantling of the division culminated in 1995 when, 16 years after it had been acquired, Parts Inc (a subsidiary of Parts Industries) was sold for $79 m [£52 m at contemporary exchange rates]. It went back to an American company, APS Holding Corporation of Houston, Texas. That was effectively the end of the venture into the automotive aftermarket. GKN retained Meineke but that was all. Meineke consistently turned in excellent profits, although – as time would show – it had a sting in its tail.

Why did the time and money devoted to Autoparts fail to deliver the hoped-for returns? Jessop's view was straightforward: "Autoparts was not connected with our auto business. People who made money out of this business did so by trading a relatively small number of parts at large volumes. Whereas we bought an amorphous collection of companies in the UK and France and businesses in the US which operated all over different states. The US just couldn't be run efficiently."

Lees reflected: "Autoparts was like steel stockholding – it's a branch operation. And GKN was never any good at running branch operations. To run one successfully, you have to do it by numbers through the branch managers. You've got to have good branch managers and have central purchasing, or economic central purchasing. You have to put a certain amount of discretion on the branch managers and you have to fire them if they don't come up to snuff, and reward them if they do well. In other words, you have to be monitoring them constantly, on a daily, weekly basis.

We were never tough enough, in my view. We never had the drive or the people capable of running the branches. We didn't have the experience, frankly."

There was an additional issue, specific to Autoparts: "The theory was that, if the OE market goes down, the aftermarket goes up. That's great, except it didn't allow for the fact that the OE product quality, reliability and durability was improving. You don't have to buy windscreen wipers every six months. Plus, you are up against Mom and Dad whose livelihood it is. Although they don't have the economies of scale in purchasing, they have the get up and go and willingness to open at 8 am on a Sunday morning, which a branch manager who's well paid simply doesn't have."

Lees thought there might have been an additional element which had led GKN in the late 1970s and early 1980s to overestimate its ability to manage a different kind of business. "Possibly we had a slight delusion of grandeur. We had been around all this time, we were a FT30 founder company and suddenly the 'K' and the 'N' were disappearing. What could we do that fitted our basic core and could beef it up? Auto was going well and Defence was going well, but Defence wasn't big. Automotive was very profitable, so there was cash and there was this drive to beef up. With the benefit of hindsight, that was a pretty bad mistake. In today's world, people would say 'We've got this wonderful auto franchise, let's build on that.'"

Disposal of the underperforming industrial services operations had the additional benefit of allowing Beresford to focus on his priorities. One challenge stood out: CHEP's success was, paradoxically, straining the relationship with

Brambles. If GKN could not repair that relationship, the group could be badly damaged.

"The relationship with Brambles was always somewhat tense, but it was particularly tense at that time because Brambles thought GKN had disadvantaged them by taking the majority holding in CHEP UK," Beresford said. "As a result, they were determined to keep the rest of the world beyond Europe and the US to themselves."

Having proved its model in both Western Europe and the US, CHEP was now ready to go global. Brambles' antagonism towards its partner therefore threatened to block GKN off from participation in important new sources of CHEP growth. "It was absolutely essential to get a global partnership agreement," said Beresford. "Without it, we'd have been progressively cut out of the emerging markets."

The strains were even affecting existing operations. "They were doing their best to stop us developing in Europe," said Beresford. Yet it was critical that CHEP Europe had a pan-European network: "You couldn't operate on a basis of individual nation states – we had to have a continental pool. That was absolutely essential."

GKN had to play hardball to bring Brambles to a reconciliation. Its lever was a loophole in the agreement to operate CHEP South Africa: "There was a mistake in the licence which gave us the ability to use all the CHEP knowhow to develop our own business in new markets out of South Africa," Beresford said. "We wouldn't have done it, but they weren't to know that." The move echoed Brookes' tactics in the bruising discussions with BHP over John Lysaght.

Along with the stick, GKN also employed a carrot – it offered Brambles an equal stake in CHEP UK, thereby satisfying the Australian demand for parity. "That did wonders for the relationship," said Beresford. "It resolved an issue which had been gnawing at them for a long time."

The approach worked: in 1994, the companies signed an agreement establishing all future CHEP ventures in any territory as joint ventures between Brambles and GKN. "After that, we went from strength to strength," Beresford said. CHEP immediately moved into Latin America and later developed in South-East Asia, setting up in Malaysia, Singapore and Hong Kong. In America, the partners made an important management change, bringing in Bob Moore from Pepsi to run the business. "He gave it a really aggressive customer focus," said Beresford."

CHEP encountered one unexpected hazard when the giant General Electric demanded that it buy a plastic pallet which had been developed by GE's Plastics division under Jeffrey Immelt [later GE's chairman]. GE put a "colossal" price tag on the plastic pallet, Beresford recalled. Speculation was rife that GE was prepared to go into competition with CHEP if the company did not buy the plastic pallet. But CHEP successfully resisted the pressure. "We were quite nervous for a time," said Beresford.

Cleanaway also benefited from a key management appointment. "Cleanaway was doing fine, but it was content at the time to be a domestic UK waste management business," Beresford said. "One of the spin-off benefits of the CHEP agreement with Brambles was that it helped our relationship with them on Cleanaway."

The two companies agreed that they should take Cleanaway into mainland Europe. "We wanted to put it on a much more aggressive growth path," said Beresford. Gerben Westra, a Dutchman, was selected to lead the expansion. He grew the recycling business in the UK and made significant acquisitions in the Netherlands and Germany. "Gerben transformed Cleanaway," said Beresford. During the rest of the decade, the business almost quadrupled in size. In the process, despite all the false starts and wrong turnings over two decades, it and CHEP vindicated the industrial services growth strategy.

In the mid-1990s, despite the Westland acquisition and the growth of CHEP and Cleanaway, the automotive businesses consistently generated about two-thirds of GKN's sales and almost 60% of its profit. This performance was sustained despite the fact that Automotive was already a very substantial business. In 1995, for instance, Automotive trading profits increased from £133 m to £181 m out of the group's total £328 m.

At the heart of this success was the continued momentum of the Driveline operations under Bonner. City analysts repeatedly forecasted that the business would run out of steam as the upsurge in front wheel drive vehicles subsided, but GKN continued to defy those predictions by finding new sources of growth.

Two key trends were becoming established. One was the desire of some car makers to outsource all or part of their in-house component manufacture in order to concentrate on their core business of designing, making and marketing vehicles. The other was the industry's continued globalisation. GKN was in the forefront of both.

"The platform for acquiring in-house manufacturing assets from customers was created back in the Seventies," said Bonner. "That was when we had given licences to the OEMs and shared production with them. Then, as a number of vehicle manufacturers began to examine their own raison d'être and manufacturing depth, they looked at more outsourcing driven by their own cash constraints in the second half of the Eighties and early Nineties. We were able to open up discussions, in most cases on an exclusive basis, about acquiring assets."

In 1994, GKN reached a milestone outsourcing deal with Fiat. It acquired Fiat's CVJ and driveshaft plant at Novoli, Florence in a deal worth a total of £50 m. That included not only the acquisition cost, but investment in a new plant 15 km west of Florence at Campi Bisenzio, working capital and the cost of relocation from Novoli. Fiat retained a 15% stake in the new operation, with GKN owning the rest.

That deal was followed by outsourcing ventures with Fiat in Poland and – later – with General Motors' German arm Opel at Kaiserslautern, and Nissan in Japan. At the same time, Bonner continued the business's push into emerging markets as an increasing number of established manufacturers set up factories in those territories while indigenous companies, such as Hyundai in Korea, emerged on the world scene. Having established a network of joint ventures and associate companies throughout the vehicle-producing world, GKN now moved into a second phase in which it increased its control of those operations.

"We were partly opportunistic," Bonner said. "But we were progressively driven by determining that we needed to be producing everywhere where there was a significant volume of local production. By the mid-Nineties, the emerging markets scenario was being further consolidated. We were seeing many of these ventures turning into significantly profitable operations. We were gaining confidence to operate in many of these countries.

"Many of the regulations and legal requirements were changing so that majority foreign ownership became possible in many countries for the first time. These ventures became an increasing part of the turnover and profit stream of the division. So, where we could, we began a policy of taking our partners out. That couldn't happen overnight – it always takes two to tango. But we were eventually able to establish 100% ownership in many countries – Brazil, Mexico, India, Thailand, Malaysia."

Thus, in 1995 alone, GKN was able to move to majority ownership of Invel in India, while increasing its stakes in both its Brazilian and Argentinian joint ventures with America's Dana Corporation to 49%, acquiring 49% of a Colombian CVJ maker and raising its interest in a Slovenian CVJ producer from 17.7% to 46.5%. The following year it raised the Slovenian stake to 74%.

That February, it bought out the minority interests in its Spanish driveline subsidiaries and reached agreement to form a CVJ joint venture in South Korea with Hanwha, with GKN holding 49%. In China – the one country which refused to allow GKN to move to full control – it nevertheless continued to expand, raising its holding in Shanghai GKN from 25% to 40% and establishing a new CVJ joint venture in Jilin Province with Norinco, of which it held 50%.

Apart from their patience and persistence in building relationships, Bonner and his team's passport to success in both globalisation and outsourcing deals was their technological leadership. In the mid-1990s, GKN Driveline produced a new generation of driveshafts – smaller, lighter, more refined but with no diminution in strength – designed to support the business through the year 2000. Driveline's worldwide market share at this stage was about 34%, and climbing.

Within the motor industry, there was widespread recognition that GKN products were technically superior. Again, the kaizen factor was crucial. As Bonner said in 1995: "GKN's leading market position is dependent on providing a continuous supply of product that meets or exceeds customers' requirements in terms of performance, quality, weight, range, cost effectiveness and global availability." It was a comprehensive recipe for world market leadership.

# CHAPTER 24

# Courtroom Battle

While Driveline advanced consistently and relentlessly on a global front, back in Cleveland Row its owner was approaching an historic changing of the guard. During the early and mid 1990s, there had been several switches in board personnel, both executive and non-executive. Jessop, Walsh and Daly had all retired or moved on to pastures new, being succeeded respectively by Beresford, David Turner and David Wright. Among the non-executives, Roy Brown, a director of Unilever, joined the board in January 1996.

The biggest move, however, was yet to come. Lees would reach the age of 60 by the end of 1996 and the board announced that from 1 January 1997 – and for the first time in the history of GKN – the roles of chairman and chief executive would be divided. Lees himself would become non-executive chairman; the company would appoint a new chief executive. The search was on.

It soon became apparent that the new CEO would definitely come from outside the company. Bonner, who clearly had the credentials for the job, made it clear that he was not a candidate. Lees had someone in mind: during the search for future possible non-executive directors, he had met C. K. Chow, who ran the industrial gases business of BOC. "CK", as he was universally known, made an impression, although he was unaware of this at the time. He only found out when he was in Taipei on BOC business: "A headhunter called me in the middle of the night. So I said to him, 'Why are you waking me up? What do you want to talk to me about?' He told me it was about the chief executive post at GKN, so I said, 'OK, that's a good enough reason!'"

Chow had another talk with Lees, and also spoke to Sir John Parker, one of GKN's senior non-executives. They asked whether he would accept the chief executive's job. Chow said he would: "The decision was relatively easy for me – it was a great opportunity. So I moved to GKN."

Chow joined GKN in July 1996, to give himself time to familiarise himself with the business before taking over the reins. Just before Christmas, he and his wife went back to Hong Kong for a holiday. They were walking down the street when they saw a headline on the front page of the *Financial Times*. It said GKN had suffered a damages award of almost $600 m after losing a lawsuit in an American court brought by Meineke franchisees. Chow had had a few hours' warning – he had been told the night before. "My wife looked at me and said, 'Is that you? And you complained about the cost of the clothes I bought yesterday!'"

The Chows were not the only people to have been taken aback by the Meineke judgment. It hit GKN like a bombshell. Beresford was asleep in a hotel near the Redditch office when he was awoken at 4 am by a call telling him that there had been a $150 m judgment against GKN. He went straight to Redditch. "By the time I got there, the judge had awarded punitive damages against us and it was up to $300 m. An hour later, that figure had been doubled by multiple damages to $600 m."

Beresford and Grey Denham, who had been up most of the night with his deputy Rufus Ogilvie Smals, then rang Lees, who was thunderstruck. Work then focused on ensuring that a Stock Exchange announcement was issued before the opening of trading. "That morning was, without question, my worst-ever moment at GKN," said Beresford.

Meineke was a true *cause célèbre*. The US Court of Appeals, which later delivered the very last judgment in the Meineke case, described it as "an ordinary contract dispute which somehow managed to become a massive tort action". The lawsuit, it said, "managed to wander beyond its legitimate origins, and at the end it spun completely out of control".

The dispute first surfaced in 1993 with complaints from a small number of Meineke franchisees that some advertising was being placed through an advertising agency, New Horizons Advertising, wholly-owned by Meineke. Under their franchise agreements, franchisees paid both a franchise royalty fee and an advertising royalty fee.

The dispute turned on whether, under US state and federal franchise laws, and under the Meineke franchise contracts themselves, the advertising royalty monies were held in trust by Meineke for the benefit of the franchisees. If that was the case, then the commission fees charged by New Horizons in placing advertising constituted a breach of trust, as the company was owned by Meineke. Under the Law of Trusts, a trustee cannot benefit from the Trusteeship.

Meineke always denied the franchisees' arguments on the grounds that its contracts with them on advertising did not create a trust. However, GKN was aware that, if a judge found in favour of the franchisees, a large damages award was possible.

A court might find that the loss suffered by the franchisees should relate not to the advertising fees paid to New Horizons – only $10m over 10 years – but to the claimed loss of earnings that would have been generated over the period had those fees been used to buy additional advertising. It was also possible that any damages could be tripled by the Court and that the jury could award punitive damages.

In mid-1994, Denham led a GKN team which tried to reach a settlement with the franchisees, but the two sides were so far apart that the attempt failed. "One alternative they suggested for settlement was that we 'give them the franchise' by transferring Meineke to them!" Denham said.

As ill luck would have it, the case in the Charlotte district court came before Judge Robert Potter, nicknamed "Maximum Bob" because of his severe sentences and judgments in cases including that of the fallen evangelists Jim and Tammy Bakker.

Judge Potter vastly extended the dimensions of the case, certifying it as a class action to include all current

Meineke franchisees and all who had held a franchise in the previous decade – about 3000 in total. He even certified the class as a "non-opt out" class, meaning that even those franchisees who did not want to sue Meineke would be included in the action as plaintiffs.

"Pre-trial disclosure was monumental," Denham recalled. "More than 1 million pages of paper were handed over, together with tape recordings of all franchise agreement completion meetings which totalled about 6000 hours."

The judgment that was handed down on the evening of 18 December, US time, was confused and confusing. In a final twist, Judge Potter ruled that GKN, as well as Meineke, was liable. In legal terms, he "pierced the corporate veil". For GKN, it was a painful act. The size of the award against the group was not clear, being either $398 m or $554 m depending on how the judgment was read, and the group duly disclosed both numbers in its Stock Exchange statement the following morning.

Almost three months later, the District Court clarified its decision: GKN was liable for $591 m plus £10 m interest, minus at least 34% in respect of the "releases" given to the group by a number of franchisees who had been included in the action. Three Meineke executives were found personally liable, with awards of more than $1 m made against each of them.

The net liability came to $397 m – £270 m at prevailing exchange rates – and GKN made that provision in its 1996 accounts. It blew a gaping hole in the year's results: instead of reporting a record pre-tax profit of more than £363 m, the group had to announce a slump from £322 m in 1995 to less than £93 m. Earnings, post the provision, came in at a loss of 12p a share instead of a record 65.2p.

Now the group's fightback began. The campaign was meticulous and far-reaching. Within two months of the court clarification, GKN filed notice of appeal to the US Court of Appeals in Richmond, Virginia. The group appointed a specialist appeal lawyer to head the team – Ken Starr, a former Federal Court of Appeals judge and at the time the special prosecutor in the Whitewater affair. Starr soon became the lead investigator in the ultimately abortive move to impeach President Bill Clinton.

A separate team led by Ted Olson, later President George W. Bush's first Solicitor General, took charge of developing *amici curiae* (literally, friends of the court – impartial advisers) and a sophisticated and high-level media campaign. Articles about the case appeared in the *Washington Post*, *New York Times* and *Wall Street Journal*. John Major, then Prime Minister, mentioned the case in a speech during a visit to North Carolina.

GKN did not know which three Appeal Court judges would hear the appeal. So it distributed to radio stations in all the towns where the judges lived a supportive interview with Dick Thornburgh, a former US Attorney-General, for transmission during morning and evening rush-hour news bulletins.

The *amici curiae* included household name corporations with extensive franchising networks, among them McDonald's, Burger King and Mobil Oil. The *amici* also included some Meineke franchisees who were happy to support the group. For the first time in the history of American jurisprudence, a State – the State of North

Carolina – joined in support of an appeal in a commercial dispute. Finally, Starr rehearsed the appeal in front of four retired Appeal Court judges of differing political persuasions, and modified his final presentation as a result of their comments.

On 5 May 1998, the appeal was heard before three judges headed by Chief Judge Wilkinson. While they were deliberating, a last attempt for an out-of-court settlement was made. GKN almost settled at that point: "You make your luck in life, but we were certainly lucky on Meineke," Lees recounted. "It had reached a stage where the appeal had been heard but they hadn't delivered the judgment. We believed the case could be settled for about $100 m." Whilst an attempt was made to settle, no figure was agreed by the time the verdict came through.

The Appeal Court verdict was delivered on 19 August, and it was withering. The suit "had come close to visiting corporate ruin on Meineke," said the judges. There was no legal basis for imposing liability on GKN, which was thereby able to write back almost all the provision. Moreover: "Because the most primary principles of procedure and the most settled precepts of commercial law were not observed here, the judgment of the district court is reversed in its entirety…". GKN and Meineke were totally vindicated. Denham, who had spent more than four years managing the case, could relax at last.

The Meineke case had overshadowed a fundamental improvement in GKN's fortunes during the mid–late '90s. Chow said: "Meineke apart, GKN was well on its way to cyclical recovery from the low point of the early Nineties. However, the structural issues were also very clear. We had one very successful product – the CVJ. Driveline was a very strong, good business. But we didn't really have any other major auto businesses. We had some positions in OffHighway and agricultural equipment.

"Then there was Defence. The problem with the defence portfolio was that, while Westland had a good order book, the armoured vehicle business was running down after a couple of big orders from the Middle East. The general consensus was that we didn't have the critical mass to succeed in the long term in the defence business. We didn't see how, in the long term, the UK helicopter business could survive as a stand-alone business."

CHEP and Cleanaway, the two big successes of the diversification into services, were in good shape, Chow thought. However, the ownership structure posed a question, given that GKN did not control the joint ventures with Brambles. "So the main issues were that Defence needed some thinking through; what should we do about CHEP and Cleanaway, which were 50%-owned; and what should we do to build on Driveline."

In parallel with his strategic analysis, Chow also set in train a cultural examination: "I hired consultants and did a survey of the GKN senior and mid-level managers. What did they expect from the new CEO? What did they think the company should do?" According to the responses: "They welcomed a new CEO because they thought hiring from the outside was the right thing to do; and their message to me was, that they were looking for change."

And change was what Chow set out to deliver, except in one key area: "In Driveline, we had just one objective – to maximise its growth." Bonner's patient positioning and incremental stake-building paid dividends again when the Asian financial crisis struck in 1997. That temporarily depressed Asian sales, but created the opportunity for Driveline to accelerate its moves to control Asian joint ventures: it established a new CVJ business in Thailand in which it had majority ownership and bought out its South Korean partner to take full control of that venture. In recognition of the rise of South-East Asia as a global production centre, it established a testing, support and engineering facility in Japan.

There was one new, genuinely equal joint venture that Driveline was delighted to form. In September, it agreed to establish a partnership company with Toyoda Machine Works (JTEKT) to develop and manufacture CVJs and driveshafts for Toyota. Toyoda was the component branch of the Toyota empire and this was a landmark agreement: a reflection of the respect GKN had earned over the decade and more since Bonner had initiated its relationship with the Japanese market leader.

Bonner and Chow had one other important decision to make: should Driveline try to expand from its status as a sub-system specialist into a full system supplier? It was not the first time such a debate had taken place within the group, but systems capability was now the talk of the industry. It was interlinked with significant consolidation among the component makers – this was the period when Lucas merged with Varity and Federal Mogul gobbled up T&N.

In GKN's case, a specific proposal arrived on its doorstep: Ford – at the time, its largest global customer – suggested that the group should acquire its own in-house component manufacturer Visteon with Ford taking a significant stake in the enlarged company. "After careful consideration, we decided that we should not try to expand from CVJs into systems," Chow said. "We didn't see any way to add value by doing that, let alone by doing it through a merger with Visteon. So we decided to go against the market and focus on the sub-system, the component. We could see many ways to take cost out of that, to improve it continuously and to gain more market share. Time has proven that we were right, because almost all of those who did go into systems failed in the end. That was a major strategic decision."

That judgment and the Toyota joint venture were fitting final acts in Bonner's distinguished leadership of the Driveline business. He retired at the end of 1998, 30 years after joining the group and 27 years after first making the journey to Lohmar as a junior accountant.

Bonner of course owed much to Bernard Walterscheid-Muller's vision in identifying him as his successor. The rest was down to him. For a British manager to transform a German-based business into a pre-eminent global concern was, and remains, a remarkable achievement. It has very few, if any, parallels in post-war British industrial history.

Driveline under Bonner was ahead of most of its non-American customers in seeing the need for a physical presence in the US; it was one of the first companies in any industry to recognise the importance of the emerging Latin American and Asian markets; and it was one of the first non-Japanese suppliers to understand that the cornerstone of competitive advantage was the relentless, incremental enhancement of product and process.

Bonner was always the first to insist that Driveline was never a one-man band. Apart from the support and strategic endorsement that he received from successive chairmen and senior GKN executives, the success of the business was a reflection of its bench strength. "In the Seventies, the management was mostly German," Bonner recalled. "But as I began to pull the total business together and make it more co-ordinated, we deliberately tried to build an international team. That of course included Germans, but became very international."

Bonner's immediate successor was an Armenian, Sarkis Kalyandjian, who had joined GKN in the early 1990s. He in turn was succeeded by Ian Griffiths – whose father was the former GKN main board director and automotive division head, Gordon. "A lot of the continuity was due to the fact that the succession was largely internal in terms of running the business," said Bonner.

"Ian Griffiths, for example, had been in the business for a significant amount of time before he took over. He did change things in a significant way. But why should he throw everything out of the window? He had been part of the strategy. We brought in people from outside – it was not that we were totally incestuous. But we didn't bring them in at the top: that's what gave us the continuity. That and the fact that a lot of the team stayed the same when the leader changed."

# CHAPTER 25

# Acquisition Drive

Trevor Bonner was not the only GKN veteran to retire in 1998. Brian Insch, who had been at GKN for 35 years and was the longest-serving of the early 1980s' executive director generation, also stepped down. Insch had cut his management teeth on the steel businesses, but his enduring achievement was to build the Human Resources function from the foundations laid by Parsons.

Parsons had been a trail-blazer in employee education and training, health and safety in the post-war years; Insch ensured that the policies and practices kept pace with the group's internationalisation, and skilfully handled the ever-widening definition of the role as it extended to community involvement and environmental responsibility.

His work in turn established a new platform from which GKN could enter the world of sustainability at the forefront of British business. What made Insch so effective was his application of the hard-edged, objective-focused operational manager's skills to the less tangible art of personnel management. His presence ensured that HR's role in perpetuating corporate success was never undervalued.

The departures of Insch and Bonner symbolised the end of the first era of GKN's transformation, the era that began with their emergence at the top of the company – following Lees and alongside Jessop and Daly – in the early Eighties.

Chow brought a very different perspective. Born in Hong Kong, management-educated in the US and having run a very large business in another major company, he was the epitome of the new-generation chief executive – a CEO for the age of globalisation.

If the thrust under Lees had been to streamline the group, to break it down into a few core, international businesses, Chow saw his fundamental objective as being to deepen that core, widen it, and unify it. To that task, he brought an MBA's systematism. Beyond his mission statement – "GKN is a global industrial company that is committed to growth and fosters entrepreneurship. We shall lead and excel in every market we serve" – he launched a series of initiatives to promote cross-fertilisation between the businesses and the territories in which GKN operated.

The emphasis was on practice, not theory: one innovation was a central procurement unit, using the Internet, with the aim of significantly reducing group-wide costs. There were four corporate learning initiatives, a Safety Award Scheme, a Green Scheme and a change programme called "The Way Forward", a series of workshops involving 500 managers each year. "One of my personal priorities has been to encourage GKN managers to see themselves as leaders, to further eradicate unnecessary rigidity, speed up decision-making and improve risk awareness," he told shareholders.

His commitment to growth was absolute. The objective was "double-double" – double sales and double profits. And GKN certainly had the wherewithal to fulfil the growth mission. Lees' years of careful husbandry, allied to the huge bonus of the AOI settlement, had created a substantial legacy. Not only had debt been eliminated, but GKN had net cash of £281 m.

For acquisitions, Chow looked first in the obvious place – automotive. GKN knew the industry and the customers. The most obvious route was to acquire another component manufacturer: "We went through the usual suspects, and we decided not to buy one of them for various reasons." The best decision was not to bid for T&N, the company that had acquired AE after GKN was blocked by the Monopolies Commission. After its acquisition by Federal Mogul, T&N was brought down by its historical exposure to asbestosis claims.

Having discarded the obvious and most direct route to automotive expansion, Chow went back to the drawing-board. He and his team devised a different answer: "We conducted a quite systematic process and came down to Powder Metallurgy/Sinter Metals. Why? Because it was an unconsolidated part of the automotive component business with growing applications because of the need to reduce cost and the general pricing environment. We decided to try to be a global consolidator of this sector."

One of the unconsolidated players in Powder Metallurgy was GKN itself. The group had been active in Powder Met for decades – its operations dated back to GKN's post-World War Two expansion into multifarious areas of the steel-related materials industry. Powder Met – the process of atomising metal (scrap steel) into powder – and Sinter Metals – the reformed components produced from the powder – seemed to fit naturally into the group and had survived the sweeping portfolio shake-out of the Holdsworth and Lees years.

With the advantages it conferred of precision formation and material-saving componentry, it promised to deliver significant growth in a cost-conscious environment – that was why there were a lot of powder met and sinter companies in the world. When Chow arrived, Powder Metallurgy in GKN was still a small division comprising wholly-owned businesses in Britain and Italy, and a 49% stake in an Indian joint venture with Mahindra & Mahindra, the engineering conglomerate.

Consolidating such a fragmented industry was going to require some hefty spending. GKN duly obliged. In May 1997, it paid an enterprise value of £337m for Sinter Metals Inc, one of the largest US sinter products businesses. At a stroke, the deal catapulted GKN into industry leadership, with a market share more than double that of its closest competitor. GKN promptly expanded Sinter's capacity while also enlarging its existing European businesses.

Through the following year, Chow used Sinter Metals to drive a series of smaller acquisitions, further expanding its range of powdered metal parts. Focusing on engine and transmission components and powder forging technology, it first acquired an Argentinian operation which provided a base in South America.

Then, in the space of three months, it bought three companies: the connecting rod production plant of America's Borg-Warner; another US business which made non-automotive bearings, expanding Sinter's presence in hand tools and domestic appliances; and a UK company, Rigby Metal Components. The total enterprise cost of these deals was £52 m.

What Chow needed now was a large powder met producer to fuel the extensive Sinter operations downstream. Late in 1998, he found what he was looking for. The Interlake Corporation owned Hoeganaes Corporation, the leading supplier of ferrous powdered metals in North America. Hoeganaes could supply both GKN's in-house needs and external customers, 60% of whom were motor component makers.

Chow was delighted: "The combination of Hoeganaes's material technologies and Sinter Metals' product expertise and manufacturing skills will lead to even more powdered metal components replacing cast and forged structural parts," he told shareholders. Interlake was not cheap – the deal cost GKN £348 m – but it looked like a dream package as it also contained two other disparate businesses: Material Handling, which complemented CHEP, and the San Diego-based Chem-tronics, which fitted with GKN's Aerospace business.

GKN was now making rich profits. The Meineke provision write-back inflated headline pre-tax profits for 1998 to an astronomical £707 m, but the underlying figure

of £459 m still represented an all-time high. The con-
temporaneous dot.com boom might have been sending
technology sector shares into orbit, but GKN was also
flying high.

Chow still wasn't finished in powder met and sinter.
In the ensuing months, GKN spent a further £131 m on
six more acquisitions, five of them in the US. In the space
of four years, it had increased the size of the business 10-
fold to annual sales of £630 m. It was now three times
larger than its nearest competitor, and the only sizeable
operator to combine both material and component technologies. In terms of attaining critical mass, it was mission
accomplished. Translating that into profitable growth
proved a different, and harder, task.

With the Powder Met/Sinter expansion well under
way, Chow turned his attention to Defence. Here, he faced
a more complex set of strategic equations: "The defence
business question was buy, sell or merge?" he recalled.
"That was the issue with both Westland and armoured
vehicles."

GKN concluded that the armoured vehicle business
had peaked and did not offer the group the kind of returns
it was seeking in the medium-to-long term, when weighed
against the amount of investment required to remain a
major player. So the alternative was either merge with a
view to eventual exit, or sell outright.

Its options were even fewer than those Daly had evalu-
ated when GKN first decided to expand into Defence a
decade earlier. There were only two other British players
of note, Vickers and Alvis. Vickers was by far the larger,
and GKN quickly decided that the logical move was to

combine forces with Vickers Defence Systems, maker of the Challenger tank and other vehicles.

The two companies were in rival European consortia competing for the only significant new order in prospect, the Multi-Role Armoured Vehicle, or MRAV, which had superseded FFLAV. MRAV envisaged a requirement for 6000 vehicles from the German, French and British armies. GKN's partners were Rheinmetall and GIAT.

"MRAV was the one big order and whoever won it would add value and whoever lost it would destroy value," said Chow. But Vickers did not want to merge with GKN Defence, and the efforts made by the group to agree a deal came to nothing. The GKN grouping, Eurokonsortium, then won MRAV: "That increased the value of our business from nil or negative if we hadn't won it," said Chow. "It gave us some value." Ironically, MRAV never actually materialised, although neither GKN nor anyone else could have known that at the time.

With Vickers out of the picture, GKN focused on Alvis. The two companies struck an imaginative deal in which GKN merged Defence into Alvis, in return for £78 m and a 29.9% stake in the enlarged group. It was a variation on the Phoenix schemes with British Steel, providing GKN with a path to eventual exit. "We decided that we should get out of the business, but we couldn't do that in one go," said Chow. "It would take two or three steps." Again, patience would be a virtue.

Westland was a bigger and more valuable business, and therefore a different proposition. For one thing, Westland was not only about helicopters: it also had the aerostructures operation, which was renamed GKN Westland

Aerospace. In Aerostructures, Chow's strategy from the outset was clear – of the three strategic options, the answer was: buy.

"Consolidation and growth within the aerospace industry is impacting the supply chain as prime contractors seek partnerships with fewer, stronger suppliers such as GKN," said Chow. When he joined, the business had annual sales of about £200 m from structures work and the supply of specific components such as engine nacelles and cockpit canopies and windows.

Over the next two years, Aerospace more than doubled in size through a series of acquisitions and organic contract wins, including new business with Boeing and Airbus and the canopy for the multi-nation Eurofighter Typhoon. Four acquisitions in 1997 were followed by two in 1998, including Dow-UT Composite Products, the world market leader in resin transfer moulding composites, and the Chem-tronics arm of Interlake, which made complex engine and airframe components.

At the same time, GKN streamlined the aerospace components portfolio by selling its 52% stake in the Normalair-Garrett environmental systems business to its partner Allied-Signal. Normalair was UK-focused and did not fit Chow's specification for building a global aerospace division.

In helicopters, GKN foresaw significant consolidation in the world industry but had no potential domestic partner – BAe was not interested and, in any case, the natural ally would be an existing helicopter manufacturer. GKN already had one clear candidate – Italy's Agusta, its partner on the EH101 programme. However, Chow wanted to assess the level of interest of the other main players. That exercise did not take long: "The Americans weren't interested in buying what they saw as a minor player – they all wanted to team up with Agusta or Eurocopter."

As for the Franco–German Eurocopter, its attitude to Westland was interesting: "It simply didn't recognise Westland as a player in the industry. We realised pretty soon that we weren't going to get far with them," Chow recalled.

Agusta, owned by the Italian aerospace and industrial giant Finmeccanica, was confirmed as the best partner. The two groups were the smallest of the six main companies in the industry – Agusta was number five, Westland six – but they were complementary in their respective product portfolios and financial profiles: "We had a very strong order book; they didn't, but they had a very strong product pipeline – which we didn't," said Chow. "So one was high in current value and the other was high in future value."

On the back of the original EH101 Merlin maritime patrol contract for the Royal Navy, Westland had built a buoyant order book worth almost £4 billion. The RAF had ordered the EH101 military utility variant; Canada had ordered a search-and-rescue version and the Tokyo Metropolitan Police had bought a civil version.

On top of that, the British Army had ordered 67 McDonnell-Douglas Apache helicopters which were being built at Yeovil and Westland was also winning new orders for the Super-Lynx variant of the original Lynx aircraft. Westland had certainly proved itself: "The Westland people were great engineers," said Lees. "They may not have been the most efficient company when we bought them, but there was no question about their engineering quality."

However, about 97% of the order book was for the UK MoD and much of that – notably the EH101 and Apache contracts – would end in the early 2000s. By contrast, Agusta had a long-term growth outlook through its civil market helicopters, a share in the European NH90 military aircraft and a new product, the AB139, developed with America's Bell, which had strong defence and civil potential.

"We didn't have the appetite to buy Agusta – we couldn't justify that without a heavy commitment to enter the helicopter business, which didn't make much sense to us. Finmeccanica had a number of defence businesses and it was more logical for them to be a helicopter company," Chow said.

The slight complication was that Finmeccanica wanted to buy Westland outright but GKN did not want to sell it: "We didn't feel a complete sale of Westland was the best way to extract value from it," said Chow. After protracted negotiations, GKN and Finmeccanica announced at the Farnborough Air Show in mid-2000 that they had reached agreement to create a 50–50 joint venture company, AgustaWestland.

By then, GKN had a new managing director of Aerospace. He had joined the group the previous November after a highly-successful 20 years at BAe. In a way, GKN's success in persuading him to join the group was the ultimate benefit of the Westland acquisition. Lees said: "If we hadn't had an aerospace business, we would never have got Kevin Smith."

# CHAPTER 26

# Parting of the Ways

Kevin Smith had not planned to join GKN. After he decided to leave BAe, he was lined up to head another UK aerospace company. However, he met and talked with Chow, who persuaded him to change his career plans. By the time he joined the group, GKN's Aerospace acquisition splurge was in full spate.

"When I arrived, I wasn't sure what they had. So I had a look around," Smith recalled. "We had to integrate these acquisitions and get some clarity into the aerospace business. I saw one investor, who asked me: 'What are you going to do with this bag of bits you call an aerospace business?' That wasn't far from the truth."

Smith set to work restructuring the aerospace interests "to create a genuine first-tier supplier of structures, components, assemblies and engineering services". Three plants – two in the US, one in the UK – were closed as he focused the operations on seven manufacturing centres in Europe and the US. A small German actuation business was sold.

"The restructuring cost about £70 m, but it was essential," Smith said. Then he set about building GKN into a front-rank aerospace business: "We cleaned out the portfolio and focused hard on two main areas: US Defence and Structures.

"From a technology viewpoint, we had done some work looking at where the aero sector was going to go in structures over the medium term. We focused on composites and on new programmes where our main opportunities lay. We didn't want too much of anything – we weren't going to bet the company balance sheet on one programme. We wanted a broad spread."

At Cowes on the Isle of Wight, the Westland Aerostructures business – hitherto a Cinderella operation always overshadowed by the helicopter arm – began to come into its own. The company had a rich heritage both as an aviation trailblazer and as an early adopter of structures work. It dated back to the late 19th century when Sam Saunders, one of Britain's aerospace pioneers, had created a lightweight laminate which he used on seaplanes.

Saunders-Roe, as the business became, subsequently ventured into rocket-propelled fighters, satellite launch rockets and hovercraft. But structures remained part of its portfolio, and became increasingly important as other activities declined and as the industry's interest in new materials intensified.

In the Eighties, composite content on aircraft – civil and military – was no more than about 3% on average by weight. Boeing used more composites on the 777. The Airbus A380 superjumbo, planned by Toulouse to leapfrog the 747 and nicknamed "the Double-Decker", would be about 25% composite; the F-35 Joint Strike Fighter would be 45%.

Dow-UT's Connecticut plant focused on a process called Resin Transfer Moulding (RTM), primarily aimed at the military market. This could produce high-strength, complex shapes to very precise tolerances – ideal for a combat aircraft airframe or engine. The Dow expertise was critical to GKN's success in securing an important position supplying the fan casing on the Pratt & Whitney F135 engine for the Joint Strike Fighter. It enabled one-piece composite structures to replace complex metal fabrications for the first time. "That impressed a bunch of people," said Smith.

When Boeing announced its revolutionary Sonic Cruiser, projected as a supersonic successor to Concorde, GKN was well positioned to be a supplier. The Sonic Cruiser never got off the ground, but Boeing instead announced what became the 787, a new technology replacement for the 767 and 757. GKN rapidly joined the programme.

Meanwhile, in collaboration with Airbus, Cowes developed a process called Resin Film Infusion (RFI). RFI was cheaper than RTM and obviated the need for autoclaves, the giant, high temperature ovens that were the conventional means of bonding composite elements on a structure such as a wing. RFI operated at low pressures and could deliver large, lightweight, high-quality structures at lower cost than the traditional methods.

RFI opened the way for GKN to secure work on the A380 worth about $2 m per aircraft. "The A380 was important," Smith said. "It was our first major design and

313

build programme with Airbus. We bought into the pro-gramme with some financial support from the Alabama Pension Fund. We had had a technology programme running with Airbus on wing composites. As a result of all this, we got the trailing edge on the A380 and most of the composite wing panels, on a design and build basis."

It was a big breakthrough – and not just because of the size of the aircraft, the largest civil jetliner in history. A second breakthrough followed, this time in Defence. "We had looked at outsourcing, which we believed was going to become a trend in the aerospace industry as it had been in automotive," Smith said. He hired Booz-Allen Hamilton, the consultancy, to study the potential market. "They interviewed a bunch of OEMs on the future. A number of them said they planned to get out of manufacturing and into systems integration."

As a result, GKN began to position itself to capitalise on outsourcing opportunities. Not a moment too soon. Boeing, which had acquired McDonnell-Douglas, was looking to divest MacDac's St. Louis fabrication plant, which supplied parts for the F18 E/F fighter and the C17 airlifter and had a strong composites business. This would be the first major plant outsourcing in the industry. It would, at a stroke, satisfy two GKN objectives because it would also significantly expand its US defence business.

Smith faced two obstacles: private equity firms were already talking to Boeing about taking over the plant, and GKN – having incurred hefty costs sorting out the results of its acquisitions in the late '90s – had imposed a ban on further aerospace purchases.

Smith – who knew the St Louis people well from his BAe days – convinced Boeing to select GKN as its preferred purchaser. Then he persuaded Chow to waive the bar on aerospace deals: "I managed to convince CK that, even if it went completely wrong, it wasn't going to be a disaster for the group," he recalled. "But I knew it would be a great move: it gave us a much stronger platform in aerospace."

GKN paid $55 m up front and committed to invest a further $65 m in the plant. First-year revenues were $240 m. "Off a small base, it gave us 30% growth," said Smith. "We got life of programme work on all defence platforms going through the plant; we negotiated a new union agreement which allowed us to create a lot of value very quickly. For everybody, it was a really good deal."

There was also a wider dimension. GKN and Boeing signed a memorandum of understanding which made GKN Aerospace a core structures supplier to Boeing and positioned the group to participate in the vast Joint Strike Fighter programme, then in its formative stages. GKN was also to become responsible for managing parts of the supply chain for Boeing's Military Aircraft and Missile Systems Group. At a stroke, Smith had secured his objective of significantly increasing GKN's presence in US military aerospace.

At the time, the St Louis acquisition was overshadowed by another development, which came within days of the American acquisition. On 15 January, GKN announced that it was in discussions about merging its industrial services businesses – CHEP, Cleanaway, Interlake Material

Handling and Meineke – with Brambles on a nil-premium basis to create a new company, dual-listed in Sydney and London.

The statement obeyed the first law of such official announcements – its length, which was relatively short, stood in inverse proportion to its significance, which was immense. Indeed, it foreshadowed the single largest shake-up in the group's structure since the steel interests were first nationalised in 1951.

The origins of the prospective demerger lay in the 1994 global agreement which determined that all future expansion of CHEP into new territories would be through the GKN-Brambles partnership. The agreement meant that one of GKN's largest growth businesses would be a joint venture over which, by definition, the group would lack total control.

Throughout the 1990s, amid the vogue for de-conglomeratisation and the pressures on corporate resources created by globalisation, GKN had increasingly faced questions about its ability to run both manufacturing and services operations at an optimum level. The question was legitimate, even if it reflected a preoccupation with GKN's patchy overall record in services rather than an acknowledgment that CHEP and Cleanaway had proved outstandingly successful diversifications.

The joint venture structure of CHEP and Cleanaway answered the question – GKN was focused on the automotive and aerospace businesses it controlled while the predominant services activities were managed by discrete and dedicated teams of their own. However, as CHEP in particular continued its rapid expansion, largely but not exclusively thanks to its American business, this structure began to concern both GKN and Brambles executives, for different reasons.

"We became increasingly uncomfortable with the 50–50 structure," said Chow. CHEP and, to a lesser extent, Cleanaway became victims of their own success. The larger they grew, the more important and valuable they were to their owners – and the more uncomfortable their owners became about not having control over such significant and lucrative businesses.

In 2000, GKN's share of CHEP's and Cleanaway's operating profits was £137 m, more than GKN's wholly-owned Aerospace business and second only to Automotive. CHEP's American venture appeared an outstanding success. It had won the endorsement of Wal-Mart, the world's biggest retailer, which was recommending that its legions of suppliers join the pool. Then Home Depot, the world's largest DIY retailer, asked its suppliers to do the same. At the same time, CHEP was expanding in South America with new operations in Brazil and Argentina and moving into Asia. The stage seemed set for its unlimited growth.

Margins on the two industrial services joint ventures were the highest of any major business in the group. As a result, their contribution was increasingly driving GKN's stock market value and rating. Given that GKN did not control the business, this factor contributed to the structural tension.

Brambles was also increasingly unhappy about the joint venture structure, for the simple reason that CHEP in particular was accounting for an ever-increasing share of

317

the Australian company's sales, profits and market worth. Brambles' reaction was to offer to buy GKN out of both CHEP and Cleanaway. But GKN did not want to sell. For one thing, Brambles could not afford to pay anything like GKN's valuation of the businesses, taking into account not just their current high profitability but their further growth potential. For another, as Lees said later: "One of the problems of a sale would have been that we had to have a natural use for the money, other than just returning it to shareholders, which was not a very popular concept at that time."

For its part, GKN did have the financial muscle to buy out its partner – but Brambles, an Australian icon, would not and could not agree to sell two of its prime assets. "They simply wouldn't talk about us buying them out," said Chow. "A hostile bid was possible, but if we hadn't succeeded, that would have hurt our share price because you would have had two partners in a mutually-important venture who had fallen out."

The catalyst for a deal came on the Australian side. A new chairman, Don Argus, took over at the head of Brambles and its CEO, John Fletcher subsequently left, along with his finance director. Argus, one of the leading figures in Australian business, was keen on a deal with GKN; the management vacuum at Brambles accentuated the urgency of agreeing one.

Initially, discussions focused on the possibility of a full merger between GKN and Brambles. Opinions differed about the viability of this option. One school of thought was that there would be an inevitable culture clash between the two companies which would undermine the merger rationale. The other contended that, since Brambles would basically comprise CHEP and Cleanaway, which came out of the GKN joint venture, any clash of cultures would be minimised.

In the end, Brambles' unwillingness to become exposed to the automotive industry killed the concept of a full merger. So the two sides concentrated on the idea of an industrial services merger. That essentially meant combining Brambles with the joint ventures. After months of negotiation during 2000 and early 2001, the two companies announced on 20 April that they had reached agreement.

Under the terms of the deal, GKN was to demerge its industrial services operations into a new company, called Brambles Industries plc (BIP), to be quoted on the London Stock Exchange. BIP would be effectively merged with the enlarged Brambles Industries Limited (BIL), the Sydney-quoted company, through a "sharing agreement" giving the owners of both Brambles companies equal rights and an apportioned economic interest in the combined assets of the businesses. The effect would be to create an Anglo-Australian Dual Listed Company (DLC).

To balance up the asset contributions to some extent, GKN injected the Interlake materials handling business and Meineke as well as its share of CHEP and Cleanaway. GKN was still the minority partner in asset terms, so its shareholders received 43% of the new DLC.

The value created for GKN shareholders was stunning. The combined market worth of the Sydney- and London-listed vehicles was £7 billion – meaning that GKN was handing its investors more than £3 billion-worth of equity along with their continuing 100% interest in GKN. That was quite something for a business that had started life just over 25 years earlier with the formation of CHEP UK.

Fittingly, the deal coincided with the collapse of the dot.com boom, during which hosts of insubstantial companies with paper-thin business models had soared to ludicrous stock market valuations. GKN-Brambles highlighted how real, long-term growth could be generated by adding value to a very basic commodity: the humble wooden pallet. Who got the best of the merger? Lees said: "It doesn't pay to think about winners and losers – we were happy with the deal."

For GKN, however, the deal had a double significance: not only was it hiving off its most highly-valued business, but it had to find a new chief executive and a new finance director: Chow and Turner respectively were moving to fill those two vacant positions at Brambles in Sydney. That posed a big question for GKN.

Lees said: "CK's retirement from GKN hadn't been on the succession planning horizon, but Brambles didn't have a CEO or an FD and CK rose to the challenge with David." Beresford, who had been planning to retire, now found himself recalled to the colours as Chow's successor in GKN while Nigel Stein, then finance director of Sinter Metals, became group finance director. The solution was welcomed by analysts: "We see this as a positive development with a strong team in charge of each business," said Merrill Lynch.

Beresford and Stein took up their new roles when the Brambles deal was consummated in August 2001. Despite the fact that GKN remained well-rated, and retained – for the moment – its place in the FTSE 100 index, there could be no mistaking the fact that the group faced a massive challenge. Brambles was seen as the (white) swan; GKN as the ugly duckling.

The *Financial Times* Lex column summed up the prevailing sentiment when it observed: "Good news for CHEP may be less good for the remaining automotive and aerospace divisions of GKN ... strip out the high growth and high margins provided by the pallet business, and GKN risks fading into that twilight reserved for mid-sized British engineers." In the event, things turned out rather differently – for both companies.

# CHAPTER 27

# Rump or Fillet

For the first time since its industrial services diversification began in the mid-1970s, GKN was now totally focused on engineering. More, for the first time since the merger of Guest and PNB 101 years earlier, it was concentrated in only two main businesses.

Group sales were still substantial, at more than £4 billion, but the £245 m profit before tax and exceptional costs was lower than at any time since 1994. As a result of the demerger, the group eventually lost its FTSE 100 status. It remained one of only two companies (the other being Tate & Lyle, which Lees coincidentally went on to chair) which had been members of the historic FT30 index since its foundation in 1935.

Lees told shareholders: "GKN has been transformed into a global engineering company, committed to growth." Beresford said the group would remain focused on growing organically in all its businesses, capitalising on additional outsourcing opportunities in Driveline and Aerospace, and seeking further consolidation moves in Aerospace and Powder Met.

"GKN faces the future from a position of strength," he said. "The management team is committed to growing shareholder value by delivering outstanding operational performance and above-average growth through the business cycle."

GKN's new CEO had one task above all: to inspire his people to share his confidence in the slimmed-down group's future. "We had to get everybody's tails up," Beresford recalled. "It was a case of galvanising hearts and minds."

Beresford held a series of team-building sessions, where he established one particular benchmark: "I made a fetish out of the relative share prices of us and Brambles. I said, 'Come on, we are going to show them'." He also employed reverse psychology. In the City, new GKN was being regularly described – somewhat disparagingly – as "the rump". Beresford said: "We used that – we said to our people: we are a lot better than that, so let's prove it. Truth to tell, they didn't need much galvanising; they had all the motivation we needed."

GKN was already facing a cyclical downturn in automotive, which particularly impacted the American powder metallurgy businesses: "Powder Met in Europe was going very well," Beresford said. "But in the US, we were chasing water downhill because of the exposure of the operations to the Detroit car-makers in general and to General Motors in particular."

On 11 September, the challenge facing Beresford's new team suddenly became much greater. GKN, in common with its peers, was hit by the dramatic fall-out in the civil aerospace industry from the dreadful debris of the 9/11 terrorist attack on the Twin Towers.

The 9/11 onslaught sent the civil aerospace world into a tailspin. As people across the Western world stopped flying, airlines slashed orders and civil aircraft makers cut back or cancelled their production programmes. "The decline in deliveries has been precipitate," Smith reported. In 2001, Boeing and Airbus had delivered a total of 850 aircraft. In 2002, they delivered 684. In common with all suppliers, GKN had to cut back. It reduced its workforce by 15% in the space of a few months, and wrote down by £50 m the value of some assets relating to design, development and tooling for new programmes.

Despite the horrific shock to the civil aerospace system, Kevin Smith kept his eyes on GKN's strategic objective of establishing Aerospace Services as a world leader. Early in 2002, the group acquired a second Boeing business, the Washington state-based Thermal Joining Centre, which produced a high-tech titanium assembly for the F-22, the leading-edge fighter being developed for the US Air Force.

GKN further extended its presence on important US military programmes by winning design and development contracts on the Comanche battlefield helicopter. Then it paid $32 m for ASTECH, a California-based leader in composite technologies for high-stress airframe and engine components. The group put down further roots in the US industry by opening a composite engineering centre in Connecticut and a Resin Transfer Moulding (RTM) facility inside the St Louis plant.

Driveline, now under Ian Griffiths, was also making progress. The group had already achieved one significant breakthrough by buying Nissan's in-house CVJ-manufacturing company based at Tochigi – the first time a Western component maker had acquired a business at the heart of the Nissan keiretsu, the family of companies owned by the vehicle maker.

Like the joint venture with Toyoda Machine Works, this deal marked a culmination and a vindication of Bonner's painstaking strategy of relationship-building with the Japanese majors. The opportunity arose because of the appointment as Nissan chief executive of Renault's Carlos Ghosn, after the French giant took a 36% stake in Nissan when the Japanese company was plunged into financial trouble and had to find a foreign car maker to support it.

Ghosn was concentrating Nissan's limited resources on its core activity of car making, and was therefore ready to sell some of the in-house component companies to outsiders. The respect GKN had earned as a long-standing Nissan supplier served it well. Tochigi was producing 1.3 m CVJ sets a year for both domestic and export supply.

GKN now supplied both Nissan and Mitsubishi in Japan, as well as Toyota, Honda and Mazda overseas. The Toyota relationship was also expanding, with Driveline being selected as sole supplier of sideshafts to the new Camry for the Asia-Pacific region. The business received successive quality awards from Toyota, accolades rarely won by Western companies. Highlighting the strength and spread of its Pacific Rim network, GKN supplied the CVJs for the Camry from plants in Thailand, Malaysia, Taiwan and Australia. The days of exporting from Germany were over, with important ramifications for Driveline which Griffiths was already pondering.

Despite the evidence that GKN was making good on Beresford's commitment to grow organically and through further outsourcing, there was no escaping the fact that, for the first time in many decades, the group was now relatively small enough to be a potential takeover target. Lees acknowledged later: "I certainly thought the demerger of industrial services would make us more vulnerable. That was partly because of the scale issue, because anybody who wanted to buy an auto business or an auto and aero business wouldn't really want to buy CHEP. The fact that it had been hived off made GKN more attractive to the potential buyer interested in the car business. But I have never been too worried about acquisition. If you are performing as well as you can, and you aren't selling the company down the river, that's life."

The natural and obvious way for GKN to fulfil many of its expansion aims – and to put itself beyond the reach of most predators – was to bulk up through a large and strategic acquisition. Both before and during the Brambles negotiations, the group came close to doing exactly that, when it considered a large transaction in the automotive sector which, ultimately, did not materialise.

But if the transformational megadeal passed GKN by, the group's long quest for a business it could build off the Driveline base at last reached fulfilment. Appropriately, given the effort that successive Driveline managements had sustained there, this related diversification was made in Japan.

Torque Management was in several respects a natural answer to the perennial question of how to expand Driveline beyond the driveshaft. It was, as one GKN manager tagged it, "CVJ-Plus". The market for advanced electronic torque management devices – systems which enhanced vehicle traction, stability and safety by generating more power for a given amount of energy and controlling that power very precisely – was expanding rapidly, for several reasons.

One was the fast-growing demand, fuelled by relatively low oil prices, for four-wheel and all-wheel drive vehicles, such as Sport Utilities and "Crossover" models combining 4WD functions with passenger car-like refinement. Another factor was the trend for rear wheel drive vehicles to use independent rear suspension, requiring power transfer from the longitudinal propshaft to transverse sideshafts. Over and above this was the fact that front wheel drive vehicle engines were now so potentially powerful that they could exceed the practical limit for conventional FWD systems, thereby requiring higher levels of stability and control.

Under Griffiths, Driveline established a Torque Systems Group in 2002 with the aim of becoming the world leader in non-CVJ driveline products by 2010. The new group set itself to develop a full range of products, from premium propshafts – highly-sophisticated descendants of the venerable propeller shaft – to geared driveline components such as PTUs (power transfer units) to actual Torque Management Devices.

A few existing Driveline businesses from Birfield days, including the venerable BRD, contributed to the torque systems venture. But what GKN really needed was a fully-fledged springboard into the market. As it happened, Japan was pre-eminent in torque management. And within Japan,

Tochigi Fuji Sangyo (TFS), GKN's partner of 16 years in the Viscodrive Japan joint venture, had established itself as a market leader.

Nissan held a stake in TFS and – as part of Ghosn's portfolio streamlining – was looking to sell it. In March 2002, GKN paid £29 m to Nissan and other investors for one-third of TFS, along with an option to increase that holding to 50.4%. With it, GKN acquired an international business – TFS employed 2000 people in Asia-Pacific including Japan and in the US – with strong growth potential.

Combining TFS with its existing operations, GKN had a business generating annual sales of £300 m to an impressive list of car makers including long-standing customers such as BMW, Ford, Toyota and Volkswagen, and newer clients like DaimlerChrysler and Porsche.

GKN believed that annual sales could be more than doubled within five years. It also reckoned that it had an edge over its rivals, none of whom had the same level of global coverage. "The combination of GKN and TFS is potentially very powerful, not only through GKN's global presence but because no other single competitor operates across the same wide range of devices and technologies," Griffiths said.

With Driveline successfully enlarging its technical and marketing footprint, Aerospace Services establishing itself at the forefront of the trends to composites and outsourcing, and AgustaWestland going strong, Marcus Beresford had achieved his objectives. He had steered GKN through what could have been a very awkward period after the industrial services demerger.

Contrary to most expectations, Brambles had the rougher ride. Chow and Turner discovered that, in the late-1990s dash for growth by CHEP, the business had lost control of its assets. It was piling more and more pallets into the network without adequately recovering those that were there already. Costs spiralled and profits slumped. The recovery took several years; during it, Chow left to head MTR, the Hong Kong-based transport giant; Turner took over as Brambles CEO and steered CHEP back to profitable growth.

At GKN, Beresford retired on 31 December 2002 and Kevin Smith (who was knighted in 2006) succeeded him. Beresford's unexpected career coda had been a "thoroughly enjoyable" 18-month stint in the hot seat. "The team did a superb job," he said later. "And David Lees was a tremendous non-executive chairman. There was absolutely no interference, but there was a mine of information and experience if you wanted to tap it."

The succession constituted a generational shift. Smith was aged 48 and in the space of four years had built the once-disparate Aerospace Services into a world leader. "Kevin Smith discovered Structures and developed it," said Lees. "It was there on the Isle of Wight and a little bit at Yeovil, minding its own business and accounting for no more than 20% of Westland's sales and profits."

While looking to the future, Smith was very conscious of GKN's heritage. One of his first acts as chief executive was to request a copy of the memo Jim Parsons had written three decades earlier to Raymond Brookes, discussing what distinguished GKN from its peers.

One item on Smith's agenda was the future ownership of AgustaWestland. GKN was in no hurry to exit what was a highly-successful venture: "It had gone pretty well and we were quite pleased with it," Smith said. "We were getting good export orders and potential for some new orders." Among them was a high-profile contract to supply the US Presidential helicopter fleet, for which AgustaWestland had teamed up with Lockheed Martin to offer the EH101 in competition against Sikorsky.

However, Smith recognised that probably GKN was eventually to exit the business. "That was more likely to be at the next stage of industrial restructuring. The potential was there for an exit, but not at any time soon." The world industry was expected to consolidate further and, in that restructuring, GKN could find itself squeezed between Finmeccanica and a new partner.

"We didn't want to be in any joint venture of such significance where we were a substantial minority," Smith recalled. "So if we ever went into that consolidation process, we would negotiate an exit with whoever the others were." GKN also felt that, if an exit were negotiated at the time of consolidation, there could be an element of competitive tension in the discussions. Finmeccanica was, after all, the only obvious buyer of GKN's 50% AgustaWestland stake and held pre-emption rights over the shareholding.

A secondary element in Smith's calculations was the group's financial position. The level of GKN's debt after the Brambles deal, together with changes in 2003 to the pension accounting rules, constrained the GKN balance sheet. The sale of the AgustaWestland stake at a good price would significantly ease those constraints.

The catalyst for a sale of the stake came out of the blue. In February 2003, barely a month into Smith's chief executiveship, the private equity firm Carlyle Group made a proposal to the GKN board to buy the company and take it private. Talks continued for several months, but during that period GKN's share price – which had been languishing when Carlyle made its initial approach – recovered. Carlyle dropped its proposal.

It was the closest GKN had come to takeover since the merger with John Lysaght. The experience brought home to the board the need to strengthen the company's defences against a predator. That put the focus on the helicopters operation – it was a large part of the group and a potential lever for someone who might want to break up the group.

So Smith opened negotiations with Finmeccanica. The Italians' initial valuation of the GKN holding in AgustaWestland was low – a mere £680 m. GKN made clear that it would not sell its stake for anything like that price. "In the end, we got there," Smith recounted. "The deal was all in cash, tax-free and it allowed us to completely recapitalise the group. It gave us the headroom to restructure and rebalance. We were able to get on and develop a few areas, pay down the debt, sort out the pension fund issue and restructure the driveline business."

On 26 May 2004, GKN and Finmeccanica unveiled the terms on which GKN had agreed to sell its Agusta Westland stake. The price was £1063.5 billion, of which £35 m was to be held in escrow and only paid if the MoD placed an order for Future Lynx – the next-generation Lynx aircraft – by the end of 2005 (after years of wrangling, GKN eventually got £17 m of that sum in 2008). It was, said Smith, "a transforming deal for GKN – the right price at the right time."

By an appropriate coincidence, the deal was unveiled only six days after Lees had retired from the group. His chairmanship had effectively been book-ended by Westland, from the acquisition of the original minority stake within months of his succeeding Holdsworth. In a way, Westland also encapsulated the abundant value that GKN had created for its shareholders during Lees' 16 years in the chair.

Apart from the industrial services demerger to Brambles, no deal in GKN's history had produced such a return. Lees signed off by recalling for shareholders his first report to them in 1988. "I am as optimistic today about the future prospects for GKN as I was then," he said. He was succeeded by Roy Brown, who had played himself into GKN thoroughly since joining the board eight years earlier.

The group over which Brown and Smith now presided looked more like its forebear, Guest, Keen & Nettlefolds, than ever. It was essentially focused on three, wholly-owned businesses: Automotive, Aerospace and OffHighway. The last link with armoured vehicles had been severed when GKN sold its residual stake in Alvis to BAE Systems for £73 m.

The group was now highly international. Employee numbers worldwide had increased from their lows in the mid-1990s to 40,500, but GKN's British workforce numbered just 5600 – a fraction of the 1979 total. For Smith,

GKN's globalism was a huge benefit. "If you've spent all your life in the defence sector, it's all about transatlantic collaboration and so on. GKN was very comfortable operating assets in North America, looking at doing business in China, Japan and India." In Automotive, he and Griffiths were already moving to maximise the value of that global footprint.

# CHAPTER 28

# Moving South, Driving East

Two months before unveiling the Westland deal, Smith surprised both the financial and automotive markets by announcing a radical reshaping of Driveline and Sinter Metals. Over three years, at a cost of about £250 m, GKN intended to transform the production footprint of both businesses worldwide.

For Driveline, the ambitious plan was partly the logical conclusion of the long march to globalisation. GKN intended to move 20% of its driveline manufacturing from the high-cost, low-growth regions of the West and the North to the low-cost, high-growth areas in the East and South, increasing capacity from those countries to around more than half the total production.

The strategy was impeccable: while vehicle output in the developed world was slowing to annual growth rates of 2% or less, production in Latin America, Eastern Europe and Asia was surging by more than 10% a year. In 2006, output in China soared by 26% and overtook that of both

Germany and Japan. Moreover, GKN estimated the labour cost differential in the emerging markets at up to 80% lower than in the West.

Smith and Griffiths were also moving to counter an increasing threat to Driveline's market position. "Through the back end of the Nineties, NTN decided to step up their attack on the sideshaft market," said Smith. "Visteon and Delphi [Ford and General Motors' component offshoot respectively] were both spun out of their parent companies and looked to expand in sideshafts, so the market became much more competitive." NTN acquired part of Renault's in-house CVJ production and attacked America; Visteon and Delphi were both benefiting from their relationship with their former parents.

The result was that Driveline's market share, though still impressive, was slipping. "We had been losing market share; the top line was falling; price pressure was pretty difficult," Smith recalled. "We had about 80% of our asset base in North America and Western Europe, which was making it very difficult to compete in a globalising industry where there was growth in Asia and some very aggressive competition. Traditionally, you bid for business in France, won it in France and made it in France. Capital expenditure was national. Now it was global, so we knew that we had to change the manufacturing strategy.

"We had to get strategically more assets on the ground where the growth was, rather than chasing the market there. We had to lower our break-even points – Mexico and Brazil were supplying more product to North America; Eastern Europe was supplying Western Europe."

The scale of the reorientation being contemplated by GKN was immense. Driveline had 49 manufacturing facilities in 31 countries, employing more than 21,000 people. "We did a review of all our plants," said Smith. "There was a 30% gap between the best- and worst-performing units. We had to compete more effectively. And we needed much stronger access to growth. So we had to reduce national country influences. The plan had quite a lot of risk attached to it."

In the course of the restructuring, Driveline closed two North American factories and one in France, opened a new forging plant in Poland and expanded its existing facilities in Poland, Slovenia, Brazil and Mexico – in the process, taking full control of Velcon 20 years after first establishing a minority stakeholding.

There were other major changes in the management system. Smith said: "It became a much more centralised approach to these key global processes like customer account management, asset allocation, task allocation – all of which had previously been owned by the various countries and regions. Now there was a very much stronger central influence, but with a continuing high level of people who had been in the driveshaft business for a long time, with a fantastic level of engineering competence."

The Sinter and Powder Metallurgy operations were extensively restructured for different reasons. Essentially, they had struggled to earn a respectable return on the very significant sums that GKN had invested in buying and building the division.

Lees believed: "The concept was good but we struggled in execution. It was a bit of a cottage industry. There is a big question about how you mop up a series of small companies to make a big one, when you have got a business but you aren't very big yourself. The theory is easy; the practice is much more difficult. But you only know that when you've tried to do it. What are the do's and don'ts? We got too many don'ts wrong in powder met."

Two elements recurrently dogged the operations. They were heavily dependent on North America, which accounted for about 60% of sales but, unlike Driveline, they did not have a significant customer base with the transplants. Directly or indirectly, 70% of Powder Met/ Sinter sales in North America were to the "Big Three" US manufacturers.

Unfortunately, by this time the "Big Three" moniker was a misnomer. All of them were losing market share to the Japanese and Chrysler had been overtaken by Toyota in absolute sales. Toyota went on to surpass Ford globally and, in 2008, GM. So, despite its success in winning new orders, the Powder Met division was under constant pressure. On top of that, the business was being hit hard by the soaring cost of scrap steel, its primary raw material, which almost doubled in price between 2003 and 2004. That pushed Powder Met into the red.

At the outset of the transformation programme, GKN wrote down the value of the Powder Met division assets by £151 m. Then it set about streamlining the complex plant configuration. Four of the 15 factories were closed and the remaining plants were simplified so that each specialised in a smaller range of components: "Fewer plants, greater focus, better individual scale" was the mantra.

In the end, the strategic restructuring programme ran slightly over time and budget – it took just over three years to complete, and cost £277 m. But Smith had no doubt that it was money well spent. GKN garnered annual benefits of more than £70 m, more than half of that in Driveline, whose market position in the emerging markets it reinforced.

In 2007, Driveline won 80% of all available new drive-shaft orders across the world, and 90% in emerging markets. Driveline margins in 2007 exceeded 8%, their highest for years. Almost one car in two built anywhere in the world now carried GKN equipment.

The market share increase was underpinned by new developments. Once more, GKN was producing the right products for the right time. A new generation of premium driveshafts – countertrack TM, with improved efficiency and reduced size, and crosstrack TM, to reduce vehicle noise and vibration. At the other end of the Driveline vehicle market, GKN was also providing low cost solutions for the new wave of ultra-low cost cars emerging from Asia, including Tata Motor's revolutionary Nano.

Throughout this pivotal period for the Automotive businesses, GKN was laying other foundations for the future. Torque Management's footprint was further enlarged by increasing the stake in TFS from a 33% minority to 84% control. Once more, the patient approach to stake-building paid off: "A one-third share was not a GKN business," said Smith. "We always had a view that, if we could make the business work, we could eventually acquire the whole company. That happened much earlier than we anticipated."

In Aerospace, GKN expanded its transparencies business in October 2003 by buying Pilkington Aerospace, the glassmaker's windows and cockpit canopies offshoot. Aerospace structures secured a prime position on the new Airbus A400M military transport aircraft for which it would produce the world's first all-composite large wing spars.

Aerospace also strengthened its increasing presence in the engine field when General Electric selected it to develop and supply the first composite large turbofan containment case for the new generation GEnx engine. Then it broke into the potentially vast future market for unmanned airborne vehicles by joining Northrop Grumman's successful bid for the X-47B UAV. "After 2001, we targeted every new programme, civil and military, and got a good position on every one," said Smith.

Advancing its composite credentials, GKN established a new centre on the Isle of Wight, in the shape of an Advanced Composite Facility combining materials R&D and leading-edge production technology. The operation was a shot in the arm for the whole UK aerospace industry, which was facing serious competition from German and Spanish rivals. They were pouring millions of pounds into composite materials R&D with a view to seizing Britain's long-held position as the centre of excellence for Airbus wings.

Smith supplemented Aerospace's organic growth with further significant acquisitions. GKN bought Stellex, a US maker of complex metal structure components, for £93 m.

Stellex was already on the Boeing 777 and had secured positions on the 787 and F-35 Joint Strike Fighter. The group's presence in aero-engine structures was advanced by the purchase of Teleflex Aerospace, another US business, which brought existing orders on the CFM56 engine, the sole powerplant for the Boeing 737, and the GE90. Teleflex had also secured a position on the F-135 engine, thereby expanding GKN's role on the F-35.

Smith was aware that, in making GKN one of the leading British aerospace players, he was pushing the outside of the envelope. "It is very rare to be able to grow a very strong aerospace business within a very strong automotive company – the odds are overwhelmingly against you. The market valuation makes it very difficult to do that," he said. Stock markets value aerospace companies much more highly than motor industry stocks, on the assumption that aerospace offers far greater long-term growth.

Smith believed cross-fertilisation was key to unifying GKN. Some of the automotive disciplines, applied to aerospace, could bring significant competitive advantage. "In automotive, if you made 130 million units of something – as in driveshafts – every euro is really important. That requires great attention to detail. Short-term management in automotive was strong. To take some of that into aerospace was important – the focus on really good manufacturing; the focus on cost, quality and delivery. Everything in automotive is right first time, deliver on time. That was much more strongly developed than in aerospace.

"In terms of manufacturing process technology, the aerospace industry was 10 years behind. It is catching up very quickly: the next generation of civil aircraft will make a huge difference to the aerospace industry. They will be built with much more automation. We are really thinking hard about the complexity of the shapes and sizes of structures. Aircraft will be built with many fewer piece parts. As the industry grows, and volume grows, the way and speed at which you move material will become of almost automotive proportions."

Smith also wanted to promote a group team spirit, which he believed GKN was lacking. "What I had been used to with BAe, probably because we were all very close to each other, was this collegiate approach, the "BAe-ness", which wasn't there at GKN. The group had been an international corporate conglomerate in the Eighties and Nineties with a range of different businesses. The main common factor was the financial reporting system.

"When we'd done the demerger, we had the engineering company left. All its divisions had been run very separately. Within the divisions, there was a high degree of fragmentation. I felt that we had got a huge amount in common in engineering and manufacturing and that we must apply that together – we couldn't afford to run these separate streams."

One way to breed group team spirit was to intensify GKN's work in the field of corporate social responsibility. Individual GKN companies had a long history of such activity in their different localities. This tradition was highlighted after the catastrophic Asian tsunami on Boxing Day 2005. A team from GKN's Thailand driveline plant in Rayong drove 1000 kilometres with money and more than a tonne of food to help the fishermen and their families in the devastated village of Kampoun. Three months later, the team returned to build new houses and help the villagers buy new boats.

This and other, less dramatic, examples of community work encouraged Smith to plan a coordinated year of community activity with Africa as the ultimate focal point. "I thought that, if we could find a way to harness all our individual company efforts and build a project which was really about GKN working with the communities, doing good within the communities and doing that bit extra for Africa, then that could have a strong influence for the company," he said.

Mission Everest was born. Its title came from the project's symbol, a record-breaking paraglider flight on 14 May 2007 over the Himalayas by the adventurer Bear Grylls. On the ground, GKN employees were challenged to raise $500,000 in money and time donations for their communities over and above their normal activities. In the event, they raised more than three times that amount.

In recognition of their efforts, the GKN headquarters contributed $500,000 through five children's charities in Africa for new school buildings, water supplies and health care. A further $500,000 was committed in 2008. "We are doing more and more in the communities with whom we've worked," said Smith. "It's like the work John Guest did at Dowlais. It's all there in the spirit of the group."

GKN was now a business with four market-leading divisions, Smith having identified the OffHighway operation as distinct from the Driveline and Powder Metallurgy businesses. OffHighway's base remained wheels, axles and drivelines for agricultural vehicles, and it was expanding into construction and mining equipment. Growth here was accelerated by the acquisition of the US-based Rockford in August 2006 and, four months later, the purchase of Liuzhou, a Chinese wheel-making company, which brought the division's first plant in the People's Republic.

As 2007 progressed, all the work since the demerger of industrial services was paying off. In April, the shares touched 400 p for the first time since late 1999, valuing the group at about £2.8 billion. Trading profits, which had been rising steadily since the sale of the Westland stake, totalled £277 m for the year. Underlying earnings climbed to just over 35 p a share. Return on average invested capital was 15.1%. Group margin reached 7.5%, lifted by Driveline and by Aerospace, where margins climbed to 10.1%. The lights seemed set at green for further growth.

# CHAPTER 29

# The Ultimate Challenge

The only cloud on the horizon as 2007 turned into 2008 was the apparently unstoppable rise in the cost of raw materials, the product of a global commodities boom fuelled by the growth of China, India and the other emerging markets.

The price of hot rolled steel coil in the US, which had stood at $500 a tonne in January 2007, more than doubled to $1100 a tonne in the space of the next 15 months.

The cost of GKN's most important raw material, scrap steel, was also going through the roof. Scrap steel prices had been volatile throughout the decade, standing at only $150 a tonne at the end of 2002 and climbing to $350 a tonne over the next two years before falling back. In the first half of 2007, scrap steel had averaged $293 a tonne. In July 2008, the spot price had soared to $825 a tonne. Driveline and Powder Metallurgy responded by negotiating new deals with their customers to pass through much of the increases.

Meanwhile, oil prices had surged through $100 a barrel and hit a peak of $147.27 on 11 July 2008. Goldman Sachs analysts predicted oil would go to $200. Gazprom, the Russian energy leviathan, forecast it would reach $250.

Then, almost overnight, the world went into reverse. Tensions had been building in the global financial system for months, as a slump in the US housing market in 2007 had triggered a collapse in the value of "subprime" loans made on the value of American properties. These loans had been recycled, via a myriad of complex derivative instruments, through the developed world's banking system. Like a narcotic, they had poisoned the financial bloodstream.

Gradually, the price of money on the wholesale markets – dirt cheap for years – began to increase, and confidence started to ebb away. A "credit crunch" took hold. Those banks most dependent on the wholesale markets found it increasingly difficult to carry on their business. In the United States and Britain, a number of large financial houses had to be bailed out by their respective governments.

The crunch became a crisis on Monday, 15 September 2008. In the very early hours of that fateful morning, Merrill Lynch – the "Thundering Herd" of Wall Street and one of the largest of all American investment banks – was rescued through a takeover by Bank of America brokered by the US government. But Lehman Brothers, a smaller but very well-known Wall Street bank, was allowed to go to the wall.

Unlike Merrills or the other companies propped up by the US government, Lehman did not have depositors. But as a highly-active trader – it did more volume in many London stocks than any rival – Lehman had a vast array of counterparties. They were all exposed to its failure. In a nano-second, the last vestiges of residual confidence in the system were swept away by fear and panic on a scale unprecedented since the Wall Street Crash of 1929.

History played its usual trick, repeating itself with a twist. This time, the crisis was not triggered by collapsing equity markets – it was caused by credit markets that froze up, like something out of the eco-disaster movie, "The Day After Tomorrow". Around the world, governments poured in billions to support their economies. By the start of 2009, government support for banks – including capital injections, loans and guarantees – totalled more than £4 trillion.

The global salvage effort worked, insofar as it staved off total meltdown of the financial system. But it could not avert the inevitable: a plunge into deep, dark recession which left parts of the developed world – notably the US and Britain – in their worst slump since at least the early 1980s.

For the world's largest manufacturing industry, the repercussions were catastrophic. The motor industry was intimately bound up with the banking sector: credit financed more than 90% of new car purchases in the US and more than two-thirds in Europe. Vehicle sales had been sliding in the US for a year, but as credit froze in the wake of Lehman, they fell off a cliff both there and in Europe.

From 2001 until 2006, US sales had averaged around 16.5 m a year. They fell to 13.4 m in 2008. But in December and January, the Seasonally Adjusted Annual Rate (SAAR) was less than 10 m – its lowest levels since the early '80s. The Big Three suffered most. In 2007, for the first time, their combined domestic market share had fallen below 50%; in 2008, it dropped to less than 45% of the shrunken market.

Over Christmas, General Motors and Chrysler sought and received emergency bail-outs worth billions of dollars from the US government. But no-one, not even the Japanese, was immune from the US slump. The annual Detroit auto show in New Year 2009 was a grim affair: "I have seen a better mood at funerals," said the president of America's largest car-dealer chain.

In Europe, sales in Spain halved in November and December 2008. In Italy, car production fell below 700,000 vehicles for the first time since 1961. In Britain, Nissan cut almost one-third of its production workforce at Sunderland – the first such redundancy programme in the plant's quarter-century existence. Honda announced that it would stop production at its Swindon factory for two months in early 2009. Then it decided to close for four months out of the first six – a quite unprecedented shutdown. Toyota forecast that it would make its first-ever annual loss. Less than a month later, it warned that the loss would be three times the size it had anticipated.

For GKN and its fellow component-suppliers, the killer impact came as OEMs worldwide slashed their schedules. In a credit crunch, failure to control working capital means disaster: the fall in sales triggered ferocious production cutbacks as the OEMs fought to bring down their bloated stocks of finished vehicles.

The group's global leadership of its automotive segment now took on a new significance. It meant that GKN was in the front line of manufacturers experiencing the full force of an extraordinary and quite unprecedented event: the first global downturn in the history of the motor industry.

In every other cyclical post-war slump, geographical or technical factors had offset the impact of the fall in output on GKN. In the early '90s, when Western Europe and the US were hit, Germany was still enjoying the reunification boom and Japanese transplants were gaining ground in America. In the early '80s, when demand dived in Britain and America, continental Europe remained robust and the trend to front wheel drive offset much of the US weakness. In the Depression of the early '30s, the UK car industry recovered quickly because it was young and still enjoying secular growth.

Now, there were no safety valves. Analysts at Citigroup reckoned that 2009 sales in Europe could fall below the trend of replacement demand for the first time since the 1950s. With commendable understatement, they described this prospect as "a historically unusual event".

For a while, commentators thought – or hoped – that the emerging markets would be relatively protected against the developed world recession. That hope was finally punctured on 24 November 2008, when GKN issued its second warning within a month about the likely level of 2008 profits. Having warned in October that underlying pre-tax profits would be around 20% lower than the previous year's £255 m, the group told the stock market that they would in fact be down by more than a third.

The reason was stark: global production schedules had collapsed. The slump encompassed not only the US and Western Europe, but Japan where GKN's schedules had tumbled 22%, Brazil was down 25%, and even China was down 25%.

Some commentators were flabbergasted. At first, the *Financial Times* motor industry correspondent did not believe GKN's numbers. To some extent, the incredulity could be justified: it took a mental effort to absorb the full dimensions of the meltdown that was taking place. Driveline profits suffered an unprecedented fall – down from £71 m in the first half of the year to a mere £2 m in the second. In the last two months, Driveline actually lost money, so far and so fast did its schedules evaporate. Its only consolation was that almost every other major auto company, vehicle maker or supplier, was also in the red.

Smith was determined to react quickly, in order to minimise the cash outflows that the group would otherwise suffer. By the year-end, GKN had cut 2800 jobs on top of the 650 shed earlier in the year in Powder Met. Most of them were temporary workers, all were from the automotive workforce where all 64 of the factories worldwide were on short-time working. But the group had to prepare a much more far-reaching restructuring plan.

In February 2009, it estimated the cash cost of that plan, which involved further short-time working, job reductions and factory closures, at no less than £140 m. It also wrote down the value of some assets – particularly in Powder Met – by £150 m. "Our restructuring actions will deliver significant cost savings, which will help reinforce the group's resilience in the face of the global economic downturn," Smith said.

A further 2400 jobs were to be cut across the group. Factories which had survived successive recessions were casualties of the industrial tsunami. One was the old BRD propshaft plant at Aldridge, which was to be merged into the former Hardy Spicer works at Erdington in Birmingham.

The writedowns pushed GKN into a full-year pre-tax loss of £130 m – its first since 1980. Even more significantly, in order to conserve cash it did not pay a final dividend – the first time it had passed a dividend on its Ordinary stock since the early 1930s.

GKN was being tested as it had been tested on only a handful of occasions in its 250-year lifetime. The share price plummetted to its lowest levels for decades. But Smith and his team held firm. The group continued to safeguard and generate cash. And, amid the motor industry mayhem and with a looming slowdown in the aerospace and OffHighway markets, GKN continued to build for the future. In June 2009, it launched a rights issue to raise more than £400m – its first cash call for 26 years.

Six months earlier, on 5 January, GKN completed its most significant aerospace acquisition since Westland. After more than a year of negotiation, it took over owner-ship of the Airbus wing component and sub-assembly making plant at Filton in Bristol for a total cash considera-tion of £136 m, phased over several years.

The deal promised to transform the size of the aero-space business, doubling its order book for large aircraft structures to $10 billion and increasing annualised sales by 25% to £1.6 billion. The addition of Filton's 1500-strong workforce increased the size of GKN's UK staff to more than 6000, over two-thirds of them now in aerospace.

Smith said: "The acquisition of Filton is a further exciting step in the development of GKN's Aerospace business. The strategic logic is compelling. It brings a strong order backlog which supports solid growth."

The purchase confirmed GKN as Britain's third-largest aerospace group after BAES and Rolls-Royce: a remarkable metamorphosis in the 15 years since the Westland acquisition. The group was still moving up the value chain. Amid the intense instability of the global downturn, the only certainty was GKN's readiness to change once more.

# Conclusion

GKN's was not the only anniversary in 2009 that testified to the power of evolution. By a happy irony, the year also marked the bicentennial of Charles Darwin, who was born in England in 1809.

Darwin maintained that: "It is not the strongest of the species that survives, nor the most intelligent, but the one most responsive to change." As an explanation for the remarkable durability of GKN, that is not perfect – the group has regularly survived economic downturns because of its financial and operational strength, and its top management has been frequently distinguished by immense business acumen.

But there can be no doubt that GKN's readiness to change when or, better still, before change was required, has been the feature that has most distinguished it from all its peers, from the iron age of the Industrial Revolution to the present day, who have fallen by the wayside of business history.

That adaptability is reflected in so many aspects of GKN's life. The group was never a great innovator, but it was always technologically astute and quick to react. It has at times been incredibly lucky – the discovery of Uni-Cardan or Westland Aerostructures, for instance. But it repeatedly had the agility to recognise what luck had brought it and to take full advantage. "You make your own luck," as David Lees observed.

Major companies generally fail when they turn inward and close their senses to the external stimuli that kept them dynamic. By contrast, through successive generations of management, GKN has remained remarkably open minded.

The company did not have a series of dominant leaders who handed down, ex cathedra, a Darwin-like doctrine on tablets of stone. Strong leadership has of course been a feature of the group's history, from the Guests on. The leadership has come in different forms – Guest and the Nettlefolds were engineer-industrialists, Arthur Keen and H. Seymour Berry deal-making entrepreneurs. But whoever was the company's driving force, he or they never created a monolith. The group has constantly been distinguished by a tension between the centre and the divisions, between the financial controls of the former and the pressures for autonomy by the latter.

Usually, that tension has been creative. To build two large and highly-profitable service businesses, CHEP and Cleanaway, from an engineering-dominated group was an extraordinary achievement. Still more remarkable was the group's metamorphosis from a UK-orientated conglomerate in 1980 to a truly international, cosmopolitan, focused organisation less than two decades later.

The result of the structural tension has been a highly constructive balance of forces. Marcus Beresford, who had top-level experience of other major industrial groups, said that in purely technical terms, GKN's financial controls were not exceptional. But Beresford found that in its all-round corporate governance, in its planning disciplines and in the standard of the work fed into its board papers, GKN was outstanding. In other words, the information on which GKN based its decisions was of the highest order. And in business, information is not only power – its quality is the key to successful decision-making.

A similar balance was personally embodied in a number of GKN leaders. Raymond Brookes noted how James Jolly's readiness to back a radical idea sat alongside his orthodoxy. More recently, three of the most outstanding executives in GKN's history – Sir Trevor Holdsworth, Sir David Lees and Trevor Bonner – combined the financial expertise derived from an accountant's training with the deep engineering knowhow gathered during a lifetime in manufacturing.

The institutionalised combination of financial and engineering skills – a combination fatally lacking in so many British companies which failed to meet the challenge of international competition – underpins GKN's remarkable capacity for self-renewal. It has given rise to the qualities of consistency, continuity and stability that have enabled GKN to weather adversity and to emerge from it – from the wars, the depressions and recessions – stronger and better-equipped not only to survive, but to grow again.

The company has anticipated opportunities and capitalised on them. It has welcomed change, not feared it. It has been determined, but flexible. It has failed on occasion, but has not been afraid to try again. It has kept its head in crises – in the Depression and each of the recessions that started in 1980, 1990 and 2008, it continued to invest both organically and by acquisition in core businesses. In the process, it has remained – as one former executive described it – "a kind company, not a hire-and-fire company, not a knee-jerk company. You knew that if you did your job, that would be fine."

GKN's story is devoid of corporate egomania or scandals of executive remuneration. Asked if one voluntarily departing senior executive might be in receipt of a large severance payment, the chairman of the day said simply, "That is not how we do things at GKN."

Above all, as befits a company in the precise and objective universe of engineering, it has always been practical. It has had no place for delusions of grandeur or ill-conceived flights of fancy. From its earliest days, GKN has been a proud company. But that pride has always been tempered by an immense realism. That is why it is still here. That is why it occupies a unique place in global industrial history.

# Select Bibliography

*A History of GKN*, Volumes One and Two by Edgar Jones, Macmillan, 1987 and 1990.

GKN Annual Reports 1946–2008.

*The Motor Makers* by Martin Adeney, William Collins, 1988.

*Chronicle of the 20th Century*, Dorling Kindersley, 1995.

*The Rise and Decline of the British Motor Industry* by Roy Church, Macmillan, 1994; Cambridge University Press, 1995.

*Lady Charlotte Guest: An Extraordinary Life* by Revel Guest and Angela V. John, George Weidenfeld & Nicholson, 1989; Tempus, 2007.

*The British Aircraft Industry* by Keith Hayward, Manchester University Press, 1989.

*Just in Time* by John Hoskyns, Aurum, 2000.

*G. T. Clark, Scholar Ironmaster in the Victorian Age*, edited by Brian Ll. James, University of Wales Press, Cardiff, 1998.

*A Fighting Chance* by Andrew Lorenz, Hutchinson Business Books, 1989.

*A History of Modern Britain* by Andrew Marr, Macmillan, 2007.

*From Empire to Europe* by Geoffrey Owen, HarperCollins, 1999.

*All Our Working Lives* by Peter Pagnamenta and Richard Overy, BBC, 1984.

*From Boom to Bust* by David Smith, Penguin, 1992.

*Business in Britain* by Graham Turner, Eyre & Spottiswoode, 1969.

*English Culture and The Decline of the Industrial Spirit 1850–1980* by Martin J. Wiener, Cambridge University Press, 1981.

# Index

9/11 terrorist attacks 325

ACS Coffee 271
adaptability of GKN 353–4
AE, takeover bids for 218–20
Aerospace business
  expansion of 308, 340–1, 351–2
  first ventures by GKN (in WW2)
    81
  GKN's entry via Westland 279
  restructuring in early-2000s 311–15
  US Defence work 313, 314–15,
    325
  *see also* Westland
AEU/AUEW (engineering workers'
  union) 128, 180, 182
Africa, community activity with 343
Agusta helicopter company 259, 308,
  309, 310
AgustaWestland 310
  sale of GKN's stake 332
Airbus A380 superjumbo 312, 313–14
Airbus A400M military transport
  aircraft 340
Airbus wing fabrication, GKN's
  involvement 314, 340, 351–2

Alamance (North Carolina, USA),
  driveline factory 194, 246
Allied Steel & Wire Holdings (ASW)
  208, 245
Alvis 217, 259
  merger of GKN Defence with 307
  sale of GKN's stake 333
American War of Independence 4
*amici curiae* (impartial advisers),
  in Meineke lawsuit 294
annual growth rates, British output
  (19th C.) 40
Arab Organisation for Industrialisation
  (AOI), compensation claim by
  Westland 277–8, 278–9
Argentina
  CHEP in 317
  Driveline manufacturing plants 287
Argus, Don (head of Brambles) 318
armoured vehicle business 103,
  215–17, 273–4
  GKN's exit 333
  strategic decisions (in late-1990s)
    306–7
Astbury, Thomas 45, 46
ASTECH composites company 325

Atlee, Clement (Prime Minster) 85
Austin, Herbert 66, 108
Australia
    automotive businesses 246, 271
    GKN steel business 79, 130–2,
        149–50, 197
    see also Brambles group
auto after-market 145
automobile parts, Sankey's production
    66–7
Automotive businesses 106, 108–10,
    223
    contribution to GKN turnover and
        profits 123, 223
    effect of 1980–82 recession 204
    effect of collapse of Communist
        regimes 266–7
    expansion of 225–32, 303–6
    outsourcing deals 285, 286–8
    see also Driveline business
Autoparts business 194–5, 196–7,
    232
    expansion of 263
    factors affecting 281–2
    structural problems 242
    UK business sold 264

Babbage, Charles 11
Baldwins 74
    merger with GKN steel interests
        74
Barber, Anthony (Chancellor of
    Exchequer) 142
Barry, Sir Charles 19
Battlefield Mobility concept 259, 277
Bayley, John (Westland's company
    secretary) 277
Bayliss, Jones & Bayliss 47, 64
Beale, Sir John Field (GKN chairman)
    73
Beale, Sir Samuel (GKN chairman)
    73, 80, 86
Bean, Jack (Garringtons chairman) 82,
    88, 105
Beck/Arnley 232, 263

Beech, Albert (Garringtons MD) 82
Beech, Jack (general manager, then
    joint-MD of Garringtons) 82, 83
Benn, Tony (Energy Minister) 186
Beresford, Marcus (head of industrial
    services business, then CEO)
    on business portfolio 280–1
    as chief executive 320, 323–4, 329
    on Cleanaway 284, 285
    as Jessop's successor 280, 289
    on Lees 330
    Meineke court case 291
    on quality of information 355
    retirement from GKN 330
Berlin Wall, demolition of 264
Berry, H. Seymour (later Lord
    Buckland) 64–5, 67–71
    death 70
    philanthropy 70
    sense of humour 70–1
    takeover of Lysaghts 65
    takeover of Sankeys 65, 67
Bessborough, Lord 58, 63, 68
Bessemer, Henry 32, 33
Bessemer process 32–3
    used at Dowlais 35
Biggs, Sir Norman 187
Birch, Claude 100
Birfield 108
    licenses granted in Japan 226–7
    stake in Uni-Cardan group 134
    takeover by GKN 118–20
Birfield Trasmissioni 120, 134, 231
Blackwell, Sir Basil 254
Blake, Geoffrey (MD of Building
    Supplies and Services subgroup)
    157, 158, 159, 163
BMW 133, 230
Boeing–GKN supplier agreement 315
Boeing Sonic Cruiser 313
Bonner, Trevor (head of Uni-Cardan,
    then of GKN's driveline business)
    accountancy background 355
    as GKN main board director 238,
        248, 253

on GKN's share of joint ventures
286–7
on Japanese motor industry 228,
229
on management succession 299
on market leadership 288
on outsourcing deals 286
retirement 298
on Sachs merger bid 175–6
successors 299
on Uni-Cardan's contribution to
GKN 211
on Uni-Cardan's reporting systems
142
Borlenghi, Michael (head of strategy
and business development) 238,
248
Boulton & Watt steam engines 5–6
Bourne, John 244
Bowlby, Sir Anthony (Tony) 79, 94,
100
Boxing Day tsunami disaster 342–3
Brambles group (Australia) 158–9
CHEP joint ventures 161, 196, 284
merger of industrial services
businesses with GKN 315–20
pallet pool business in Australia 159
relationship with GKN 282–4,
317–18
waste management business joint
ventures 212–13, 284–5
Brambles Industries Limited (BIL)
chief executive(s) 320, 330
finance director 320
formation of 319
slump in profits 330
Brambles Industries plc (BIP),
formation of 319
branch operations, GKN's ability to
run 281–2
Brazil
CHEP in 317
Driveline manufacturing plants 247,
287, 337
BRD 104–6, 108–9, 220, 328

British Aerospace (BAe)
as possible Westland buyer 256,
275
Royal Ordnance bid 244
British Bright Bar 208, 245
British Leyland (BL) 170, 190, 204
British Motor Company (BMC) 108,
110–11
British Steel Corporation (BSC) 124
Brookes as non-exec director 125
GKN Dowlais Ltd sold to 140
joint ventures with GKN 208,
237–8, 245, 271
national strike 203
sale of GKN's stake in UES to 279
British Vending Industries 238
Brittan, Leon 256
Broken Hill Proprietary (BHP),
partnership in Lysaghts
Australia 130–2, 149–50
Bromsgrove (Worcs) forging plant 88,
89
Brookes, Raymond (GKN chairman –
*latterly* Lord Brookes)
background and education 114–15
on Birfield takeover 118, 119
BRD and 105–6, 108–10
on Brymbo steelworks 125–6, 271
disagreement with Holdsworth over
steel businesses 139, 141, 237
Garringtons and 81–4
as GKN chairman 113
on government policies 121, 122,
127, 143
on James Jolly 92–3, 355
legacy to GKN 151–5
as life president of GKN 155
Lysaght Australia and BHP 130–2,
149–50
on nationalisation of steel companies
123, 124
retirement 155
on UK economy (1970s) 129,
146–7
Uni-Cardan and 120, 134–8

Brown, Roy
  as non-executive chairman 333
  as non-executive director 289
Bruce, Henry 26
Bruce-Gardner, Sir Douglas 162
Brunel, Isambard Kingdom 16, 17, 25
Brymbo blast furnace (mid-1790s) 5
Brymbo steelworks 89–90, 97, 208
  closure of 271
  nationalisation of 91, 124–5
  reacquisition of 97, 140
  in UES joint venture 237
Buckland, Lord see Berry, H. Seymour
Building Supplies and Services (BSS)
  subgroup 157
Bullock committee (on "industrial
  democracy") 186–90
Bute, (2nd) Marquis of 15–16, 20
  negotiations with Dowlais Iron
    Company 16, 18–19

Callaghan, Jim 123, 127
Callard, Sir Jack 187
Canford Manor (nr Wimbourne,
  Dorset) 19
car body panels 66
car imports 127–8, 170, 190
car manufacturing industry in UK
  decline of 127, 170, 190, 204
  effects of strikes 117
  growth 108
car wheels 66–7
Cardiff docks, steelworks near 41
Carlyle Group (private equity firm),
  proposal to buy GKN 332
cartels
  German law on 172, 173
  steel rails 57
  woodscrews 54, 77
Carter & Co. (accountants) 55
chairman of GKN
  (Sir John Field) Beale 73
  (Sir Samuel) Beale 73
  (H. Seymour) Berry 70
  (Lord) Bessborough 58, 63

(Raymond) Brookes 113
(Roy) Brown 333
(Barrie) Heath 149, 152
(Trevor) Holdsworth 193
(James) Jolly 86
(David) Lees 248, 251, 289
(Kenneth) Peacock 93
  separation from role of chief
    executive 289
(Edward) Steer 68
see also individual name entries
Chamberlain, Joseph 50, 52–3
  marketing approach 52
  political career 52, 53
  see also Nettlefold & Chamberlain
    (N&C)
Chartism 12–13
Chem-tronics 305, 308
CHEP (Australia) 158–9
CHEP Europe 196, 245, 283
CHEP South Africa 283
CHEP UK 159–65, 195, 245, 354
  Brambles' stake in 161, 196, 284
CHEP USA 271–2, 284, 317
CHEP ventures
  global rollout of 284, 317
  ownership structure 161, 196, 283,
    284, 296, 316–18
chief executive of GKN
  (Marcus) Beresford 320
  (C.K.) Chow 290
  cultural survey as to role 296
  separation from role of chairman
    289
  (Kevin) Smith 330
child workers (mid-19th C.) 34
China
  Driveline joint ventures 246–7, 287
  OffHighway division plant 344
Chow, C. K.
  background 302
  as Brambles chief executive 320
  on CHEP and Cleanaway ventures
    317, 318
  compared with Lees 302

on Defence business 296, 306, 307,
    308, 309, 310
on Driveline business 296, 297
expansion strategy 303–8
as GKN chief executive 290
strategic analysis of GKN's position
    in late-1990s 295–6
on Westland 308–9, 310
Chrysler 177, 199, 229
Churchill, Sir Winston 85, 92
Civic stores 144, 145
Clark, George (chief executive of
    Dowlais) 23, 24, 25–7, 28, 29,
    41
    contributions to community 26–7
    death 44
    experience 25–6
    retirement 43
class action, Meineke lawsuit as 292–3
Cleanaway waste management
    business 212–13, 354
    in Europe 285
    new management appointment
    284–5
    ownership structure 213, 296, 316
Cleveland Row (London) offices 236,
    237
coal trade 29, 40, 68–9, 76
Coalbrookdale 2
Cold War, end of 265
collieries
    GKN-owned 76
    ownership by ironmasters 29
commodities, price rises 345
community activity 342–3
competition authorities 172–4,
    218–29
composite leaf spring 233, 270
composites technology 260, 312–15,
    325
Conservative governments 92–116,
    127–51, 190
constant velocity joints (CVJs) 110–13,
    231
    see also Uni-Cardan

Controlled Establishments (in WW1)
    59
corporate learning initiatives 302–3
corporate social responsibility 342,
    343
Cort, Henry 4, 6
(F.W.) Cotterill 47, 63
counter-inflationary policies 103, 143,
    147, 201
    effect on UK industry 143–4,
    201–2
Crawshay, Richard 5
"credit crunch" 346, 347
credit restrictions, removal (in 1971)
    143
Crimean War 23
Cripps, Sir Stafford (Chancellor of
    Exchequer) 91
cross-fertilisation between automotive
    and aerospace disciplines 341–2
Cuckney, Sir John (Westland
    chairman) 254, 255, 256
Custis, Paddy (GKN Finance
    Director) 169, 193
Cwmbran ironworks 46, 48, 57, 103
Cwmbran nut and bolt factory
    60, 61
Cyfarthfa ironworks 5, 13
Czechoslovakia 265

Daly, Alec (head of Sankey) 213–16,
    217
    as GKN main board director 238,
    248, 253
    on Westland bid 257, 259–60, 261,
    262
    as Westland director 261–2,
    277–8
Daniel, Bob (UTC chairman) 276
Darby, Abraham 2
Darby, John Henry 90
Darwin, Charles 353
Datsun 170
    see also Nissan
deconglomeratisation 280, 316

Defence businesses 67, 80, 103, 217,
257–8
effect of collapse of Communist
regimes 265–6
search for expansion opportunities
(in late-1980s) 258–60
strategic decisions (in late-1990s)
306–10
see also Sankey; Westland
Deming, W. Edwards 230
Denham, Grey (GKN Legal
Counsel) 208, 209, 211
Meineke court case 291, 292, 293,
295
Depression see recessions
Desert Storm (military operation)
272–3
devaluation of pound 90, 122
Disraeli, Benjamin 10
distribution services 145, 195, 196
divestments programmes 197–8, 208,
237–8, 270–1
Divett, Edward 23
dividends paid by GKN 146, 198,
203, 245, 264, 270, 351
Donald, Ian 144, 193, 228, 238, 248
dot.com boom, collapse of 320
Dow-UT Composite Products 308,
313
Dowlais–Cardiff steelworks see East
Moors steelworks
Dowlais collieries 22–3, 69–70
Dowlais Iron Company
"acid" steel process used 36–7, 42
attempts to sell company (1792,
1854) 5, 23
Bessemer process used 35
capital investment programmes
(mid-19th C.) 22, 28, 31–2
closure of Dowlais works 74–5
cut-back on investment (mid-19th
C.) 18
disadvantages 40–1, 42
East Moors steel works 41–3, 44
effect of works closure 42–3, 75

expansion 5–6, 13, 30–1
failure to meet Egyptian rail contract
74
first strike 8
formation of 1–2
Goat Mill 31
Ifor Works 13
John Guest as works manager
(1767) 3
King George V's visit 56
lack of investment (late-18th C.)
4–5
lease on mineral rights 2, 13, 15,
16, 18–19, 21
number of employees 17, 34
output 2, 4, 7, 17, 28, 30, 32, 35,
39
profits 4, 8–9, 32, 39–40, 48–9
rail manufacture 9, 17, 31, 34
raw materials supply 28–9, 36, 59
sale of company to Keen 44, 48–9
Siemens open-hearth process used
36, 41
steel output 35, 39
winding down of works (1847/48)
20
working conditions (mid-19th C.)
34
Dowty aerospace group 275
Driveline business
centralised management reporting
system 337
effect of oil price rises 148
global expansion of 177–8, 232,
246–8, 296–7, 298–9
importance to GKN 141, 211, 220,
223
market share 288, 336, 339
move of manufacturing operations
335–7
profitability (1986) 241
profits collapse (2008) 350
proposal to expand into full systems
supplier 297–8
restructuring of 335–7

start of 108–10, 118–20, 133
torque management businesses
327–9, 339
*see also* Birfield; Uni-Cardan
Dual Listed Company (DLC),
GKN–Brambles partnership in
319
Dyno-Rod, joint venture with GKN
239, 264

earnings per share 146, 198, 245, 264,
270, 294, 344
East Moors steelworks (Cardiff) 41–3,
44
acid steel process used 42
conversion to basic open-hearth
process 59
expansion of capacity 59
nationalisation of 91
orders fall in late-1920s 74
reconstruction of 76
Eastern Europe, Driveline's expansion
into 266–7
Edwardes, Sir Michael 202
EEPTU (electricians' union) 180, 181,
182
EH101 helicopter 254, 274, 309,
331
*see also* Westland helicopter group
Emitec (joint venture in Germany)
238
employee numbers (in GKN) 98, 116,
198, 207–8, 270, 275–6, 325,
333, 350, 352
in UK 116, 198, 207, 270, 275–6,
333, 352
Employment Acts 220–1
Engineering Employers' Federation
(EEF) 128, 184, 221
Eurocopter, attitude to Westland
309
European Commission, competition
issues 145–6, 172, 174
European Economic Community
(EEC) 101–2, 128

European Exchange Rate Mechanism
268
Evans, John (works manager at
Dowlais) 7, 22, 24
Evans, Moss (of T&GWU) 128
Evergreen Association 155
Exors of James Mills 77, 157

F-22 fighter plane 325
F-35 Joint Strike Fighter 313, 315,
341
Falklands War 254
fast moving consumer goods (FMCG)
distribution system 159–61
Fasteners businesses
contributions to group profits 57,
60, 78–9
divestment to management buyout
235
Holdsworth's experience running
138, 194
loss in market share (late-1970s)
195
rationalisation in 1970s/1980s 198,
210
Ferguson, Harry 88–9
Ferguson Agricultural System 88–9
Fiat
GKN's acquisition of CVJ and
driveshaft plant 286
in Poland 266, 286
stake in Westland helicopter group
256, 260
Fichtel & Sachs 171
Filton Airbus wing fabrication facility
351–2
*Financial Times* 201, 203, 290, 321,
350
Finmeccanica
Agusta helicopter business 309, 310
purchase of GKN's stake in
AgustaWestland 332
First World War (WW1) 57, 58–62,
67
post-war boom 63–9

Firth Cleveland 144
London office 236
"Follow the Customer" approach 246, 266–7, 335
Ford 108–10, 177–8, 183, 213, 229
in-house component manufacturer 297–8
Forgings and Castings business
effect of car industry strikes 117
*see also* Garrington(s);
Smith Clayton
Foundations business 157, 270–1
four-wheel drive vehicles, transmission systems for 233, 328
France, driveline factory 120, 134
franchising *see* Meineke ...
front-wheel drive vehicles 148, 177, 204
breakthrough design 111, 231

(John) Garrington & Sons 47, 104
strike at 179–82
in UES joint venture 237
WW2 shell production 81–4
Gelenkwellenbau 133, 134
Gelenkwellenwerk Mosel 266
General Electric, CHEP and 284
General Motors 199, 229
General Strike (1926) 69–70
George, Tony, on Kingsway offices 236
Germany
driveline businesses in 134–8
effect of unification (East+West) 267
*see also* Uni-Cardan
Ghosn, Carlos (Nissan chief executive) 326, 329
GKN
in British Steel Corporation joint ventures 208, 237–8
coal mining businesses 69, 76
corporate aircraft fleet 168–9
corporate ethos 154, 356
debenture stock issue 129

demerger of industrial services business 315–16, 319–20
diversity 130
dividends 146, 198, 203, 245, 264, 270, 351
earnings per share 146, 198, 245, 264, 270, 294, 344
employee numbers 98, 116, 198, 207–8, 270, 275–6, 325, 333, 350, 352
formation of 55–6
management structure 101, 104, 152–3, 194, 248, 253, 289
merger with Lysaght and Sankey 68
mining companies 68–9, 76
mission statement 302
nationalisation and 86, 87, 91, 97, 123–6
new company name 234–5
operating margins 103, 198, 344
profits warnings (2008) 349
profits/(loss) 56, 60, 78–9, 98, 101, 103, 116, 129, 147, 151, 198, 202–3, 232, 245, 264, 269–70, 293–4, 305–6, 323, 344, 351
proposed merger with Lucas 242–3
proposed takeover of AE 218–20
proposed takeover of Sachs AG 171, 172–4
return on net assets 98, 103, 198, 245, 264
rights issues 218, 278
Royal Ordnance bid 243–4
sales/turnover 101, 116, 129, 147, 151, 198, 232, 323
search for chief executive 289–90
separation of roles of chairman and chief executive 289
share price changes 241, 242, 344, 351
shares listed on European exchanges 171
shares listed on Tokyo Stock Exchange 264

steel companies merged with
    Baldwins 74
  Westland bid 253, 260–2, 276,
    278–9
GKN–Brambles dual listed company
    315–16, 319
  value created for GKN shareholders
    319–20
GKN Contractors 209–10
GKN Dowlais Ltd
  sale to BSC 140
  see also Dowlais; East Moors
GKN Universal Transmissions
    company 178
Glaenzer Spicer 120, 134, 231
Glamorganshire Canal 5
Griffiths, Gordon (GKN director,
    automotive businesses) 175, 181,
    299
Griffiths, Ian (head of Driveline
    businesses) 299, 325, 328
Guest, Lady Charlotte (Josiah John
    Guest's second wife) 10–24
  death 44
  management roles at Dowlais 11,
    22, 23
Guest, John (works manager at Dowlais,
    1767–1786) 2–3
Guest, Sir (Josiah) John (John Guest's
    grandson) 7–22
  death 21, 22
  education and training 7
  first wife 8
  as MP 10, 12
  obituary 7
  second wife 10–24
Guest, Thomas (John Guest's son) 3,
    5, 7
Guest, Keen & Co.
  attempts at acquisition of
    Nettlefolds 49–50, 51–2,
    54–5
  formation of 49
  takeover of Nettlefolds 55–6
Guest, Keen & Nettlefolds

change in company name 234–5
  formation of 55–6
  see also GKN
Guest Keen Baldwins (GKB) Iron &
    Steel Co.
  formation of 74
  GKN in full control 97
Guest Keen, Williams (India) 78, 87,
    197
  sale of GKN stake in 279
Gulf War (1990) 259

Hadley Castle, Shropshire
  N&C ironworks 51
  Sankey factory 66–7, 215–16, 264,
    273
Hanson industrial conglomerate, stake
    in Westland helicopters 257, 261
Hanson, Lord 257, 261
Hardy Spicer 108, 110, 171, 220,
    231–2, 246
Heath, Barrie (GKN chairman)
  on Bullock Inquiry 187
  on character of GKN 154
  corporate aircraft fleet 168–9
  European expansion and 171,
    172–4
  as fighter pilot 167–8
  as GKN chairman 149, 152
  Norwich Union visit 169
  pallet pool business and 162, 165
  personal characteristics 167–8, 194
  Sachs takeover bid 171, 172–4
  on UK economy 170
Heath, Edward (Prime Minister) 127,
    151
Heath Street works, Smethwick 50,
    51, 53, 60, 95
  obsolescence 100–1
helicopters business
  search for potential partners 308–9
  see also Westland helicopter group
Heseltine, Michael (Secretary of State
    for Defence) 217, 256, 257
Hill, H. G. (Lysaghts director) 65

Hill, Herbert (Birfield chairman) 108, 109, 118, 134
Hoeganaes Corporation 305
Holdsworth, Trevor (GKN chairman) 107, 138–9
  accountancy background 355
  automotive business strategy 139, 145
  as chairman 193, 355
  choice of successor 248
  compared with Lees 251, 268
  disagreement with Brookes over steel businesses 139, 141, 237
  early experience 138, 194
  on GKN's overall strategy 212
  internationalisation strategy 232, 238
  Japanese visits 228
  post-recession (1983/1984) reports 217–18, 232
  retirement 248
  symbolic changes made by 234–6
  on the Thatchers 222
  on UK economy 202
  on Uni-Cardan 139, 140, 141
Honda 227, 230, 246
  licence for CVJ production in Japan 227
  UK factory 230, 348
  US factory 246
Hooke, Robert 111
Hookes joints 111–12
Hoskyns, Sir John 119
Howard, John (GKN company secretary) 146
Howe, Sir Geoffrey (Chancellor of Exchequer) 201
Hughes, Geoffrey (GKN lawyer) 112–13
  on Birfield takeover 118–19, 120
  on Miles Druce takeover 146
  on Sachs deal 172, 173–4
  on Uni-Cardan 134, 136
Human Resources function, role of 301

*In Place of Strife* 127
incremental improvement approach, driveline operations 231
India
  driveline joint venture 247, 287
  Independence 87
  steel business 78, 87, 197, 279
"industrial democracy" 186
  Bullock committee on 186–90
industrial relations
  at Dowlais Iron Company 8, 22–3
  at Garringtons 180–2
  at Sankey 128
  decline in UK 127, 142, 143, 184–5
  McFarlane's views 180–3, 184–5, 185–6
  reforms 126–7, 220–1
industrial services businesses
  demerged into Dual Listed Company 315–16, 319–20
  discussions on merger with Brambles 318–19
  divestment of underperforming operations 282
  effect on GKN's stock market value 317
  expansion of 196, 232–3, 239, 283–4
  GKN's first ventures 145, 157
  ownership structure of joint ventures 161, 196, 283, 284, 296, 316–18
  rationalisation of portfolio 264, 280–1
  *see also* Autoparts; CHEP; Cleanaway; Vending
inflation 126, 129, 146, 148, 170, 201
  effect on investment levels 129, 143–4
Insch, Brian 238, 248, 301–2
Insch, James 131
interest rate rises 147, 201, 268
Interlake Corporation 305

Interlake Material Handling business
305, 315–16, 319
internationalisation strategy 232, 238,
267
investor relations 252
Iran, Khomeini regime 199
Iran–Iraq war 209
Iraq
GKN contracts in 209–10
invasion of Kuwait 268, 272–3
Iron & Steel Corporation 91
Iron & Steel Holding & Realisation
Agency 92, 95
Iron & Steel Institute 38, 48
Isle of Wight, composites research and
production facility 260, 312, 340
Issigonis, Alec 110–11, 231
Italy
car production in 348
driveline factory 120, 134

Jaguar–GKN joint venture 245
Japan
Driveline testing facility 297
torque management expertise 329
Japanese motor industry 225, 227
GKN's relationships with 228–9,
297
imports into UK 170
imports into USA 226
manufacturing philosophy 230
transplants (factories) 226, 229–30
Uni-Cardan licensees 227–8
Jeans, J. Stephen, on British steel
industry 40
Jenkins, Clive (of ASTMS) 186
Jessop, John (head of industrial services
businesses) 157, 238, 248
on Autoparts 281
on business portfolio 157–8
CHEP pallet pool and 159–65,
196, 271
Cleanaway waste business 212–13
as GKN main board director 238,
248, 253

on Ray Brookes 156
retirement 280
joint consultative committees 188
Jolly, James (chairman of GKN) 63,
73, 79, 80, 86
Brookes on 92–3, 355
expansion of GKN steel interests
89–90
on nationalisation of steel
companies 86, 87, 90–1
retirement 92
Jones, Jack (of T&GWU) 186

kaizen (continuous improvement)
concept 230, 231, 248, 288
Kalyandjian, Sarkis (head of Driveline
businesses) 299
Kartelamt (West Germany)
influence of US competition law
173
on Sachs–GKN merger 172–4
Keen, Arthur 45–58
background 45
bid approaches to Nettlefolds
49–50, 51–2, 54–5
death 57
partnership with Watkins 46–7
personal wealth 49, 58
public appointments 47–8
Keen, Arthur T. 58
Kingsway (London) offices 236
Kwikform (scaffolding) 233, 245
divestment of 279

Labour governments 85–92, 116–27,
151–90
Laycock (automotive clutches) 119
Lea, David (of TUC) 186
Lees, Sir David (Finance Director, then
chairman of GKN)
on (1990s) recession 267, 269
accountancy background 355
on Autoparts 281–2
on Barrie Heath 169, 174, 193
as chairman 248, 251

Lees, Sir David *(cont.)*
compared with Holdsworth 251, 268
on Defence business 257, 265–6
on demerger of industrial services 318, 320, 327
as Finance Director 252
on inflation 268, 269
on Meineke lawsuit 291, 295
as non-executive chairman 289
overall (group) strategy 253, 257, 279–80, 323
personal characteristics 238, 251
retirement from GKN 333
shareholder communications 252
on Sinter Metal and Powder Metallurgy operations 338
on steel-making joint ventures 237–8
on takeover vulnerability 327
on Westland bid 257, 261, 277
Lehman Brothers investment bank 346–7
Levene, Sir Peter 217
Llewellyn, David 64, 65
Lloyd, Thomas (Heath Street's general manager) 95
Lofts, Ken (Sankey designer) 215
Lohr & Bromkamp 133, 231
London & North Western Railway 34, 45, 66
London Works, Smethwick 46
Lucas Industries 242–3, 297
Lysaght 65
contributions to GKN profits 79
merger with GKN 68
Lysaght Australia 79, 130–2, 149–50
sale of GKN's stake 197–8

McCarthy, Mike (CHEP USA) 271
McDonnell-Douglas Apache helicopter 309
McDonnell-Douglas' St. Louis plant 314–15

McFarlane, Jim (MD of Garringtons) 179
on 1980–82 recession 210
at EEF 184, 213
on industrial relations 180–3, 184–5, 185–6
on Mrs Thatcher 221
on Ray Brookes 155
on Sankey 213–14
McLennan, Ian (MD of BHP) 131, 149, 150
Major, John (Prime Minister) 294
management structure (of GKN) 101, 104, 152–3, 194, 248, 253, 289
Marsh, Richard (Industry Minister) 124, 125
Martin, Edward (General Manager at Dowlais) 38–9, 41, 48
Massey-Ferguson 89
Material Handling business (part of Interlake Corporation) 305, 315–16, 319
Maxwell-Holroyd, Leslie 106, 112, 113
Meineke Discount Muffler Shops 232, 263, 281
lawsuit brought by franchisees 290–5
in new GKN–Brambles company 316, 319
Menelaus, William (General Manager at Dowlais) 27–36, 37, 38
Merrill Lynch investment bank 346
Merthyr Board of Health 26, 27
Merthyr Tydfil
death rate (in mid-19th C.) 26
iron and steel industry 1–40
unemployment (1930s) 75
Merthyr Tydfil Waterworks 26–7
Merthyr-to-Abercynon tram-road 6
Mexico, Driveline manufacturing plants 247, 287, 337
micro-management of national economy 102–3
Mid-America Industries 263

Midland Bank 47, 56
Miles Druce 145–6
Mills, James 77
Mini car 110–11, 231
Ministry of Defence (MoD)
    contracts/orders 103, 215, 216,
        217, 274, 310, 332–3
    Options for Change programme
        265
    procurement procedure 217
    Royal Ordnance sale 243–4
    on Westland helicopter group 254,
        260
Ministry of Munitions (in WW1)
    58–9, 61
Ministry of Supply (in WW2) 80
Mission Everest 343
mission statement (of GKN) 302
Mond, Sir Alfred 71
monetarist theory 201
Monopolies & Mergers Commission
    218–19
Moore, Bob (head of CHEP USA)
    284
Morley, Freddie 100–1
Morris, William 66, 108
motor industry
    expansion 107–13, 118–20
    strikes in UK 117
MOWAG armoured vehicles 273–4

nationalisation of UK steel companies
    86–7, 90–1, 123–6
Nettlefold, Edward 50, 54, 55
Nettlefold, Frederick 53
Nettlefold, John Sutton 50
Nettlefold, Joseph Henry 51, 53
Nettlefold & Chamberlain (N&C)
    50–3
    bid approach from Guest, Keen
        51–2
    expansion 51
    exports 52
    Hadley Castle ironworks 51
    Heath Street factory 50, 51, 53

output 51
    Rogerstone steelworks 53
Nettlefolds 53–5
    bid approaches by Guest, Keen
        49–50, 51–2, 54–5
    contributions to GKN profits 57,
        60, 78–9
    formation of 53
    profits 54
    takeover by Guest, Keen 55–6
    see also Fasteners division
New Horizons Advertising 292
newspaper owners 64
Nicol, Bill (GKN company secretary),
    on Ken Peacock 95
Nissan 170, 326
    chief executive of 326, 329
    licence for CVJ production in Japan
        227
    UK factory 229–30, 348
    US factory 226
Normalair-Garrett environmental
    systems business 308
North Sea oil production 200
Northrop Grumman X-47B UAV
    340
Norwich Union 169
NTN Toyo Bearing 226–7, 336

OffHighway division 89, 123, 241–2,
    243–4, 296, 333
    expansion of 343–4
oil embargoes 122, 147
oil price rises (2008) 346
oil price shocks 110, 147–8, 199,
    268
    consequences for GKN 148
oil production by UK 200
Olson, Ted 294
open-mindedness of GKN's
    management 354
operating margins 103, 198, 344
Orconera Iron Company 36, 42
Organization of Petroleum Exporting
    Countries (OPEC) 147, 199

outsourcing
  in aerospace industry 314–15
  in automotive industry 286

pallet pool 157–65
  see also CHEP
Parsons, Jim (GKN Personnel
    Director)
  employee information systems
    developed by 187–9, 301
  on Ken Peacock 93–4, 95, 100
  memorandum on character of GKN
    154, 333
  on Ray Brookes 114–15
  response for Bullock committee 189
  retirement 189
  on Sankey strike 128
  on worker directors 187
Parsons, Ted 95–6
Parts Industries Inc. 195, 232, 242
  sale of subsidiary 281
Patent Nut & Bolt Co. Ltd (PNB) 46
  disposal of remaining part 198
  merger with Dowlais Iron, Steel &
    Coal Company 48–9
Peacock, Kenneth (Tom's son –
    chairman of GKN) 80, 93–6, 97,
    101–2
  retirement as chairman 113
Peacock, Tom (joint-MD, GKN) 63,
    73, 79, 80
pension fund/scheme 95, 331
Penydarren Ironworks 28–9
petrol rationing 110, 148
Phoenix ventures 208, 237–8
Pilkington Aerospace 340
plastic pallets 158, 284
Plastics Machinery businesses, sale of
    208
plate steel 42
  collapse of price 68
Poland, Driveline manufacturing plants
    266, 286, 337
Ponsonby, Edward, Earl of
    Bessborough 58, 63, 68

Potter, Robert (judge in Meineke
    lawsuit) 292
Powder Metallurgy division 303–4
  effect of 2000s downturns 324,
    350
  expansion of 305, 306
  restructuring of 337–8
Powell Duffryn, merger with GKN
    mining companies 76–7
Prices & Incomes Board 116
profits/(loss)
  21st century 323, 344, 351
  1900s–1950s 56, 60, 78–9, 98
  1960s 101, 103, 116
  1970s 129, 147, 151, 198
  1980s 202, 232, 245, 264
  1990s 269–70, 293–4, 305–6
propshafts 108–10
puddling and rolling process 4–5, 6
  capacity limitations 30, 32

rails
  collapse of price 68
  manufacture of 9, 17, 31, 34, 74
  price of steel vs iron 35
  steel 35, 39
railway accessories and sleepers 39,
    103
railway boom (mid-18th C.) 9
Rapid Reaction Force concept 259
raw materials costs 345
raw materials supply 28–9, 36, 59
rearmament, pre-WW2 79
recessions 73–5, 199–205, 267–71,
    347, 356
  effect on GKN 74–5, 204, 207–10,
    275, 348–51
Redditch (Worcs), admin HQ moved
    to 236, 237
Redland Purle 212–13
Reese, A.J. (general manager of East
    Moors steelworks) 75–6
Renault 326, 336
resin film infusion (RFI) technique
    313

resin transfer moulding (RTM)
technology 308, 313
responsiveness to change 353–4
return on investment, factors affecting
185
return on net assets (RoNA) 98, 103,
198, 245, 264
Rhondda, Viscountess 65
Richter, Oliver 158, 159, 161
Roberts, Roy 162, 193, 238, 248
Robertson, Joe (head of GKN patent
department) 112
Rockford, acquisition of 344
Rogerstone steelworks (South Wales)
53–4, 66
Rolls-Royce aero-engine company 100,
104, 145, 179
Royal Ordnance (RO), bid for 243–4
"running-out" furnace 13

Sachs AG 171–2
proposed takeover by GKN 171,
172–4
sales/turnover, GKN 101, 116, 129,
147, 151, 198, 232, 323
Sanford (North Carolina, USA), GKN
driveline factory 178
Sankey 213–16
contributions to GKN profits 78
core product range 215
MoD contracts/orders 103, 215,
217
productivity 214
strike at 128
Sankey, George 65–6, 67
(Joseph) Sankey & Sons 65–7
merger with GKN 68
Saunders-Roe 312
Saxon armoured personnel carrier 103,
215–16
scaffolding businesses 157, 158,
232–3, 279
Scottish Stampings 88
strike at 128
scrap steel prices 338, 345

Scunthorpe steelworks 65
nationalisation of 91, 124
reacquisition of 97
Second World War (WW2),
rearmament prior to 79
secondary strikes and picketing 220,
221
Servotomic 157–8
share price changes, GKN shares 241,
242, 344, 351
shell forging project (in WW2)
82–4
shipbuilding industry, as market for
plate steel 42
Siemens open-hearth steel process
35–6, 41
Siemens, Sir William 35
Sikorsky helicopters 255
Sinter Metals division 304
expansion of 304–5, 306
restructuring of 337–8
Skoda 267
Slovenia, Driveline manufacturing
plants 287, 337
Smith Clayton forgings business 179,
183
in UES joint venture 237
Smith, Kevin (head of Aerospace
business, *then* CEO of GKN)
310, 311
on AgustaWestland 331, 332
as chief executive of GKN 330
as head of Aerospace business 310,
311, 330
on rationalisation and expansion of
Aerospace 311–15, 325
soldiers' helmets 67
Somerset Wire Co. 80
South Korea, Driveline business 287,
297
Spain
car sales 348
CHEP in 245
Driveline business 176, 246, 287
iron ore from 37, 42, 59

speed limits on roads 148
Spitfire aircraft 81
Starr, Ken (US lawyer) 294, 295
steam engines 5–6, 31
steam locomotives 6
steel industry, nationalisation of 86–7,
    90–1, 124–5
steel making
    "acid" process 36–7, 42
    "basic" process 37, 42
    Bessemer process 32–3
    closure of Dowlais works 74
    profitability 86–7, 117–18
    Siemens system 35–6
    UK compared with US industry
        75–6
steel-making businesses
    divestment programmes 197, 208,
        237–8
    nationalisation of 91, 124
steel rails 35, 39
steel stockholding businesses 145–6
    sale of 238
Steer, Edward (GKN chairman) 68
Stein, Nigel (Group Finance Director,
    GKN) 320
Stellex 340–1
Stenman AB (Swedish screw maker)
    77
Stern Osmat 196
stock markets
    1929 crash 73
    GKN shares listed on European
        exchanges 171
    GKN shares listed on Tokyo Stock
        Exchange 264
    view of aerospace vs motor industry
        341
stockbroker's lunch 252
"stop–go" economic policies 102,
    122
strikes 8, 22–3, 99, 122, 127, 128–9,
    180–2
    effect on GKN 117, 126, 128, 181,
        198, 203

subprime loans, collapse of 346
Suez crisis (1956) 110
supplier–customer relationships
    183–4

Taff Vale Railway Company 17
Taitt, William (John Guest's
    son-in-law) 3, 5, 6, 7
takeover target, GKN as 327
team spirit, promotion of 342–3
Teleflex Aerospace 341
telephone callboxes 234
Telford, Shropshire
    armoured vehicle production
        215–16, 273
    autostructures production 264
    composite leaf spring production
        233, 270
Thailand, CVJ business 297, 342
Thatcher, Denis 222
Thatcher, Margaret (Prime Minster)
    190, 200, 201, 221, 254, 256
Thermal Joining Centre (former
    Boeing company) 325
three-day working week 150, 151
tin plate mills 39
Tochigi-based CVJ-manufacturing
    company, purchase from Nissan
    326
Tochigi Fuji Sangyo (TFS) 233–4,
    329, 339–40
Tokyo Stock Exchange, GKN shares
    listed 264
torque management businesses 327–9,
    339–40
Toyoda, Eiji 226
Toyoda Machine Works, GKN
    partnership with 297
Toyota
    effect of 2008 recession 348
    GKN driveshafts supplied to Japan
        246, 326
    global sales 338
    licence for CVJ production in Japan
        227

UK factory 230
US factory 226, 246
Toyota Production System 230
Translite KK (joint venture in Japan)
  233
Transmissions operations
  in Europe 134, 138, 140, 171, 176
  in USA 177–8, 194
Trevithick, Richard 6
Trimmer, William 65
Turner & Newall (T&N) 219, 220,
  297, 303
Turner, David
  as CEO, Brambles 330
  as Finance Director, Brambles 320
  as Finance Director, GKN 253, 289

UK
  car manufacturers 127, 170, 190,
    204
  economy (1970s) 129, 146–7, 170
  economy (1980s) 200, 201, 202
  industrial productivity 40, 129,
    142, 170, 185
  Japanese-owned car factories
    229–30
  manufacturing output decline 200
undercut-free joint 231
unemployment levels 68, 69, 78, 200
Uni-Cardan 120, 133–8, 354
  continuous improvements in design
    and manufacturing 231
  contribution to GKN's profits 141,
    211, 223, 267
  expansion of 171, 176
  financial system 142
  GKN's stake in 134, 138, 140,
    246
  joint ventures 238, 246, 247
  licenses granted in Japan 227–8
unions, immunity from legal action
  220, 221
United Engineering Steels (UES) 237,
  245, 271
  sale of GKN's stake 279

United States Steel Corporation 49
United Technologies Corporation
  (UTC)
  Sikorsky helicopter arm 255
  stake in Westland helicopter group
    255, 256, 260–1, 276
universal joints 111–12
US Court of Appeals, on Meineke case
  291, 295
US Defence business 313, 314–15,
  325
USA
  autoparts distribution operations
    195, 197, 232, 242, 281
  decline in car sales 199, 267, 347–8
  early (18th C.) exports to 4
  GKN driveline operations 177–8,
    194
  Japanese car imports 226
  Japanese-owned car factories 226
  steel production volumes 40
  vehicle manufacture 177, 199

Vandervell engine bearings
  business 123, 218, 220, 246
Velcon 247, 337
vending service businesses 238, 245,
  271
  divestment of 279
Venture Pressings (VP) 245
Vickers 258–9, 306–7
Victoria Cross (VC) awards 61
Viscodrive 233–4, 246
Visteon (component manufacturer)
  298, 336
Volkswagen 133, 230, 266, 267

wages freeze policies 103, 143
Walsh, Brian (GKN Finance Director)
  248, 253
  on Westland board 262, 277
Walterscheid-Muller, Walter 133, 135,
  136–8, 178, 298
Warrior tracked personnel carrier 215,
  216–17

wars
  iron and steel industry affected by
    4, 5, 8, 59–61
  see also American War of
    Independence; Crimean War;
    Falklands War; First World War;
    Gulf War; Iran–Iraq War; Second
    World War
Watkins, Francis 45, 46, 47
Watkins & Keen 46
  see also Patent Nut and Bolts (PNB)
Wedderburn, Lord [LSE lawyer]
    186–7
Welding businesses, sale of 208
Welsh Associated Collieries (WAC)
    76
  merger with Powell Duffryn 76–7
Westland Aerostructures 260, 307–8,
    312, 354
Westland helicopter group
  claim against Arab Organisation for
    Industrialisation 277–8
  crisis 254–6, 257
  EH101 helicopter orders 274, 309,
    331
  European consortium's bid 256
  Fiat's stake in 256, 260
  GKN's stake in 253, 260–2, 276,
    278–9
  in joint venture with Agusta 310
  takeover bid by GKN 278–9
  UTC/Sikorsky's stake in 255, 256,
    260–1
  see also AgustaWestland

Westra, Gerben (head of Cleanaway)
    285
Wheeldon, Howard, on Ray Brookes
    156
Wilkinson, Isaac 3
Williams, Owen 77, 78
Williams, Peter (CHEP USA) 271
Wilson, Harold (Prime Minister) 116,
    117, 126
Wimbourne, Lord 24, 41, 43, 44, 48,
    63
"Winter of Discontent" (1978–1979)
    190
Wolseley Tool & Motor Co. 66
women in workplace 34, 60
Woods, Basil 145, 161–2, 193
worker directors, Bullock report on
    186, 187, 189
workforce numbers (in GKN) 98,
    116, 198, 207–8, 270, 275–6,
    325, 333, 350, 352
  in UK 116, 198, 207, 270, 275–6,
    333, 352
Worldparts Corporation 197
Wright, David, as Alec Daly's successor
    289
Wright, George (of AUEW) 128
wrought iron
  compared with steel 35
  manufacture of 4–5

Yom Kippur war 147, 278

Zaire, GKN contracts in 209